The Social Studies Curriculum

SUNY Series, Theory, Research, and Practice in Social Education

Peter H. Martorella, Editor

The Social Studies Curriculum

Purposes, Problems, and Possibilities

EDITED BY

E. Wayne Ross

State University of New York Press

Published by
State University of New York Press, Albany

For information, address State University of New York
Press, State University Plaza, Albany, N.Y. 12246

Production by Diane Ganeles
Marketing by Hannah J. Hazen

Library of Congress Cataloging-in-Publication Data
The social studies curriculum : purposes, problems, and possibilities
    / edited by E. Wayne Ross.
        p. cm. — (SUNY series, theory, research, and practice in
social education)
    Includes bibliographical references and index.
    ISBN 0-7914-3443-5 (hardcover : acid free paper). — ISBN
0-7914-3444-3 (pbk. : acid free paper).
    1. Social sciences—Study and teaching (Elementary)—United
States—Curricula. 2. Social sciences—Study and teaching
(Secondary)—United States—Curricula. 3. Interdisciplinary
approach in education—United States. 4. Curriculum planning-
-United States. I. Ross, E. Wayne, 1956– . II. Series.
LB1584.S6373   1997
372.83'043—dc20   96-36305
                                                              CIP

10 9 8 7 6 5 4

For
Colin and Rachel

Contents

Acknowledgments   ix

Introduction   xi
    E. Wayne Ross

Part I: Purposes of the Social Studies Curriculum

1. The Struggle for the Social Studies Curriculum   3
    E. Wayne Ross

2. History as the Core of Social Studies Education   21
    Michael Whelan

3. The Unique Mission of the Social Studies   39
    David Warren Saxe

Part II: Social Issues and the Social Studies Curriculum

4. Social Studies and Feminism   59
    Nel Noddings

5. Gender in Social Education   71
    Jane Bernard-Powers

6. Against the Sovereignty of Origins: Contradictions
    in the Experience of Racial Inequality in
    Education and Society   91
    Cameron McCarthy

7. Multicultural Social Studies: Schools as Places for
    Examining and Challenging Inequality   107
    David Hursh

Part III: The Social Studies Curriculum in Practice

8. Crafting a Culturally Relevant Social Studies Approach   121
     Gloria Ladson-Billings

9. Social Studies and the Arts   137
     Terrie L. Epstein

10. Science in Social Studies: Reclaiming Science for
     Social Knowledge   165
     Stephen C. Fleury

11. Infusing Global Perspectives into the Social Studies
     Curriculum   183
     Merry M. Merryfield

12. Teaching Social Issues: Implementing an
     Issues-Centered Curriculum   197
     Ronald W. Evans

13. Assessment in Social Studies: Moving toward
     Authenticity   213
     Sandra Mathison

Notes   225

References   229

Contributors   259

Name Index   263

Subject Index   269

Acknowledgments

I would like to thank each of the authors who wrote chapters for this volume. Each contribution reflects sound and serious reflection upon the often times confounding issues of curriculum work in social studies education. I have learned much from each of these individuals in the past. In working on this project I found that I still have much more to learn from them about social studies curriculum and pedagogy.

There are many persons who have over the years greatly influenced my thinking and work as a social studies educator. In particular, I am deeply indebted to Jeffrey W. Cornett, Stephen C. Fleury, and Perry Marker for their profound insights on the social studies curriculum and teaching. I appreciate their critical but supportive responses to my work. In their work as scholars and teachers, as well as in their everyday lives, each of them are models of a commitment to and action for social justice, democracy, and the dignity and worth of every individual.

I am especially grateful to my colleagues in social studies education with whom I have worked in many different ways to advance and transform social studies curriculum, teaching, and scholarship: Susan Adler, Jane Bernard-Powers, Lynne Boyle-Baise, Jim Elliott, Terrie Epstein, Ron Evans, S. G. Grant, David Hursh, Joel Jenne, Marilyn Johnston, Gloria Ladson-Billings, Jim Nehring, Susan Noffke, Valerie Ooka Pang, Walter Parker, Lynda Stone, Steve Thornton, Bruce VanSledright, Michael Whelan, and many others. I am truly thankful and proud to have the opportunity to work with such extraordinary colleagues and friends.

I would like to thank Linda Biemer, Dean of the School of Education and Human Development at the State University of New York at Binghamton for the opportunity finish work on this volume while on sabbatical leave. Ellen Boesenberg and Verik J. Probst, my graduate assistants were invaluable in completing work on the manuscript. Lois Patton, Acting Director of SUNY Press, has been, as usual, a source of encouragement and support. I greatly appreciate her belief in this book, editorial expertise, and patience.

The most important influence in my life is Sandra Mathison. As I worked to complete this project, she provided me with the encouragement, criticism, and assistance that I needed, always at just the right time. Her sustenance both intellectually and emotionally is the source of any success I have experienced. She has shown me vistas that I never knew existed and for that I thank her with all my heart.

E. W. R.

Introduction

E. Wayne Ross

Social studies has had a relatively brief and turbulent history as one of the core subjects in the school curriculum. The fundamental content of the social studies curriculum—the study of human enterprise across space and time—has always been at the core of educational endeavors. Recent scholarship has raised questions about the traditional account of the origins of the social studies curriculum, however, it is generally accepted that the formal introduction of social studies to the school curriculum was marked by the publication of *The Social Studies in Secondary Education* in 1916. This was the final report of the Committee on Social Studies of the National Education Association (NEA) Commission on the Reorganization of Secondary Schools, which included an emphasis on the development of citizenship values in students. The Committee on Social Studies was heavily influenced by earlier commissions of the NEA and the American Historical Association. Their respective aims were the reform of secondary education and the inclusion of history as a core school subject. The roots of the contemporary social studies curriculum, therefore, can be traced to two distinct curriculum reform efforts: the introduction of academic history into the curriculum and citizenship education.

Since its formal introduction into the school, social studies has been the subject of numerous commission and blue-ribbon panel studies, ranging from the sixteen-volume report of the American Historical Association's Commission on Social Studies in the 1930s to the recent movement for national curriculum standards. Separate and competing curriculum standards have recently been published for no less than six areas of the social studies curriculum:

United States and global history, economics, geography, civics, and social studies.

Throughout the twentieth century the social studies curriculum has been an ideological battleground in which such diverse curricular programs as the "life adjustment movement," progressive education, social reconstructionism, and nationalistic history have held sway at various times. The debate over the nature, purpose, and content of the social studies curriculum continues today, with competing groups variously arguing for a "social problems approach," or the "disciplinary study of history and geography" as the most appropriate framework for the social studies curriculum. All participants in this debate agree, however, that social studies curriculum and instruction plays a crucial role in the conceptions and understandings of our social, political, and economic roles as public citizens and the actions we take based on those conceptions.

The purpose of this book is to present a substantive overview of the issues in curriculum development and implementation faced by social studies educators. The book was written for professional educators and those preparing to enter the profession as teachers, curriculum workers, and administrators. And each chapter is written to be accessible to the lay reader interested in educational issues. *The Social Studies Curriculum: Purposes, Problems, and Possibilities* presents contemporary perspectives on some of the most enduring problems facing social studies educators. It has strong emphasis on concerns for diversity of purposes and forms of knowledge within the social studies curriculum. This collection of essays provides readers with a systematic investigation of a broad range of issues affecting the curriculum. Enabling inservice and preservice teachers and other curriculum workers to better understand the nature, scope, and context of social studies curriculum concerns in today's schools is a primary goal of this collection.

The book is organized into three thematic sections representing contemporary areas of concern and debate among social studies teachers, curriculum workers, and scholars. Part I—Purposes of the Social Studies Curriculum—focuses on the purposes identified for social studies education in North America. This section provides background on disciplinary struggles to control the social studies, as well as ways in which state departments of education, textbook publishers, and others have influenced the curriculum. Particular emphasis is placed on the "history versus social studies" debate and opposing viewpoints are presented. In the opening chapter, I present a broad overview of the struggles for the social studies curriculum, describing a series of tensions and contradictions that have functioned to define the debates over the social studies curriculum since its inception. The two chapters that follow are written by historians of social studies education. They represent the diverse perspectives on the origins and purposes of the social studies curriculum. Michael Whelan argues for history as the core of social studies education. David W. Saxe outlines the unique mission of social studies as an interdisciplinary study of social problems.

Part II—Social Issues and the Social Studies Curriculum—examines social issues in the curriculum, with an emphasis on issues of diversity. The scope of social issues relevant to the study of human enterprise across space and time is mind-boggling. The fundamental question faced in all curriculum development work—What knowledge is of most worth?—is, for social studies educators, a question whose response carries with it social, political, ideological as well as epistemological consequences. It is not possible to present a comprehensive overview of all the important issues related to social studies content areas. While many significant areas of concern for social studies educators are not covered here, this section does address several of the most frequently raised concerns regarding issues of social diversity (for example, Eurocentrism vs. Afrocentricism, gender, race, class).

Nel Noddings provides a provocative analysis of how form and content of the social studies can be reconstructed through feminism. Noddings argues that the next wave of feminism should be directed toward the articulation of women's culture and that feminists should resist the total assimilation of this material into the mainstream curriculum because such assimilation could be tantamount to destruction. In "Gender in Social Education," Jane Bernard-Powers provides a historical account of the gender equity movement in social studies education. Bernard-Powers examines how gender equity concerns have transformed social science scholarship and the subsequent affects on textbooks, curriculum frameworks, and teacher education. While Bernard-Powers documents significant changes in the curriculum as a result of gender equity work, like Nodding she identifies significant work yet to be done.

The second half of Part II focuses on issues of race, culture, and class. In "Against the Sovereignty of Origins," Cameron McCarthy examines the racial inequalities in society and education, and the contradictions that are embedded within the experience of racial inequality. David Hursh examines schools as public arenas for understanding diversity. He provides examples of how a multicultural perspective assists students and teachers in engaging in an analysis of society that leads to the development of a more sophisticated understanding of social studies disciplines as well as their own lives.

The final section of the book examines the social studies curriculum in practice. The focus in Part III is on issues in social studies that are currently demanding the attention of teachers and curriculum workers as a result of initiatives to transform social studies curriculum and pedagogy. The authors in this section examine current practices against a backdrop of possibilities for what social studies curriculum and pedagogy might be. Each chapter offers new ideas that can grow out of or be grafted onto current realities experienced in the social studies classroom. As in the other sections of the book, a plethora of perspectives is offered. But there are many important issues and initiatives (economic education, sexuality education, geography) that are not directly addressed because of space limitations. Curriculum themes addressed in this section represent those that are particularly significant for social studies at the turn of the century.

In "Crafting a Culturally Relevant Social Studies Approach," Gloria Ladson-Billings describes an approach to teaching social studies that empowers students to critically examine the society in which they live and to work for social change. In order to do this, students must possess a variety of literacies: language-based, mathematical, scientific, artistic, musical, historical, cultural, economic, social, civic, and political. Ladson-Billings describes what teachers can learn from culturally relevant teaching based upon case studies of the successful work of teachers in a largely African-American and low-income community.

Terrie L. Epstein presents an arts-based approach to social studies curriculum and instruction. In describing her work with high school students, Epstein illustrates in detail how student engagement with the arts (as interpretive and creative) can assist students in constructing complex historical understandings and increase the equity in educational experiences and outcomes. In "Science in Social Studies," Stephen C. Fleury explores the interrelationships of science and technology in society, and the role of scientific and technological topics in the social studies curriculum. Fleury's emphasis is placed on ways in which the social studies curriculum might better prepare students for the complexities of a scientific technological society.

Merry M. Merryfield describes how teachers can infuse global perspectives into the social studies curriculum. Global education is an integral part of the K-12 social studies curriculum in many states and local school districts across the United States. This approach to social studies emphasizes human experience as transnational, cross-cultural, and multicultural interactions among a variety of actors (for example, individuals, states, multinational corporations, and the like). Merryfield describes how a variety of teachers are infusing global perspectives by using strategies such as comparisons across cultures and linking knowledge over time and space.

Ronald W. Evans describes an issues-centered social studies curriculum, based upon the perspective that social studies is a broadly defined interdisciplinary field devoted to the examination of social issues and problems. Evans provides a rationale for issues-centered social studies and examples of issues-centered curricula and teaching.

The final chapter addresses a central issue that affects social studies curriculum and instruction: student assessment. Sandra Mathison distinguishes assessment practices from tests and measurement, and analyzes both the technical and social aspects of assessment. In social studies, as in other school subject areas, the recent trend is away from traditional means of assessing student knowledge and skills and toward more "authentic" assessment practices. Mathison provides examples of both the limitations and possibilities of innovative performance assessment practices in social studies and the dilemmas inherent in assessment reform in social studies.

It is my hope that these essays will stimulate readers to reconsider their assumptions and understanding about the origins, purposes, and nature of the social studies curriculum. As is evident in the chapters that follow, curriculum is much more than information to be passed on to students—a collection of facts and generalizations from history and the social science disciplines. The curriculum is what is experienced by students. It is dynamic and inclusive of the interactions among students, teachers, subject matter, and the context. The true measure of success in any social studies program will be found in its effects on individual students' thinking and actions, as well as the communities to which students belong. Teachers are the key component in any curriculum improvement. It is my hope that this book provides them with perspectives, insights, and knowledge that are beneficial in their continued growth as professional educators.

PART I

Purposes of the Social Studies Curriculum

CHAPTER ONE

The Struggle for the Social Studies Curriculum

E. Wayne Ross

Introduction

The content of the social studies curriculum is the most inclusive of all school subjects. Stanley and Nelson define social education as "the study of all human enterprise over time and space" (1994, p. 266). Determining the boundaries of the social education taught in schools, what most people know as the social studies, requires decisions about what social knowledge is most important, which skills and behaviors are most valuable, what values are most significant and what sequence of content and skills best fits the subject matter and the students (Stanley and Nelson 1994). Given this, it is not surprising that social studies has been racked by intellectual battles over its purpose, content, and pedagogy since its inception as a school subject in the early part of the twentieth century. To top it off, even the historical accounts of the origins of the social studies as a school subject are now under dispute.

Three questions form the framework for this chapter: (1) What is the social studies curriculum? (2) Who controls the social studies curriculum? (3) What is the social studies teacher's role in relation to the curriculum? These may seem to be simple and straightforward questions, but, as we shall see, there is debate and controversy surrounding each. Even the most basic aspects of the social studies—such as its purpose in the school curriculum—have been contested since its inception. As each of the above questions are addressed, fundamental tensions and contradictions that underlie the social studies curriculum will be identified. My intention is to present this series of tensions and contradictions as a heuristic for

3

understanding the dynamic nature of the social studies. It would be a mistake to treat them as definitive oppositionals, however; it is the struggles over these contradictions that have shaped the nature of the social studies curriculum in the past and continue to fashion it today.

The first section of this chapter examines the origins and purposes of the social studies curriculum. The historical analysis presented in this section does not attempt to be exhaustive, but is intended as a context for understanding the contemporary social studies curriculum and current efforts to reform it. Both the contradictory origins of social studies in schools and the long-standing dispute over the relative emphasis of cultural transmission and critical thinking will be examined. The following section examines the question of curricular control, with particular emphasis on the historical tensions between curriculum centralization and grassroots curriculum development in the social studies. The current movement toward curriculum standards in social studies is addressed in this section.

Social studies curriculum and instruction cannot be considered in isolation. The teacher is the most critical element in the improvement and transformation of the social studies curriculum. In the final section of this chapter, the role of the social studies teacher in relation to the curriculum is examined. In this section, the role of teachers as curriculum conduits is contrasted with the a more professional activist view of teachers as curriculum theorizers.

What is the Social Studies Curriculum?

Origins of Social Studies in School: Academic History and Social Improvement

Social studies in the broadest sense—that is, the preparation of young people so that they possess the knowledge, skills, and values necessary for active participation in society—has been a primary part of schooling in North America since colonial times. The earliest laws establishing schools in the United States specified religious and moral instruction. In the Latin grammar schools of New England, instruction in catechism and Bible was the core of schooling, while geography and moral philosophy were also taught.

Nationalistic education, intended to develop loyal patriots, replaced religion as the main purpose of social education following the American Revolution. From the late eighteenth century, when Webster began to include nationalistic material in his geography texts, up to the present day, nationalistic education has permeated the social studies curriculum (Stanley and Nelson 1994).

The traditional view of the origins of the contemporary social studies curriculum is that the National Education Association (NEA) 1916 Committee on Social Studies introduced the term *social studies*. It also created the scope and sequence of courses that define the contemporary curriculum.

As mentioned above, the origins of the contemporary social studies curriculum has recently become a flash point between advocates of a history-centered social studies curriculum and those calling for a curriculum based on the interdisciplinary study of current social issues. (The history of the early years of social studies is the focus of the Michael Whelan's chapter in this volume.) Whelan (1992 and in this volume) points out the contemporary social studies has roots in both the movement to include the academic study of history in the schools (through the work of the NEA 1893 Committee of Ten and the American Historical Association (AHA) 1899 Committee of Seven) as well as ideas drawn from social welfare and social improvement movements of the nineteenth and early twentieth centuries, which influenced the report of the NEA 1916 Committee on Social Studies. Whelan suggests that both sides (for example, Ravitch 1989; Saxe 1991) in the debate over the origins of social studies have drawn somewhat extreme and misleading portraits of the roles and differences between historians and progressive social meliorists in the development of social studies as a school subject. Nonetheless, the contemporary social studies curriculum does have at least two sources—academic history and social improvement.

The tensions and contradictions inherent in the establishment of social studies in schools, while perhaps not as extreme as represented by some scholars, may still help to explain the internal conflict that has shaped the field since its beginnings. Disagreement over curricular issues in social studies has characterized the field since its birth and, as Whelan notes, these disagreements and diversities of opinion regarding the nature, purpose, and organization of social studies have served to energize the field.

The Purposes of the Social Studies Curriculum: Cultural Transmission and Critical Thought

There is widespread agreement that the proper aim of social studies is *citizenship education* or the preparation of young people so that they possess the knowledge, skills, and values necessary for active participation in society (Barr, Barth, and Shermis 1977; Fullinwider 1991; Longstreet 1985; Marker and Mehlinger 1992; McCutchen 1963; Shaver 1977; Stanley 1985; Thornton 1994). Most social studies educators justify the subject on the grounds of citizenship. However, there is no consensus on what *citizenship* means nor on the implications of citizenship for curriculum and instruction. As Marker and Mehlinger note in their review of research on the social studies curriculum:

> The apparent consensus on behalf of citizenship education is almost meaningless. Behind that totem to which nearly all social studies researchers pay homage lies continuous and rancorous debate about the purposes of social studies. Some believe that social studies should focus primarily on history and geography; others have argued that social studies should examine "closed areas," topics that are more or less taboo in polite society (Hunt and Metcalf 1955), decision making (Engle 1963), public policy (Oliver and Shaver 1966), environmental competence (Newmann 1977), moral development (Kohlberg 1973, 1975), and adult social roles (Superka and Hawke, 1982). While a few think that the purpose of social studies is to make students astute critics of American society (Engle and Ochoa, 1988), others believe . . . that the purpose of social studies is mainly socialization into the values, habits and beliefs that permit youth to find a niche in adult society. [1992, p. 832]

Various schemes have been used by researchers to make sense of the wide ranging and conflicting purposes offered for social studies. The most influential of these was worked out by Barr, Barth, and Shermis (1977). They grouped the various positions on the social studies curriculum into three themes: citizenship (or cultural) transmission, social science, and reflective inquiry. Morrissett and Haas (1982) used the categories of conservative cultural continuity, the intellectual aspects of history and the social sciences, and the process of reflective thinking. Both sets of researchers essentially agree that social studies is used for three primary purposes: (1) socialization into society's norms; (2) transmission of facts, concepts, and generalizations from the academic disciplines; and

(3) the promotion of critical or reflective thinking. While these re-searchers come down on differing sides (with Barr, Barth, and Shermis favoring *reflective inquiry* and Morrissett and Haas argu-ing for the *intellectual aspects of the academic disciplines*), they both agree that *citizenship transmission* or *conservative cultural continuity* is the dominant approach practiced in schools (Marker and Mehlinger 1992).

A third analytic framework of the purposes of social studies is offered by Stanley and Nelson (1994). They argue that the key element in the dispute over the purpose of social studies in the school curriculum involves the relative emphasis given to cultural transmission or to critical or reflective thinking. When cultural transmission is emphasized, the intent is to use the social studies curriculum to promote social adaptation. The emphasis is on teach-ing content, behaviors, and values that reflect views accepted by the traditional, dominant society. This approach is politically con-servative, valuing stability and common standards of thought and behavior. When critical or reflective thinking is emphasized, the intent is to use the social studies curriculum to promote social transformation. The emphasis is on teaching content, behaviors, and values that question and critique standard views accepted by the dominant society. This approach is a more progressive view, valuing diversity and the potential of social action to lead to the reconstruction of society.

It is within the context of the tensions between the relative emphasis on transmission of the cultural heritage of the dominant society or the development of critical thought that the social stud-ies curriculum has had a mixed history—predominately conserva-tive in its purposes, but also at times incorporating progressive and even radical purposes. Stanley and Nelson organize the variations in social studies curriculum and instruction into three broad and not necessarily opposing categories: subject-centered social studies, civics-centered social studies, and issues-centered social studies.

Subject-centered approaches argue that the social studies cur-riculum derives its content and purposes from disciplines taught in higher education. Some advocates would limit social studies cur-riculum to the study of traditional history and geography, while others would also include the traditional social sciences (for ex-ample, anthropology, economics, political science, sociology, psychol-ogy). Still others would include inter- and multidisciplinary areas such as ethnic studies, law, women's studies, cultural studies, and gay/lesbian studies. The glue holding these various curricular views together is that each seeks to derive an organizing framework for the social studies curriculum based upon disciplinary knowledge from higher education. Some subject-centered advocates argue for cultural transmission, without multiculturalism (Ravitch 1990; Schlesinger 1991), while others are for using the disciplines as a means for stimulating critical thinking and diversity (chapters by Whelan and Epstein in this volume). For both groups, subject matter knowledge is paramount.

Civics-centered social studies is concerned with individual and social attitudes and behaviors more than with subject matter knowledge. Civic competence—or the ability and responsibility to interpret, understand, and act effectively as a member of one's society—is the unifying theme in this approach. As within the subject-centered approach, there are a wide spectrum of views from inculcating cultural traditions to promoting social action. They differ on the relative emphasis that should be given to uncritical loyalty, socially approved behaviors, and to social criticism and improvement. But they share the view that social studies is more than subject matter study and must be tied to civic competence. Examples of this view are Engle and Ochoa (1988) and Saxe (in this volume).

Issues-centered approaches propose that social studies is the examination of specific issues. Social as well as personal problems and controversies are the primary content of the curriculum. The views in this category range from personal development to social problems as the purpose of the social studies curriculum. Some would advocate the study of only perennial issues, while others emphasize current or personal issues, such as moral dilemmas and values clarification. Some advocates argue that social criticism or activism is the main reason for studying issues (for example, Evans in this volume), while others view this approach as a way to help students adapt to the society.

The three approaches to social studies described by Stanley and Nelson are not necessarily separate or opposing. Knowledge from the disciplines is used in each; none disagrees that one purpose of the social studies is citizenship education; and each accepts social studies as a valuable construct.

> Each of these approaches has at least one strand that advocates social studies as the transmission of socially approved ideas and another strand that advocates independent critical thinking or action. The three orientations differ in how each would approach either transmission or criticism: one primarily uses subject knowl-

edge; one uses character development; and one uses issues. [Stanley and Nelson 1994, p. 269]

These are important differences and it is likely that a mix of these orientations would be evident within a school and across individual teachers' careers.

Who Controls the Social Studies Curriculum?

Any response to this question hinges on your conception of curriculum. Curricular issues cannot be usefully discussed or analyzed apart from teachers' pedagogical practices (Ross, Cornett, and McCutcheon 1992). Indeed, as Whelan (chapter two) points out, even the curriculum commissions of the late nineteenth century recognized the crucial role of social studies teachers in achieving curricular goals. As will become evident in this and the following section, however, agreement on the importance of the teacher's role does not translate into consensus regarding the appropriate actions to take to improve or transform the curriculum.

While there are a myriad of definitions of *curriculum,* there is a single fundamental distinction that is useful in any analysis of curriculum—that is, the difference between the *formal* and the *enacted* curriculum. The formal curriculum is the explicit or official curriculum, embodied in published courses or study, state frameworks, textbooks, tests, or more recently curriculum standards efforts (for example, National Council for the Social Studies 1994). The enacted curriculum is best understood as the curriculum experienced by students. Cornbleth calls this the *social process curriculum.* Unlike the formal curriculum, the enacted curriculum is "not a tangible product but the actual day-to-day classroom interactions of teacher, students and ideas" (Cornbleth 1985, cited in Marker and Mehlinger, p. 834).

The current debates for the purpose and organization of the formal social studies curriculum are only the most recent waves in a sea of tensions between centralized and grassroots curriculum development that has marked the history of education in the United States. Curriculum development and reform efforts have long harbored a tension between approaches that rely on centralized efforts leading to a standard curriculum and grassroots democratic efforts that provide greater involvement for teachers, parents, students, and other local curriculum leaders in determining what is worthwhile to know and experience. Curriculum centralization has resulted from three major influences: legal decisions, policy efforts by governments, professional associations, and foundations, and published materials. Examples of the latter two influences will be sketched below.[1]

The centralizing influence of educational policy on curriculum can be seen as early as 1839 in Henry Barnard's first annual report as secretary to the Board of Commissioners of Common Schools in Connecticut, which raised the question of what the common school curriculum should be (Schubert 1991). Educational reform efforts in the 1890s attempted to define the nature of the school curriculum and featured efforts by both intellectual traditionalists (for example, W.T. Harris and Charles Eliot) and developmentalists (for example, Charles DeGarmo and Frank McMurry) to exercise control through a centralized curriculum (Kleibard 1987).

The social studies curriculum has been heavily influenced by policies of curriculum centralization. The roots of the contemporary social studies curriculum are found in the 1916 report of the NEA Committee on the Social Studies as well as the NEA Committee of Ten (1893) and AHA Committee of Seven (1899), which preceded it. The current pattern of topics and courses for secondary social studies is largely the result of recommendations of the 1916 committee. The pattern of course offerings in social studies, which has been consistent for most of the twentieth century, reflects a time in which many students completed only elementary or junior high school, thus United State history is offered in grades 5, 8, and 11 (Marker and Mehlinger 1992). Despite the changing demographics of school attendance, the pattern of course offerings have remained essentially unchanged:

K Self, school, community, home
1 Families
2 Neighborhoods
3 Communities
4 State history, geographic regions
5 United States history
6 World cultures, Western hemisphere
7 World geography or world history
8 United States history
9 Civics or world cultures

10 World history
11 United States history
12 American government

Efforts to centralize the curriculum through government mandates also have a long history. The debate over vocational education in the early 1900s embodied rhetoric similar to today's concerns for economic competitiveness. One assessment of the educational situation at the time argued that schools were failing to provide students with "industrial intelligence" and called for a shift in the orientation of secondary schools from "cultural" to vocational education (Krug 1969). The subsequent campaign for vocational education was modeled after Germany's dual system and ultimately produced the Smith-Hughes Act of 1917. Smith-Hughes fostered the transformation of the American high school from an elite institution into one for the masses by mandating that the states specify training needs, program prescriptions, standards and means for monitoring progress.

The dual system of education created by Smith-Hughes was reconceptualized in 1990 with the passage of the Perkins Vocational and Applied Technology Act. This provides a major incentive for the development of work education programs that integrate academic and vocational studies. The new law supports grassroots curriculum development by allocating 75 percent of its funds directly to local schools, rather than to the states, and giving priority to communities with the highest rates of poverty. This approach supports local grassroots initiatives of people who know best the needs and characteristics of economically distressed communities (Wirth 1992).

Curriculum frameworks produced by states are often accompanied by mandated standardized tests that insure the alignment of classroom practices with state frameworks (the Regents Examinations in New York state are one of the oldest examples). These frameworks are intended to influence textbook publishers and establish standards by which students, teachers, and schools will be assessed. In many cases, state curriculum frameworks represent a major step toward state control of what knowledge is of most worth (Cornbleth and Waugh 1995; Mathison 1991; Ross 1992). Although states (and, as we shall see, current curriculum standards projects) deny that these frameworks amount to "curriculum," their practical effects are the equivalent. This is particularly true when frameworks, standardized tests, and textbooks are aligned (Brooks 1991).

I have just hinted at the large-scale centralizing influence of education policies on curriculum. Resistance to curriculum centralization has always existed. There is a strong tradition of local school control in the United States and this has generally extended to curriculum development and implementation. The influence of John Dewey's philosophy of education has been a major resource for the resistance. Dewey argued that acquaintance with centralized knowledge must derive from situational concerns—that is, disciplinary knowledge must be attained by inquiring students in ways that have meaning for them.

William H. Kilpatrick's project method is an example of a grassroots approach to curriculum development that is clearly different from centralized curricula and based upon Dewey's philosophy (Kilpatrick 1918). The project method is very similar to the contemporary notion of thematic units, in which learning is approached as integrative, multifaceted, collaborative, responsive to students' varied needs and organized around a particular theme. In the project method, students and teachers took on a greater role in determining the curriculum because they were deemed in the best position to understand the personal and contextual foundations from which a meaningful and relevant curriculum could be constructed. Projects were pursued in small groups or as whole-class experiences:

> Knowledge from the disciplines would be brought to bear on the project when it was perceived as relevant. The essence of the project required that teachers and students develop the idea together. If students were fascinated by zoos, for instance all subjects (traditional and modern) could be related to a deepened understanding of zoos. [Schubert 1991, p. 107]

PUBLISHED MATERIALS

Textbooks have also been a major force standardizing the curriculum. For more than sixty years teachers have relied on textbooks as a primary instructional tool. In 1931, Bagley found that American students spent a significant portion of their school day in formal mastery of text materials (Bagley 1931 cited in McCutcheon 1995). A 1978 study of fifth-grade curricula found 78 percent of what students studied came from textbooks. A 1979 study found textbooks and related materials were the basis for 90 percent of instructional time in schools. In their review of research on the social studies curriculum, Marker and Mehlinger (1992) found about half of all social studies teachers depend upon a single textbook, and about 90 percent use no more than three.

Many states adopt textbooks on a statewide basis (Marker and Mehlinger 1992), and three large "adoption states" (California, Florida, and Texas) exert an enormous influence on the content of textbooks used nationwide. The textbook industry is highly competitive and the industry is dominated by a small number of large corporations; textbook companies modify their products to qualify for adoption in one of these states. As a result, the values and politics of adoption committees in those states influence curriculum nationally (Black 1967; Bowler 1978; Cornbleth and Waugh 1995).

In attempting to reach the widest range of purchasers, textbook publishers promote values (overtly and covertly) that maintain social and economic hierarchies and relationships supported by the dominant socioeconomic class (Apple 1986). James W. Loewen (1995) illustrates this at length in his analysis of United States history textbooks. For example, in a discussion of how history textbooks make white racism invisible, he notes:

> Although textbook authors no longer sugarcoat how slavery affected African Americans, they minimize white complicity in it. They present slavery virtually as uncaused, a tragedy, rather than a wrong perpetrated by some people on others. . . . Like their treatment of slavery, textbooks' new view of Reconstruction represents a sea change, past due, much closer to what the original sources for the period reveal, and much less dominated by white supremacy. However, in the way the textbooks structure their discussion, most of them inadvertently still take a white supremacist viewpoint. Their rhetoric makes African Americans rather than whites the "problem" and assumes that the major issue of Reconstruction was how to integrate African Americans into the system, economically and politically. . . . The archetype of African Americans as dependent on others begins . . . in textbook treatments of Reconstruction. . . . In reality, white violence, not black ignorance, was the key problem during Reconstruction. [Loewen 1995, p. 151]

In his analysis of the history of curriculum centralization, Schubert notes 1958 as a key turning point in educational policymaking. That year the National Defense Education Act helped to import disciplinary specialists to design curriculum packages for schools. In the social studies, these curriculum innovations were collectively called the New Social Studies. The purpose of the New Social Studies was to "capture the main ideas and current approaches to knowledge represented by the academic disciplines" (Marker and Mehlinger 1992, p. 838). These curriculum projects focused on inquiry methods and the *structure of the disciplines* approach. Although social studies specialists helped in the development of New Social Studies materials, the curricular focus was on the academic disciplines. These materials were not teacher proof, but they are exemplars of teachers-as-curriculum-conduit thinking (Ross 1994). Developers, who were primarily experts in academic disciplines, viewed teachers as implementors not active partners in the creation of classroom curriculum. Strategies for promoting the New Social Studies as well as other subject matter projects from this era, focused on preparing teachers to faithfully implement the developers' curricular ideas. For example, schools could not adopt and use the project *Man: A Course of Study* unless teachers were specially trained (Marker and Mehlinger 1992).

While the development and dissemination of the 1960s curriculum projects were well funded, they failed to make a major impact on classroom practices. Some have argued that the "failure" of the projects is attributable to technical problems, such as inadequate training of teachers to use the packages or lack of formative evaluation. In contrast:

> Proponents of grassroots democracy in curriculum offered the explanation that the failure was due to the blatant disregard of teachers and students in curriculum decision making. This is especially ironic inasmuch as those who promoted inquiry methods with the young neglected to allow inquiry by teachers and students about matters most fundamental to their growing lives, that is, inquiry about that which is most worthwhile to know and experience. [Schubert 1991, p. 114]

It is clear that in the past thirty years support for educational reform from industry, private foundations as well as the federal government, has produced a more capitalistic, less educator-oriented, and ultimately less democratic network of curriculum policy-makers.

CURRICULUM STANDARDS

It is still too early to assess the full impact of the current curriculum standards movement on the social studies curriculum. However, it is clear that curriculum centralization efforts are successfully transforming the formal curriculum in all areas and particularly in social studies (Ross, in press). The standards movement is a massive effort at curriculum centralization. Virtually all of the subject matter–based professional education groups have undertaken the creation of curriculum standards in recent years. Encouraged by the positive response to the development of standards for the mathematics curriculum and the availability of federal funding for such projects, social studies educators have taken up the development of curriculum standards with unparalleled zeal. There are now separate and competing curriculum standards for United States and global history, geography, economics, civics, and social studies.

Because the aim of these projects is to create a national educational system with uniform content and goals, ongoing debates and divisions within the field of social studies has intensified. The curriculum standards movement is a rationalized managerial approach to issues of curriculum development and teaching that attempts to define curricular goals; design assessment tasks based on these goals; set standards for the content of subject matter areas and grade level; and test students and report the results to the public. The intent is to establish standards for content and student performance levels.

The primary tension, today and historically, in curriculum reform efforts is between centralized and grassroots decision-making. When there are multiple participants and competing interests in the curriculum-making process, the question arises, Where does control reside? The curriculum standards movement in social studies represents an effort by policy elites to standardize the content and much of the practice of education. Operationally, curriculum standards projects in social studies are antidemocratic because they severely restrict the legitimate role of teachers and other educational professionals as well as the public in participating in the conversation about the origin, nature, and ethics of knowledge taught in the social studies curriculum. The curriculum standards movement ignores the most striking aspect of the teacher's role in curriculum development, which is its inevitability (Thornton 1991). Resources that might have been directed to assisting teachers to become better decision-makers have instead been channeled into a program dedicated to the development of schemes for preventing teachers from making curricular decisions.

The circumstances described above leads to the final question addressed in this chapter:

What is the Social Studies Teacher's Role in Relation to the Curriculum?[2]

With regard to curriculum development, the claim that "teachers make a difference" has most often meant that teachers make or break implementation efforts and consequently must receive the proper training to make it rather than break it (Parker 1987). This is the language of teachers as *curriculum conduits*, and it has been the dominant language of curriculum development this century. A fundamental assumption of most curriculum centralization efforts is that means (instruction) can be separated from the ends (curricular goals and objectives). Many teachers have internalized the means-ends distinction between their pedagogy and the curriculum. As a result, they view their professional role as instructional decision-makers not as curriculum developers (Thornton 1991).

What is clear from studies of teacher decision-making, however, is that teachers do much more than select teaching methods to implement formally adopted curricular goals. As Thornton argues, teacher beliefs about social studies subject matter and student thinking in social studies, as well as planning and instructional strategies, together function to create the enacted curriculum of the classroom—the day-to-day interactions among students, teachers, and subject matter.

The difference between the publicly declared formal curriculum and the curriculum experienced by students in social studies classrooms is considerable. The key to the curriculum experienced in social studies classrooms is the teachers:

> Teacher's beliefs about schooling, his or her knowledge of the subject area and of available materials and techniques, how he or she decides to put these together for the classroom—out of that process of reflection and personal inclination comes the day-by-day classroom experience of students. This is not to say that social studies classes are not affected by factors such as the characteristics of the students enrolled, but only to emphasize that the teacher plays the primary structuring role. [Shaver, Davis, and Helburn 1980]

Although powerful cultural and institutional forces work to shape the professional role and identity of teachers, we know that teachers are not merely passive recipients of the culture of schooling (and the means-ends distinction found within it). Teachers are actively involved in shaping the culture of schooling. For example, the New Social Studies was unsuccessful largely because teachers did not use the material or the innovative practices in their classrooms (Marker and Mehlinger 1992; Shaver, Davis, and Helburn 1980; Schubert 1991). This example illustrates the importance of focusing on the development of the enacted curriculum instead of the formal curriculum. The teachers' role in relation to the curriculum is more properly understood as "user-developer" rather than "users of teacher-proof curricula" (Ben-Peretz 1989).

There are three possible roles for teachers in curriculum implementation (Ben-Peretz 1989). First, teachers can use teacher-proof materials (designed to minimize the teacher's influence). This view of teachers was adopted at the turn of the twentieth century as history was becoming established as a school subject. "Good textbooks . . . were the basis of good teaching and the good textbook, in order to be published, prudently followed the guidance of the two preeminent national history committees" (Saxe 1991, p. 29). Arthur Schlesinger, Sr., a preeminent American historian in the early part of this century, put it this way: "whether we like it or not, the textbook not the teacher teaches the course" (Saxe 1991, p. 29). Schlesinger's thinking was adopted by many subsequent curriculum reformers as described above. This is clearly not a desirable role for professional teachers.

A second possible role for teachers in relation to the curriculum is as *active implementors*. In this role teachers are assumed to have impact on the implementation of curricular ideas, and curriculum developers create implementation strategies aimed at helping teachers understand the curricular innovation. The New Social Studies is an exemplar of this role for the teacher. Teachers were viewed as active implementors but not as full partners in the creation of the curriculum. Strategies for promoting the use of the New Social Studies materials focused on preparing teachers to faithfully implement the developers' curricular ideas. For example, schools could not adopt the MACOS program unless teachers were specially trained (Marker and Mehlinger 1992).

A third and most desirable role for teachers is as curriculum user-developers. From this perspective teachers are assumed to be full partners in development of the enacted curriculum. Teacher inquiry is a key element in the success of the curriculum, because it is inquiry directed at discovering curriculum potential that leads to the change and transformation of formal curriculum materials, and most importantly the development of new alternatives that are best suited for circumstances the teacher is working within.

The current curriculum standards movement highlights the contradiction between the views of teachers as active implementors or a user-developers. Ultimately, however, curriculum improvement depends upon teachers being more thoughtful about their work (see, for example, Cornett et al. 1992; Parker and McDaniel 1992). The most effective means of improving the curriculum is to improve the education and professional development afforded teachers. As Whelan has argued elsewhere, teachers need to be better prepared to exercise the curricular decision-making responsibilities that are an inherent part of instructional practice.

Early in this century John Dewey identified the intellectual subservience of teachers as a central problem facing progressive educators in their efforts to improve the curriculum. Dewey saw the solution to the problem as the development of teaching as professional work. Prospective teachers, Dewey argued:

> Should be given to understand that they not only are permitted to act on their own initiative, but that they are expected to do so and that their ability to take hold of a situation for themselves would be a more important factor in judging them than their following any particular set methods or scheme. [Dewey 1904, pp. 27–28]

In the context of the curriculum standards movement, Dewey's diagnosis and treatment are still appropriate today.

Conclusion

In this chapter I have posed three fundamental questions about the social studies curriculum: (1) What is the social studies curriculum? (2) Who controls the social studies curriculum? (3) What is the social studies teacher's role in relation to the curriculum? In responding to these questions I identified a series of tensions and contradictions that have shaped the field of social studies historically and that still affect it today.

In response to the first question, I identified the tension between the study of academic history and efforts of social meliorists as setting the stage for a long-standing conflict between advocates of subject-centered and civics or issued-centered social studies. In addition, it was argued that the purposes of the social studies

curriculum have essentially been defined by the relative emphasis given to cultural transmission or critical thinking in the
curriculum.

The second question led to an examination of the long-standing tensions between curriculum centralization and grassroots curriculum development. The recent curriculum standards movement
was discussed in this section and used as a bridge to the consideration of the final question regarding the role of the social studies
teacher in relation to the curriculum. In the closing section I argued that teachers are the key element in curriculum improvement
and that curriculum change in the social studies will be achieved
only through the improved education and professional development
opportunities for teachers.

My intention has been to present this series of tensions and
contradictions as a heuristic for understanding the dynamic nature
of the social studies. It would be a mistake to treat them as definitive oppositionals, however, it is the struggles over these contradictions that has shaped the nature of the social studies curriculum
in the past and continues to define it today.

CHAPTER TWO

History as the Core of Social Studies Education

Michael Whelan

Introduction

Disagreement about curriculum issues in social studies education is not new or reason for undue concern. On the contrary, since social studies emerged as a school subject early in the twentieth century, its development has been characterized, and indeed often energized, by a diversity of opinion regarding its nature, its purposes, and, as a result, its most appropriate curriculum organization (Hertzberg 1981; Lybarger 1991). Fundamental questions—whether social studies is a unified field of study or a cluster of separate disciples, for example—have been considered and contested for decades.

The debate that has erupted recently, however, between advocates of a history centered curriculum and those calling for a curriculum based on the interdisciplinary study of current social issues has become so adversarial as to threaten the field with factionalism and thereby undercut the pluralism from which social studies has frequently benefited. Rather than engaging in a critical yet constructive discussion of their respective positions, prominent spokespersons for both history and issues-centered curriculum models have taken rigid, uncompromising stands, devised historical interpretations to bolster their competing claims of legitimacy, and assailed each other's proposals as antiintellectual, anti-egalitarian, and a threat to the nation's basic institutions (e.g., Bradley Commission 1988, 1989; Evans 1989b, 1989c; Nelson 1992; Ravitch 1985, 1989b).

Furthermore, like many educational policy disputes, this debate is increasingly becoming an end in itself and, as such, of little practical consequence for social studies teachers. It is not that the issues involved are inconsequential, but that they have been confused and obscured by people on both sides of the question pressing ever more arcane or irrelevant arguments in an effort to gain some dubious debating advantage. The recent spat (Barth et al. 1991) about the relative merits of history and social studies as academic disciplines, for example, has done little but lend credence to James Leming's (1989) contention of a growing, dysfunctional gulf between social studies theorists and classroom practitioners.

In this chapter, I address the central issue of this debate directly, but, hopefully, in a constructive, less contentious manner that draws on strengths of both history and issues-centered positions. Specifically, I argue for the adoption of a history-centered curriculum, but also argue that such a curriculum should be consistent with traditional ideals of social studies education, including, above all, social studies' special responsibility for citizenship education. To this end, the chapter is divided into two sections: in the first I analyze the early history of social studies education in an effort to clarify the balance between historical study and the study of current issues that the first curriculum committees in social studies sought to strike; and in the second I suggest some guidelines for social studies teachers today to follow in implementing a history-centered curriculum true to this original vision of the subject.

The Origins of Social Studies Reconsidered

As mentioned above, each side in this debate has turned to history to substantiate its position. Each, that is, has sought "to prove" through historical analysis that the curriculum model it proposes is more in accord with "the original intent" of the founders of social studies education. Like most history written to justify a preconceived conclusion, however, both interpretations are somewhat misleading. Furthermore, and perhaps not surprising considering their adversarial balance, both suffer from similar analytical problems. Two are particularly telling. The first involves a question of periodization and the second a *thin,* over simple notion of social studies' theoretical foundations.

With regard to the first problem, the question is whether the report of the Committee on Social Studies in 1916 or two reports written during the 1890s—one by the subcommittee on History,

Civil Government, and Political Economy of the Committee of Ten (1893) and the other a follow-up report by the American Historical Association's Committee of Seven on History in Schools (1899)—better represents the seminal turning point from which social studies subsequently developed as a core component of the school curriculum. The second problem stems from a tendency on the part of both sides in this debate to concentrate on the ideas of a few curriculum theorists while ignoring those of others who also contributed to social studies' original conceptualization.

Diane Ravitch (1985, 1989a, 1989b) presents the most detailed historical argument in support of the history-centered position.[1] In general, her analysis consists of a blistering critique of the Social Studies Committee report, which she says recommended a greatly diminished role for the study of history in schools. This, she argues, was part of a broader reform movement in education intended "to make the work of schools more practical" by having them assume "custodial" and "vocational" responsibilities for "the vast horde of poor . . . immigrant children" who crowded into classrooms during the decades prior to World War I (1985, pp. 124–25). Specifically, Ravitch says the Social Studies Committee called on schools to eliminate the programs in history education proposed by the Committees of Ten and Seven, programs she considers exemplary. In fact, she refers to the widespread adoption of these programs during the first fifteen years of the twentieth century as the "high-water mark" for historical study in schools (1985, p. 124). Had "the story" ended then, she laments, "most high schools would [currently] be offering at least three years of history, including ancient history, European history, and American history." Such a curriculum, in her judgment, if "brought up to date . . . [to] include histories of non-Western societies," would certainly represent "good news" for history education in schools today (1985, pp. 123–24).

But, unfortunately, according to Ravitch, the news has been anything but good since 1915. The Committee on Social Studies, dominated by "educational progressives" who thought of schools "in terms of their social function" more than their educational function,[2] recommended that schools replace existing programs in history education with a new program of social studies education. The progressives, Ravitch argues, thought the study of history "useless" for the large majority of students not intending to go to college. They therefore insisted that all students study social studies, a subject whose goals and content were specifically designed to meet the progressives' crass "utilitarian [test of] social efficiency." Accordingly, Ravitch says socialization skills and citizenship training displaced the chronological study of history in schools (1985, pp. 124–29). Subsequent efforts to reexamine the social studies curriculum," she continues, bringing her argument up to date, have done "little to resuscitate the position of history" because "the ideology of social efficiency" still prevails among curriculum theorists and educational policy-makers (1985, p. 130). Thus, she concludes that history's "rightful place in the schools" has been denied throughout most of the twentieth century, much to the educational detriment of the country in general (1985, pp. 130–31).

David Warren Saxe (1991, 1992a, 1992b) presents the most comprehensive counter-argument in support of the issues-centered position. He agrees with Ravitch that social studies was intended by its founders as an alternative to history education, but vigorously disputes her evaluation of the relative merits of the two subjects. Like Ravitch, he argues that a group of "social studies insurgents" (his term for those Ravitch refers to as "educational progressives") sought a "complete reformation" of existing history programs, but believes that this effort, though never fully realized, was enlightened, not ill-advised.

If possible, Saxe is even more emphatic than Ravitch in drawing a distinction between history and social studies education. He unequivocally asserts that social studies is not derivative of history education, but arose instead from "its own set of unique beginnings" (1991, p. 1). Early in the twentieth century, Saxe maintains, leading social studies insurgents sought to supplant, and not merely revise, the history curriculum that had been "imposed" on schools during the 1890s by the Committees of Ten and Seven whose members were interested only in the intellectual development of the college-bound elite. In its place, the insurgents, who Saxe says dominated the Social Studies Committee proceedings, proposed an entirely new course of study, one that was grounded in the social sciences, not history; that was inspired by the activist spirit of the social welfare movement; and most important, that was intended to instill in every student a worthy sense of social consciousness through the study of current social issues (passim). Thus, for Saxe (1992a), the endorsement of this radical curriculum initiative by the Social Studies Committee, which he says "launched [the subject] into the mainstream of public education" (1992a, p. 161), represents a real revolution in the field and not a program of piecemeal reform (1992a, passim).

In sum, therefore, while Ravitch and Saxe strongly disagree about the merits of social studies education, their respective interpretations of its emergence as a school subject are remarkably similar. Both claim that the Social Studies Committee recommended the disestablishment of history education in schools and the institution in its place of an entirely new course of study. This analysis is simple and straightforward, and therefore appealing to partisans in the current debate about the social studies curriculum. It is also inaccurate, however, especially with regard to two fundamental issues, and therefore misleading.

First, the composition of the Social Studies Committee was much more diverse, both professionally and philosophically, than either Ravitch or Saxe admits. In this regard, it reflects the heterogeneity of educational reform in general during the progressive era (Hertzberg 1989; Kliebard 1986). Second, and more important, the Social Studies Committee did not recommend the disestablishment of history education, but rather a series of reforms in the way history was organized for instruction.

Unlike the Committees of Ten and Seven, which were composed chiefly of history professors from colleges and universities, the Social Studies Committee included teachers and administrators from public and private schools around the country; teacher educators from normal schools and colleges of education; representatives from the United States Bureau of Education; and subject matter specialists from various academic disciplines, not just history. Some members, as Ravitch and Saxe maintain, sought to lessen, if not eliminate, history's place in the curriculum. But others, including the only two women to serve on the Committee, were active members of regional history teachers associations who wanted to reform, but certainly not dispense with, the study of history in schools. Still others were more concerned with pedagogical issues, especially as they related to nascent notions of child development, than issues of curriculum content. The influence of each of these groups is evident in the Committee's final report: that of the social studies insurgents in recommendations to institute two new courses in civics education; that of the history reformers in proposals to redesign existing courses in history education; and that of the pedagogy experts in suggestions, often illustrated by specific examples, to improve methods of teaching (passim). For the purposes of this chapter, however, the courses the Committee proposed for adoption and their arrangement are particularly important because these recommendations reflect the Committee's efforts to reconcile the ideas of the insurgents with those of the history reformers.

In an innovative break with customary curriculum patterns, the Social Studies Committee did not recommend a unified sequence of courses, but instead a six-year program divided into two distinct cycles: a "junior cycle" for grades 7–9 and a "senior cycle" for grades 10–12 (pp. 11–13).[3] At the end of each cycle, the Committee proposed a culminating course in civics: "community civics" in grade 9 (pp. 22–34) and a course about the "problems of democracy" in grade 12 (pp. 52–56). The aim and organization of these civics courses—to cultivate the habits of intelligent and active citizenship (pp. 23, 52) through the study of concrete social problems (pp. 34, 53)—were clearly drawn from the curriculum paradigm advanced by the insurgents.

The courses recommended for the other grades, however, (i.e., grades 7 and 8 in the junior cycle and grades 10 and 11 in the senior cycle) were just as clearly drawn from the curriculum ideal envisioned by the history reformers. For the most part, these courses involved the study of European and American history. As the Committee repeatedly emphasized (pp. 11–12, 15–22, 35–52), however, such study was intended to be thoroughly integrated within the overall cyclic curriculum structure. In other words, the Committee intended the study of history to be adapted as fully as possible to the aim and organization of the capstone courses in civics (pp. 21–22, p. 37).

To facilitate this integration, the Committee spoke at length about the principles underlying its conception of history education (pp. 21–22, 36–52).[4] First, it defined the ultimate purpose of historical study as helping students understand the relationship between the past and the present, and not simply understand the past (pp. 21, 41, 42). Accordingly, it said the primary theme of the history courses it recommended should be the evolutionary development of a society or a culture, with special emphasis placed on those aspects of the past that helped make the present intelligible. Second, the Committee declared that it was "high time" history education were brought into "the closest possible relation with the actual life and future duties of the great majority of those who fill [the] public schools" (p. 50). Thus, it strongly advised that the "selection of a topic in history and the amount of attention given to it should depend . . . chiefly upon the degree to which such topic can be related to the present life interests of the pupil, or can be used by him [sic] in his present process of growth" (p. 44).

Through the years, this sentence has probably been the most controversial—and misunderstood—in the entire report. Apologists and critics alike have singled it out, claiming that the curriculum standard it established represents all that is right with the report or all that is wrong with it. Recently, for example, some in the issues-centered camp (e.g., Evans 1989a; Saxe 1992b) have argued that this standard obviously endorses a presentist, sociological approach to social studies education. Others, in the history-centered camp (e.g., Jackson and Jackson 1989; Ravitch 1985), have complained that it legitimizes a curriculum based on little more than students' immediate personal interests. Neither interpretation is wellfounded, however. As evident in the three examples the Committee offered to illustrate its standard—the relevance, respectively, of the war of 1812, the architecture of ancient Athens, and the development of medieval craft guilds to some of the more pressing international, urban, and labor issues the country faced at the time the report was written (pp. 44–47)—the Social Studies Committee clearly intended students to study history, but believed that the educational merit of such study was the extent to which it enlightened the present (and the future) as well as the past. Knowledge of the past, in other words, was not valued by the Committee as an end in itself, but as a means of helping students understand "the most vital problems of the present" (p. 41). Studied in this way, the Committee was convinced, history would contribute to the ultimate objective of social studies education, which it defined as intelligent and active citizenship. In fact, its members believed that the study of history had a special potential in this regard, because no other subject contributed so directly to the development of a clear conception of American nationality, a strong sense of patriotism, a keen understanding of civic responsibility, and a just and sympathetic attitude toward other nations and their peoples (p. 39).

Clearly, the curriculum the Committee envisioned was different than that typically taught in schools at the time. The standard the Committee suggested for the selection of curriculum topics called for teachers to expand the focus of historical study far beyond the customary limits of political issues and military campaigns. Specifically, the Committee advised the inclusion of many additional topics about the history of "common men and common things" (pp. 50–52). Such curriculum expansion, the Committee understood, would necessitate a synthesizing, interdisciplinary approach to historical study in which students and teachers regularly drew upon concepts and methods of inquiry developed in the social sciences (p. 36). But the study of history, along with the study of civics, remained the central component of the curriculum the Social Studies Committee recommended.

Thus, the Social Studies Committee report, despite the arguments by Ravitch and Saxe to the contrary, is misunderstood as a revolutionary document. It called for significant reforms in the history programs proposed by the Committees of Ten and Seven, but not their elimination. In fact, a comparative analysis of the three reports reveals considerable continuity, especially with regard to fundamental recommendations (Whelan 1989). All three reports, for example, recommended that history or social studies hold a central place in secondary school education; that it be studied by students in every year of their secondary schooling; that it be considered equal in value and importance to other required subjects; and that it be organized around major themes of European and American history (Committee of Ten, passim; Committee of Seven, passim; Committee on Social Studies, passim). In addition, all three identified a broad social purpose to which history or social studies should contribute as the underlying rationale for its inclusion in a secondary school curriculum. The Committee of Ten referred to this purpose as "prepar[ation] for the duties of life" (Committee of Ten, p. 51), the Committee of Seven as "a sense of the duties and responsibilities of citizenship" (Committee of Seven, p. 17), and the Social Studies Committee as "social efficiency," which it defined more specifically as "the cultivation of good citizenship" (Committee on Social Studies, p. 9).

There is no question that the Social Studies Committee attached greater significance than the earlier committees to the development of citizenship values. But this discrepancy in emphasis can hardly be considered revolutionary. Rather, the real revolution in history and social studies education—and in secondary school education in general—is more properly associated with the report of the Committee of Ten (Whelan 1991, 1992). Prior to this landmark report, secondary schools were clearly the weakest link in the nation's educational system. Few students attended, mostly those planning to go to college, and the curriculum as a result was largely defined by college admission standards, which emphasized the study of "classical" subjects. Within this curriculum framework, history was widely regarded as but an adjunct to instruction in the languages and culture of ancient Greece and Rome. Very few schools offered students the opportunity to study history for more than a semester or perhaps a year. Furthermore, the most common method of teaching history was rote recitation.

The Committee of Ten, in measured yet unambiguous terms, rejected this system as wholly inadequate (pp. 162–65, passim). Its members unanimously recommended that the study of "history and kindred subjects" should be a substantial part of every student's secondary school education (pp. 170–74); that such study should include significantly more subject matter about "modern" historical topics (pp. 174–83); and that teachers should rely on a variety of "improved methods" of instruction that would regularly require students to exercise their powers of critical judgment (pp. 185–201). The subsequent reports of the Committee of Seven and the Social Studies Committee reaffirmed these fundamental principles; but, because the study of history was more firmly established in schools in 1916 than it had been earlier, it was less urgent for the Social Studies Committee to justify history's place in the curriculum. Thus members felt free to clarify the type of history most conducive to the "conscious and constant . . . cultivation of good citizenship" (p. 9, passim).

All three committees, however, understood that the successful implementation of the curriculum and instructional reforms they recommended would depend to a great extent on the efforts of individual teachers. "Above all," as the Committee of Ten advised, "the teacher must keep up with [developments in the field] . . . and . . . also [pay] special attention to effective methods of imparting instruction" (pp. 186–87). In less explicit but no less forceful terms, the Committee of Seven (pp. 113–18) and the Social Studies Committee made the same basic point (pp. 51–52). In other words, the members of all three committees understood that curriculum and instructional reform would succeed or fail on a classroom-by-classroom basis.

Some Guidelines for Instituting a History-Centered Curriculum

Teachers are "key" in determining the curriculum that students experience (Shaver, Davis, and Helburn 1980; Thornton 1991). If the myriad decisions they make in this regard are divided into two broad categories—instructional strategy decisions and decisions about curriculum content—research indicates that social studies teachers feel more responsibility for the former than the latter

(Thornton pp. 241–45). Decisions about the curriculum, most believe, are properly the province of "official" educational agencies, school-district committees or, by default, textbook publishing companies. As teachers, they see their role as simply "teaching" the curriculum, not "defining" it. Unfortunately, research also indicates that the teaching strategies social studies teachers rely on most often—teacher-dominated, textbook-driven lecture and discussion—often fail to stimulate high-level cognition among students (Thornton p. 245).

The implementation of a history-centered curriculum consistent with social studies' ultimate objective of active, enlightened citizenship will require considerable reform of this pattern of instructional practice. Teachers must assume more responsibility for the content of the courses they teach, and also alter classroom routines, so that students are regularly engaged in activities that promote complex, critical thinking.

Such reform, however, at least according to some social studies educators (Evans 1992; Nelson 1990, 1992) will be difficult, if not impossible, to achieve if the curriculum is history-centered. History, they claim, is peculiarly predisposed to ineffective teaching practice, and tends therefore to result in inappropriate educational experiences for students. Ronald Evans, for example, says that the study of history "inspire[s] didactic forms of teaching in which knowledge is passively accepted by students and stored away for [some uncertain] later use"; that it "devalues the lived experiences of students and teachers and the cultural knowledge that all parties bring to the classroom"; that it serves as a "forum for a great deal of non-critical chronicling" in which "knowledge [is valued solely] for the sake of knowing"; and, perhaps most damning, that history "frequently serve[s] as a subtle means of oppression by emphasizing the stories of dominant elites, glorifying national heroes, minimizing the contributions of persons of color and de-emphasizing or omitting controversial questions" (pp. 313–14).

While these generalization may accurately describe the way history is taught in many schools, there is nevertheless no reason to suppose that the cause of these problems is rooted in the subject matter of history. Neither logic nor research supports such a conclusion. To suggest that ineffective teachers will somehow become more effective if they simply teach something other than history is an oversimplification of the complexities involved in organizing classroom instruction. Curriculum reform, in other words, whether history-centered or not, is highly unlikely by itself to transform what is widely regarded as sterile, uninspired classroom practice in social studies education (Engle 1990; Goodlad 1984; Shaver, Davis, and Helburn 1980; Superka, Hawke, and Morrissette 1980). Research, though sketchy, moreover, indicates that social studies teachers have varied their teaching styles very little, if at all, as curriculum emphases have changed through the years (Cuban 1991; Franklin 1990; Shaver 1987; Wiley 1977). Rather, a "few key patterns" of instructional practice have dominated the field throughout the twentieth century (Cuban p. 203). To attribute this "pervasive constancy" to the single factor of historical subject matter is again a simplistic analysis that challenges both research-based and experience-based knowledge about social studies teaching (pp. 205–6).

Still, the critique by Evans underscores two points of fundamental importance: first, that history's potential to promote worthy citizenship values is undermined if it is taught in a way that contradicts sound pedagogical practice; and second, that a history-centered curriculum in which controversial questions are avoided or deemphasized, or the experiences and perspectives of certain groups of people are ignored or misrepresented, is more akin to indoctrination than a justifiable conception of social studies education. Research about instruction in history (Downey and Levstik 1988, 1991) demonstrates that students learn best when they are active, not passive; creative, and not merely receptive; and when they are put in positions to exercise their powers of critical judgment, and not simply required to recall (and periodically regurgitate) bits of factual information. In other words, students studying history should be involved in the interrelated processes of constructing knowledge and meaning for themselves. Such practice is not only grounded in sound pedagogical principle, but also entails intellectual skills and attitudes consistent with the goal of active, enlightened citizenship.

Effective instructional practice, though necessary, is nevertheless insufficient, however. Curriculum content must also contribute to social studies' citizenship goals. To do so, as the Social Studies Committee explicitly advised, students should study those aspects of the past that continue to affect their lives as individuals and as members of social groups. Classroom teachers, therefore, in light of their close, personal contact with students, must take ultimate responsibility for curriculum decisions. As they do, at least four interrelated considerations should guide their decision-making process.

First, a history-centered curriculum should not be centered solely on the past. Rather, students studying history should ask questions of the past that are related to issues presently affecting their daily lives. If teachers are to facilitate such a "dialogue" between the past and the present, they cannot teach the "same old stuff" year after year, but must revise curriculum content on a regular basis. As the conditions within which students live inevitably change, the topics teachers include in a history-centered curriculum must change accordingly. Some topics—such as slavery and immigration in a United States history course, for example—will rarely, if ever, be omitted; but the emphasis and perspective these "perennials" receive, and the decisions teachers make about other topics to include will depend to a great extent on ever-changing social circumstances. While it is true that the past never changes, it is also true, and more important for instructional purposes, that the present significance of the past is continually evolving. Thus, a historical issue that may be essential for students to study today, may just as well be a matter of mere antiquarian curiosity sometime in the future. The historical significance of the international crises involving the Quemoy and Matsu Islands during the 1950s is admittedly an extreme example, but one that highlights the fundamental point: many curriculum decisions appropriate for one time or one group of students are not necessarily appropriate for all times or all students.

Teachers' responsibility to adjust the curriculum to meet the needs of students also raises questions about the advisability of establishing national curriculum standards for history education. Such standards, in all likelihood, will restrict the curriculum flexibility so essential to a meaningful course of study.[5] "No one [historical] account," as the Social Studies Committee wisely observed, can possibly "meet the needs of all [students]" (p. 41). And the advice implicit in this sage observation is no less true today than it was in 1916. Indeed, in the ever-increasing complexity of modern life, it seems the more things change, the more things change more. Any effort to standardize the content of a history-centered curriculum, therefore, no matter how well-intentioned those defining the standards may be, assumes, and erroneously so, that all students will always need to ask the same types of questions of the past.

While it may be worthwhile to consider the adoption of national standards regarding the skills involved in asking and answering historical questions (that is, the basic investigative skills needed to engage in historical study), the establishment of curriculum content standards would clearly be shortsighted. Decisions about what a particular group of students should study are best left to classroom teachers, and not some remote national committee.

At least one generalization about curriculum content is appropriate, however: if a history-centered curriculum is to inform issues of present concern to students, it should include a wider range of topics than has typically been the norm. The Social Studies Committee made the same point more than seventy-five years ago, but it was not until the last quarter-century or so that historians began to produce the type of scholarship needed to make a more inclusive conception of history education a real possibility (Grob and Billias 1987; Kammen 1980). Now, however, new scholarship in many areas of study previously ignored or poorly apprehended by historians—issues about women's history, ethnic history, cultural and intellectual history, community and local history, urban history, family history, and many other topics often categorized under the general heading of "social history"—hold the potential to transform the traditional history curriculum. No longer must so much attention be focused on questions about military and political decisions viewed from the perspective of the decision-makers. Instead, students may study many other issues often of more immediate import to their lives.

Furthermore, this new historical scholarship often involves innovative interdisciplinary methods of investigation and analysis, and, in many cases, also entails or encourages the consideration of historical phenomena from more than one point of view. Thus, the infusion of the curriculum with topics arising from this scholarship may enhance history's educative potential in a number of ways. In addition to helping students better understand a wider and more relevant range of historical issues, it may also help them appreciate the central role of interpretation in historical study and the crucial relationship between empathy, tolerance, and the maintenance of democratic institutions. Provision should be made therefore for students to become familiar with the content and methods of inquiry of this new historical scholarship. To do so, a history-centered curriculum should include numerous opportunities for students to study nontraditional topics (crime, health care, and formal education) and traditional topics from nontraditional points of view (e.g., from the "bottom-up," as well as the "top-down").

Provision should also be made for students to study things that never happened. This may sound odd, perhaps even absurd, in a history-centered curriculum, but it is nevertheless important. If the study of history is to contribute to the goal of active, enlightened citizenship, students, as Shirley Engle (1990) has suggested, should regularly consider history in the "hypothetical mood." In other words, they should consider how things might have been, and not simply study how they actually were. Such reflection is particularly valuable when analyzing political or public policy issues, which are likely to remain, and rightfully so, at the heart of a history-centered curriculum. In many cases, however, these issues cannot be understood fully or evaluated fairly without considering the likely consequences of possible alternatives.

Some may criticize this sort of inquiry as mere speculation and inappropriate therefore to historical study; but counter-factual analysis can often be very instructive. How, for example, is one to evaluate the policies of Lincoln or Franklin Roosevelt without considering the range of possible options open to them? Or how is one to understand historical decisions that have been made about transportation, immigration, and weapons production, to cite but a few public policy issues, without asking questions about how these things might have been decided differently? Choosing among options on the basis of rational inquiry is the essence of democratic citizenship; the systematic study of historical alternatives should therefore be an essential part of a history-centered curriculum.

There is, however, a still more basic understanding about the nature of human existence that the study of historical alternatives can illuminate. Ironically, this understanding is often lost in the course of more conventional history instruction. The past, it is essential for students to understand, was not preordained and could have been otherwise. It was determined to a great extent, much as the future will be determined, by decisions people made or failed to make. Studying history without considering its possible alternatives can obscure this fundamental point, and leave students with the profoundly mistaken impression that the past was somehow determined apart from human volition. Such an impression can contribute to feelings of alienation, powerlessness, and disaffection, feelings clearly antithetical to the citizenship goals social studies seeks to instill.

Finally, a history-centered curriculum should be organized around the study of historical conditions, and not just historical events. Disproportionate attention to the latter can quickly degenerate into superficial chronicling of little educative value or meaning to students. The analysis of conditions underlying historical events can lead quite naturally, however, to enlightening comparative studies of similar or analogous conditions in the present. Questions about gender and familial relations that developed in rural/frontier environments in the United States during the nineteenth century, for example, will likely raise questions among students about the way these relations have developed in urban/suburban environments during the twentieth century. The educational values involved in comparative studies are similar in many ways to those involved in analyzing historical alternatives; but such comparisons also help resolve a more practical curriculum problem in history education. Too often the study of current or recent social issues is confined to the last two weeks of the year in a history program based on adherence to rigid chronology or restricted to a weekly "current events day" in which issues are considered in an ad hoc, decontextualized fashion. Neither option is satisfactory. Comparing social conditions through time is certainly preferable, for it provides students with a meaningful framework within which to consider current issues on a regular basis.

Chronology should not be abandoned in the interest of relevance, however. To do so would not be wise and is not necessary. Many of today's most urgent social issues have long histories and can be addressed within a chronologically ordered course of study that allows for regular historical comparisons. Moreover, social issues are historical phenomena and therefore, in most cases, best studied within a history-centered framework. To do otherwise, to study social issues seriatim apart from their historical context—to study environmental issues during the first half of the 10th grade and issues about war and peace during the second half, for example— will only add to the inauthenticity of social studies education. Issues that affect students' lives, like all other social issues, do not occur in isolation; each is always part of a crowded social agenda and as a result must compete with others for public attention and the allocation of scarce resources. Within this context, different issues, even those seemingly quite distinct, are inevitably linked: decisions about one affect the range of possible decisions that can be made about others.

Such interrelated complexity is the reality of human existence, and the social studies curriculum should be organized in a way that embraces this reality and thereby helps students to understand it. Urban violence, for example, is a long-standing social problem that is part of a far-reaching web of social issues; if it is studied apart from this web, it is likely to appear less complicated than it actually is and lead students to believe that it can be solved by some simplistic scheme or, even more mistakenly, that it is caused and sustained by some nebulous conspiracy. "For every complex problem," H. L. Mencken cautioned in typically acerbic fashion, "there is a simple solution that is usually wrong." Studying social issues apart from their historical context would seem such a solution.

Conclusion

No matter how the social studies curriculum is constituted, whether history-centered, issues-centered, or otherwise, it will never be problem-free. Certain curriculum dilemmas—breadth versus depth, chronology versus themes, dominant culture versus particular culture, teacher as advocate versus teacher as neutral—are either unique to or particularly acute in social studies education. They will never be fully or finally resolved. The point, therefore, to paraphrase Winston Churchill, is not that a history-centered curriculum is perfect, only that it is better than any other arrangement.

History's claim to a central and unifying position in social studies education, however, is based on more than relative expediency. It stems instead from the more profound understanding that the nature of human existence is essentially historical. Some may quickly counter that human existence is social, cultural, political, economic, and geographic as well; but these aspects of human existence are but abstractions if considered apart from the course of human history. The complex relationships within and among groups that is the subject matter of sociology, for example, are in fact historical phenomena. The same is true of the subject matter of anthropology, cultural geography, economics, and political science. All analyze historical phenomena, phenomena understood most fully as they actually happened, within a historical context. Indeed, whatever meaning life may hold is largely derived from reflecting upon experience; and human experience, in all its variability and developmental complexity, is the subject matter of history. Perhaps, that is why all peoples have always studied history. In one way or another, it explains who they are.

History, in other words, is the only social subject open to the whole range of human experience and its development through time. It is distinctively disposed, therefore, to draw upon and synthesize knowledge and ideas from all other fields of study. For these reasons, it is also the most natural and best suited subject around which to organize social studies education. If historical study is based on a few fundamental principles—specifically, that students should actively construct meaning for themselves; that the study of history should focus on the relationship between the past and the present, and not just the past; that history's significance is ever-evolving; that its meaning is often a matter of perspective; and that things that never happened are often as important as things that did—a history-centered curriculum can provide students with a most insightful, authentic, and enlightening course of study.

CHAPTER THREE

The Unique Mission of Social Studies

David Warren Saxe

Social studies is ideally suited for those public schools that have identified the need to further the developing civic competence of elementary, middle, and secondary school students. In these settings, civic competence (activated as something students both practice and consciously work to acquire) becomes the goal and social studies the primary means to achieve the goal. Loosely constructed, social studies for civic competence has two overlapping central aims: to provide experiences for students:

- to acquire as well as to have access to knowledge necessary for competent, active citizenship within local, state, regional, national, and international settings; and
- to become familiar with and to practice the skills and dispositions required for liberal-democratic citizenship.

Liberal-democratic thinking rests upon several key principles. Although the precise working order or application of liberal-democratic principles are certainly debatable, the general spirit of liberal-democratic thinking has been relatively consistent throughout the history of the United States. Because actual teaching contexts and conditions vary widely in the United States, you might want to approach the construction of your personal foundation for the teaching of social studies for civic competence with a strong measure of flexibility. In order to explore the possibilities for teaching about civic competence, the following list represents an overview of liberal-democratic principles that embrace the knowledge, skills, and dispositions that are necessary for students to both understand and practice. In brief, social studies for civic competence:

- enables open participation on public issues that includes a meaningful voice and role in community and societal affairs;
- ensures access to information for the purpose of responsible decision-making, to develop an educated electorate;
- acknowledges the diversity of human forms and ideas, including an awareness toward various creeds, religious beliefs, capacities, opinions, and other personally held convictions;
- supports equal treatment and consideration of all citizens on matters with social implications;
- desires maintenance of and a reasoned respect for law, property, and human rights;
- highlights the acceptance of social obligations to reciprocate service and loyalty to society in exchange for the protection and promotion of individual liberty.

Why Do Young Citizens Need Civic Competence?

Civic competence is a critical part of every citizen's education. The primary question for social studies teachers to grapple with is what makes civic competence so important. As found in the principles above, liberal-democratic thinking rests upon two competing concepts: freedom and control. Although the community must support and defend the freedom of its citizens, individuals must agree to follow rules that permit the community's existence. As much as individuals may aspire toward liberal-democracy, one cannot be simultaneously free while being held under control. The juxtaposition of freedom and control generates paradoxical conditions for individuals of the community. For public schools, in particular, there is an obligation to promote both the freedom of the individual, as well as to reinforce the individual's responsibility toward the community. The exercise of these twin obligations creates problems for teachers as well as students. A sampling of questions:

- How do I help students learn about their freedom, if they refuse to sit still?

- If I make students sit still (with threats of punishment or penalties), will they ever learn how to express their freedom?
- If I allow students to study what they want, what happens if they study things that go off the subject?
- If I force students to complete activities from prepackaged worksheets, am I stifling creativity?

When I began teaching twenty years ago, I believed that the good teacher was one whose classes showed no outward signs of discipline problems. The bad teacher was the one who had a noisy classroom of students moving about without apparent reason. Controlled students implied that the acquisition of knowledge, skills, and dispositions was taking place; uncontrolled students indicated the failure of such acquisitions. Following the lead of my mentor-teachers, the way a social studies teacher taught about freedom was to *tell* students about freedom of expression, independence, decision-making, and critical thinking. The way a social studies teacher taught about control was to demonstrate it directly with students. Thus, both freedom and control were supposedly taught by benign imposition. The idea of creating situations or conditions where students could explore freedom *and* learn about control was not only unhealthy for students, but teachers. It seems the culture of the school supported the belief that those new teachers who remained employed could "control" their students; those who permitted too much freedom were fired.

Either as a participant or observer, since your earliest recollections of school, you have been engaged in teaching and learning situations. By now you should know that the exercise of freedom with students has as many drawbacks as constantly telling students what to do. To reconcile the differences as well as to reduce tensions between freedom and control, it seems logical to work toward balancing freedom and control. That is, to permit students freedom with restraints. However, the notion of balancing freedom and control is problematic. Because paradoxes cannot be fully resolved (freedom and control cannot occupy the same space at the same time), our best hope is to work at reducing the tensions between freedom and control. To reconcile the paradoxes between freedom and control is to realize when to exercise freedom and when to apply control. John Dewey's simile of the pendulum is instructive in understanding how this paradox can be reconciled.

The Simile of the Pendulum

As teachers, part of our responsibility is to expand the intellectual and creative capacities of students. Another responsibility for teachers is to help students understand the need for controls (rule and law). For social studies teachers these responsibilities capture much of what social studies is all about. Although John Dewey (1926) argued that all teachers need to consider the application of freedom and control, Dewey's simile of the pendulum is of particular interest to social studies teachers. Depending upon the school and teachers involved, Dewey argued that the act of teaching was either centered on freedom or focused upon teacher imposition. On the freedom side, many schools failed to cultivate in students a responsibility toward the community; on the control side, far too many schools completely abdicated the fostering of freedom of thought and action. To correct the exploitation of freedom and the imposition of external controls on students, what was needed was the ability to move like a pendulum from one side or the other as necessary.

Thus, to reconcile the paradoxes of freedom and control, Dewey held that teachers needed to be ready to read the context and conditions of the classroom as well as to gain a greater understanding of their students. Having gauged classroom realities as well as the needs of the students, the teacher then determined what was needed: more freedom or more controls. As the intellectual leader of the class, the teacher is uniquely qualified to decide when students require activities that may lead to an understanding of responsibility and when students need activities that can highlight the practice of freedom of thought and action. In practice, it is not simply that teachers randomly sponsor "free-time" on Monday and Friday (when students can think and do as they wish), and "control-time" on Tuesday, Wednesday, and Thursday (when students complete assignments). Teachers must be ready to devise freedom and control experiences and opportunities as necessary. With civic competence as a primary goal, social studies teachers need to be prepared to work both sides of the paradoxes, to move like a pendulum (depending upon conditions and other variables) between models of freedom and models of control.

In exercising our classroom decisions as we work through the paradox of freedom and control, it must be understood at the outset that teaching and learning cannot take place in a state of chaos. No government, whether a democratic-republic, communist dictatorship, or constitutional monarchy can maintain law and order in a state of chaos. Taking a stand on order and discipline as a first requirement of teaching does not mean that liberal-democratic teaching and learning cannot take place. The creation of a stable classroom environment is central to our work.

In the creation of such a classroom, social studies teachers need to support the notion of core-knowledge through a common language. In the United States this means instruction in English for all students and a reliance on a set of common core-knowledge facts centered on the history and geography of the United States and its contacts throughout the world. Making such a educationally conservative demand does not imply that politically conservative outcomes will follow. Throughout our history there are many examples of individuals who have challenged so-called conservative policies and practices. Taking examples from recent history, it is significant to note that the United States Supreme Court that ended legal discrimination of public schools in 1954 were products of public schools. Both Martin Luther King and Malcolm X were products of public schools, as was George Wallace and Strom Thurmond. Our school systems prepared both Bill Clinton and Bob Dole. The notion that educationally conservative practices such as reliance upon a common language and common core-knowledge as a basis for liberal-democratic education works to reproduce the "status quo" is patently false.

For our purposes learning through educationally conservative practices such as reliance upon memory, acquiring factual knowledge, and domain-appropriate procedures *increases* the intellectual capital of students (see Hirsch, 1996). With such knowledge, skills, and dispositions, students are truly empowered to chart their own course as citizens. Concurrently, the teaching of liberal-democracy through educationally progressive practices may actually inhibit the acquisition of liberal-democracy itself. E. D. Hirsch, Jr. (1996) argues that there is an *inverse* relationship between educationally progressivism and social progressivism. That is

> the best practices of educational conservatism are the only means whereby children from disadvantaged homes can secure the knowledge and skills that will enable them to improve their condition. (Hirsch, p. 7)

If Hirsch is correct, the only way social studies teachers will succeed in the quest to inject and improve civic competence is by applying knowledge, skills, and dispositions that are centered in educationally conservative practice. Hirsch is not the first to advocate such a bold plan. The notion of a common knowledge base as a means toward acquisition of political, social, and economic power was articulated by such unlikely companions as William C. Bagley, John Dewey, and Antonio Gramsci (see Hirsch 1996).

Setting a Context for Activating Civic Competence

Throughout the twentieth century, social studies as a means to activate civic competence has remained a singularly unique curricular enterprise. Nonetheless, despite the central goal of civic competence, many public schools have taken the responsibility to present content-centered courses based largely on historical topics in place of social studies for civic competence. The rhetoric surrounding these courses often explicitly connects history-centered subjects to civic competence. That is, we are often told that history-centered instruction contains the knowledge, skills, and dispositions required for civic competence—indeed that academically centered instruction directly leads to civic competence. In practice, however, there is little evidence to suggest that learning about history *promotes civic-minded behaviors* (acting in the behalf of community interests), *increases direct civic participation* (joining groups and becoming actively engaged in discussion/action on political, economic, and social issues), or *boosts either voter registration or actual voting* in local, state, or national elections. Similarly, civic competence claims made for such subjects as geography, sociology, anthropology, other social sciences, or other related subject matters are difficult to prove. Although knowledge from these subjects may help students to become oriented to historical and geographical contexts, issues, personages, and perspectives, alone, such subject matters do not necessarily advance the cause of civic competence.

While civic competence can be practiced and learned in many situations and contexts outside schools, public schools are ideally suited to create planned as well as to foster spontaneous opportunities/experiences for young citizens to consider and practice liberal-democratic ideas in a nurturing, developmental, and reflective environment. What should be the basis for education of citizens in public schools? It is logical to expect that the civic education of young citizens among schools supported by public monies should reflect the prevailing principles and objectives of the particular nation's governing structure. In an American context, citizenship education should reflect liberal-democratic ideals. In other contexts, citizenship education might reflect different perspectives on community and state life.

For example, it is logical to expect that Swedes learn about community and state living from a Swedish governing perspective, Israelis from an Israeli perspective, Chinese from a Chinese perspective, and so forth. Although we may reject and vigorously protest the application of a particular system of political, economic, and social life, based upon our liberal-democratic traditions, we should not expect that our values and dispositions will be accepted by citizens of other sovereign nations.

In specifics, due to the nature of our American political organization (democratic-republic), the teaching of social studies in public schools should directly involve experiences that foster and support the principles of government as found in such documents as Paine's *Common Sense*, the Declaration of Independence, the United States Constitution, the Bill of Rights, the Federalist Papers, among many other important documents. As we simplify the term *government* to the notion of how people living in the same area get along with one another, we may reduce these documents to two interconnected concepts: rights (freedoms) and responsibilities (controls). According to America's founding documents (and the continuing and expanding interpretations of these works), *all* citizens of the nation are accorded certain rights that others may not take away (except, of course, when an individual abuses these rights or works to take the rights away from another citizen).

Simultaneously, each citizen has a responsibility to contribute to furthering the public good as well as practice a respect for the rights of other citizens. Because our country's founders thoughtfully left vague exactly those rights that citizens should expect and those responsibilities citizens should practice and support, each generation of Americans must interpret and determine the nature, limitations, and expression of these rights and responsibilities. It is upon the notion of interpretation and determination of rights and responsibilities that (which also includes the notion of original intent) social studies education rests.

In the effort to help our students come to know and understand the workings of rights and responsibilities, social studies teachers may draw upon any number of sources. Although traditional academic areas of study such as history and geography (each complete with well-defined curricula) offer much to the practice and learning of civic competence, social studies teachers must be prepared to offer students opportunities to deal directly with issues of community life.

In short, teachers need to prepare and present experiences that have civic competence as the primary goal. The goals of subject-centered instruction in history and geography all too often become ends themselves rather than critical components of social studies. That is, what is typically expected from students in history-centered classrooms is the memorization of factual information alone, not the true practice of civic competence. Students are treated not as active participants in their own learning, but rather as placid receptacles of data, where they are literally fed with boring lectures, mindless worksheets, brain-numbing tests as they plow through the entire history of the United States from prehistorical times to the present in nine months or, in the guise of geography, embark on a fact-based whirlwind "tour" of exotic foreign lands.

The nature and practice of history-centered or subject-centered teaching is not in itself bad; students need exposure to historical concepts, trends, and data in order to achieve civic competence. The root problem of history-centered teaching is that its *delivery* is almost always from the control side of the pendulum. A secondary issue, but no less problematic, is that the history-centered curriculum is typically worked out in advance as lecture-telling, standardized-objective tests, prepackaged curricula, and other regiments. Such things are important. But a pattern of didactic teaching alone creates a teacher-to-student atmosphere that sharply reduces opportunities to explore freedom of thought and action. Teachers who practice social studies for civic competence recognize the importance of teacher-directed instruction. However, teachers of social studies for civic competence must also apply methods that support the freedom side of the paradoxes/pendulum.

As much as critics (from all sides) complain about emphasis upon facts, dates, and memorization, we cannot expect social studies teaching to improve as long as subject-centered teaching alone is the order of the day. Throughout this century, history-centered or subject-centered teaching has driven social studies teaching. Originally, students in public schools were taught about practical subjects (3Rs). Then in the 1890s professors of history and allied subjects worked to bring academically centered subject teaching into public schools for the expressed purpose of improving the academic quality of university students. The direct teaching of citizenship was not a primary goal. Since this time, goals of social studies curricula have been disputed by those who continue to view public schools as preparatory institutions for universities and colleges on the one hand, and those who view public schools as institutions where young citizens should be given opportunities to practice and learn about civic competence. To understand social studies then and now, one must come to grips with the difference between these two views.

Since schools are supported by public monies, the first obligation of the school is to support social studies for civic competence that would include but is not limited to subject-centered teachings for academic advancement. The community should be held accountable for providing adequate resources for social studies for civic competence; to support the teaching of freedom of thought and action as well as the importance of instilling a keen responsibility toward the general welfare of community. However, the community should not be made responsible, nor divert a disproportionate share of resources for subject-centered curricula designed to serve primarily those who seek entrance into institutions of higher learning. As much as it is important to advance the intellectual capacities of certain individuals, in a liberal-democracy, the goal of civic competence is to elevate the intellectual growth and capacities of each citizen with curricular experiences that highlight both sides of the twin paradoxes.

No other area of the school curriculum or segment of any other public institution has as its primary purpose the development of civic competence among young citizens. Given this task, what is it that young citizens need to know? Be able to do? Should be exposed to? Should consider? Should practice? Should make decisions about? Should act upon? In sum, what is the stuff of social studies? As a social studies teacher, what activities should you design for your students? What knowledge, skills, and dispositions should you include in your teaching? What opportunities and experiences should you create, foster, and sustain for and with your students? What goals or aims are appropriate? What do you hope students will be able to do (or do better) as a result of your teaching?

Whether you are supplied with a predetermined, prepackaged curriculum or you have generated a curriculum of your own, your challenge is to design lessons that provide the greatest opportunities for students to practice and acquire liberal-democratic skills, dispositions, and knowledge. Once you have determined your goals, what teaching methods should you consider? Should you lecture? Show films? Assign readings? Filmstrips? Lead discussions? Create projects? Have students complete worksheets? Book reports? Give quizzes, tests? Complete portfolios? Use original documents? Plan activities? Stage plays? Create art work, videos? Take fieldtrips? How much exposure is required? Will you focus on depth or coverage? Will one brief lecture do? A simple reading? Will students need repetition? What should you do if students do not appear to be "getting it"?

As you begin your teaching career, consideration of these questions may work more to overwhelm you than to guide your thoughts and actions. Although possibilities and alternatives are discussed in the many chapters of this book, ultimately you will be responsible not only for the instruction delivered in your class, but for whatever decisions are made. For example, a curricular guide might dictate that you present the Revolutionary War. In addition, among other things, the guide might also outline that students should be able to identify certain events or personalities, that students should be prepared to compare and contrast the Articles of Confederation with the United States Constitution, that students should become aware of the lives of different American groups, or that students study economic and social contexts of the Revolutionary War period. While decisions on the parameters and topics of the curriculum may be imposed upon you, in many cases, such curricular decisions are typically very broad. In this setting, your task is to implement and activate the civic competence curriculum; to not only make logical and supportable teaching decisions based upon your assessment of the teaching situation, but to be certain that both sides of the twin paradoxes are represented in your teaching.

Patterns of curricular decision-making and teacher empowerment vary widely in public schools of the United States. In some schools you might be responsible for the generation, implementation, and assessment of the curriculum. In others, teachers are accountable for only the implementation and assessment, and still in others, perhaps just the implementation. Whatever the case, teachers are held accountable to exercise thoughtful judgment and measured action. To successfully introduce liberal-democratic principles to young citizens, you need to carefully consider the foundation of your teaching activities. If you accept the responsibility for fostering civic competence in young citizens, then your instructional activities must work toward this stated goal.

A Framework for Teaching about Civic Competence

Social studies lessons from kindergarten through twelfth grade should be designed to engage students directly with experiences and opportunities from both sides of the twin paradoxes. Students of all ages need to know about our nation's history, geography, and other cultural, economic, and political information; to know about the world; to gain an understanding of the issues that affect our lives now and in the future. Students also need to have opportunities to experience freedom of thought and action; to gain a sense of what liberal-democracy is all about by becoming directly engaged with the practice of liberal-democratic principles.

Given these goals, social studies teachers must begin their work actively helping to socialize students into the community. The socialization process is the critical element of early social studies development. In fact, socialization is the cornerstone of community life. Without proper socialization, freedom of thought and action is meaningless. That is, if individuals of the community do not accept the responsibility for maintenance of the community, freedom is not possible. Citizens of the community must agree to and routinely apply basic standards of public conduct. If citizens cannot walk to the corner store without fear of being shot or molested; if citizens are not permitted to speak out; if citizens are prevented from exercising the freedoms annotated in the nation's founding documents, then it is apparent that a breakdown in basic socialization behavior has occurred. By now, you realize that this breakdown has already occurred in a number of American communities. Far too many Americans live in fear, have lost the freedom of movement, speech, and action. *And* far too many Americans have rejected socialization and have failed to abide by even the basic standards of liberal-democratic conduct.

Given these realities, one would think that subject-centered instruction, with curricula and methodologies directed toward the control side of the paradoxes/pendulum, would have helped students to understand the need for socialization conduct. Indeed, in totalitarian states, control side curricula and methodologies have worked extremely well in creating passive citizens. Yet, ironically, the breakdown in civic behaviors in the United States (because many citizens have an incomplete notion of liberal-democratic rights and responsibilities), is rooted in the failure of many young citizens to understand how to apply freedom of thought and action. Again, the key to achieving civic competence in schools rests with the social studies teacher's ability to foster and apply socialization processes. Although students need to practice and consider such things as decision-making skills, independent thinking, problem-solving, and individual action, students must first begin by learning about such things as sharing, acting in cooperation with others, the art of compromising, considering the convictions and beliefs of others, and respecting the property of others.

The First Context of Schooling

Although adults may not realize it, children know much about the world and community life by the time they begin school. Many children enter kindergarten after two or more years of child-care programs. In addition, media such as books, magazines, television, computers, internet, video tapes, and a variety of music forms have influenced young lives. Finally, children have had exposure to family, street, and community life, perhaps even church, formal sports, and other organizational patterns. Whether or not adults have recognized the intellectual growth of preschool children, children have formed generalizations about the basics of community life. Either from direct involvement or merely from watching from a parent's lap, children realize that rules are a part of organized activities; that adults give directions, often yelling at children to sit still or to be quiet. They have observed that sometimes adults hit or punish children. Overall, children have noted that adults act as commanders.

Struggling to find a place in the world, children are eager to please, difficult to handle, spontaneous, precocious, clever, and wonderful all at once. Typically, the first day of class, from kindergarten to sixth grade to twelfth grade, is spent learning about the rules of the class (from the teacher's perspective) among other routine things. Control is the primary goal. While teachers understand the need to be heard as instructions are being given, that certain behaviors will not be tolerated, that children will respect one another, and more, teachers often become so preoccupied with controlling measures, that freedom is lost or only provided for in a context of control.

For many teachers, as well as children, few have had experiences dealing with issues from the freedom side of the paradoxes. The thought of introducing freedom into class combined with the fear of losing class control is too much to bear. Let teachers in the later grades introduce freedom activities. The problem with this thinking is that teachers throughout the grades routinely function on the control side. Meaningful freedom activities are rarely, if ever, introduced at any level. One great paradox of our liberal-democratic nation is that our educational institutions call for the development of freedom, but do not support its actual practice. "Of course, we support the principles of freedom and democracy, we tell our children all about it!"

The practice of telling things to children is implicit in subject-centered teaching. Yet, perhaps more than that, teachers are conditioned and predisposed to control-side activities. Thus, with predetermined objectives, content, activities, and assessments, teachers easily fall into the pattern (or trap) of teacher talks while children listen, teacher directed activities, and basic teacher domination. All this is important as a basis of social studies. In this context though, at what point do students practice and learn about freedom, when they become the teacher? Children need to understand rules, yes, but they need to explore and experience the feeling of freedom, the idea of creating, to explore both inside and outside traditional contexts.

Teaching a child about rules and responsibility doesn't mean much without the child feeling and applying freedom and independence. Is the bringing together of freedom and control difficult? Yes! That is why the juxtaposition of freedom and control is paradoxical. The application of curricula that work to both ends is one of the greatest challenges of education; a challenge that social studies for civic competence is uniquely designed to accept.

Social Skills

The first priorities of the teacher are the safety and well-being of the child; all else follows. Social skills acquisition not only make the classroom a safer environment for children, social skills also add to the confidence and potential of each child. Social skills are linked to behaviors that help children to practice and learn:

- to build constructive relationships with others
- to recognize and appreciate others
- to identify problems and challenging situations or contexts
- to practice making decisions
- to work out suggestions and test alternatives
- to plan and execute ideas
- to apply findings to everyday life situations

Teachers that apply social skills acquisition with children work to help children find competent ways to interact with other children and adults. The skills of sharing, listening, taking turns, keeping hands to yourself, thinking about the feelings of others, respecting the property of others are all important social skills that lead to meaningful social intercourse. As children practice and gain a sense of getting along with others, teachers can introduce experiences that represent the freedom side of the paradoxes.

Thought and Action

Since the practice of control side teaching is so well known and used, I have focused on the other side of the twin paradoxes. Founded on the freedom side of the paradoxes, thought and action experiences involve eight intellectual processes that occur naturally among children. Thought and action activities enable students through the introduction and practice of the processes of discovery, inquiry, challenge, exploration, and imagination. Additionally, thought and action highlights the ability to engage in problem-solving, decision-making, and reflective thinking. Teachers using thought and action practices can help children to think, act, and deal with new situations, problems, issues, and decisions with greater effectiveness and efficiency. The following are descriptions of the eight individual abilities of thought and action.

Discovery—place students into new situations, creating or stimulating an experience by which students can interpret, react, define, describe, compare-contrast, or explain the event in their own terms, by their own means.

Inquiry—create or stimulate experiences where children will pursue answers to questions, search for clarity on an issue, or seek out information that sheds light on or permits a better understanding of ideas, issues, or questions that are either posed or revealed through experience.

Challenge—develop experiences that cast doubt or raise questions about supposed truth and status quo issues with the intention of seeking truth or more honest conclusions.

Exploration—provide for experiences where students can create/generate possibilities, probabilities, alternatives for a particular question, problem, issue, idea (or set of same), or factual data. All ideas/responses are considered.

Imagination—plan experiences that highlight opportunities for children to create/generate possibilities, alternatives, and scenarios without constraint or limit by known laws, rules, beliefs, conventions, or theories.

Problem-Solving—presentation, recognition, or revelation of a concrete or abstract problem where children work to identify a potential solution as well as possible alternative solutions. Additionally, teachers stimulate students to recognize and analyze various consequences or each proposed solution.

Decision-Making—given a variety of individual choices and alternative possibilities to select from, provide opportunities for children to craft a specific decision or reach a definite conclusion of their own making. This action should include appropriate attention to potential or forecasted consequences of the decision or conclusion. In addition, by creating experiences for students to practice how competent and thorough decisions are made, teachers should also help children to practice articulating and documenting reasons for decisions.

Reflection—given an issue, decision, problem, statement, teachers create or stimulate an experience where students work to determine if a conclusion or action (either developed by the student or given to the student to think about)—as well as the process used to deliver the conclusion or action—represents the best, most ethical, most truthful, or logical move. Reflection is literally a pause when you take time to think back upon something. A special focus should be placed upon student learning to develop and support judgments with conviction based upon available and reliable data.

Toward a Scope and Sequence

The thoughtful combination of social skills development for acceptance and responsibility, together with specific practice with thought and action for freedom, offer excellent opportunities for students to explore both sides of the twin paradoxes. Nonetheless, because children and teaching situations are unique, to achieve the greatest possible effect, you need to prepare yourself to adjust lessons and experiences as necessary. In applying the simile of the pendulum—moving toward freedom or toward control—given your teaching goals, you determine what experiences are required, how these experiences should be designed, presented, readjusted, and assessed.

The scope and sequence of any particular social studies program is not something that can be determined outside the context or actual conditions of the class, particularly without an acknowledgment and understanding of the abilities, needs, and capacities of your students. Although a fixed scope and sequence may be prepared in advance, the successful achievement of civic competence does require that social studies teachers carefully consider what knowledge bases and experiences pose the greatest opportunity for students to practice and acquire the skills and dispositions required of a liberal-democratic nation.

The usual knowledge bases for civic competence include information, problem sets, derived issues, and methodologies from the academic fields of history, geography, sociology, political science, psychology, anthropology, and economics. Allied sources also include the academic areas of literature, language, the natural sciences, contemporary issues and events, the media, and many others. The key to civic competence is not the acquisition of knowledge from any one of these academic areas alone, nor knowledge from any particular combination of these areas. Rather, social studies for civic competence involves the application and manipulation of knowledge from the traditional academic areas and other contemporary sources of social, political, and economic issues for the expressed purpose of furthering liberal-democratic ideals. Again, it is not the knowledge of these academic areas that is the only goal, but the student's ability to apply the knowledge to affect liberal-democratic goals.

Summary

The mission of social studies for civic competence is unique. No other subject area or public institution is expressly designed to promote citizenship. This chapter is an introduction to social studies for civic competence. It is intended to stimulate thought about these ideas and promote action. Because a fuller explanation of the ideas contained would exceed the space available, I encourage you to explore the issue of civic competence with peers, instructors, colleagues, or students. You may also want to consult sources that more fully explicate these ideas—for example, Hirsch (1996), Engle and Ochoa (1988), and Evans and Saxe (1996).

In sum, social studies teachers need to explore the use of both subject-centered/control-side teaching as well as process-centered/freedom side teaching. It is assumed that for optimal teaching of civic competence, all students should be given instruction in and competence with the common language of this nation. Moreover, to learn and practice civic competence, all students should be given exposure to a common core knowledge base that would include commonly held skills and dispositions. While educationally progressive techniques are recognized as possible aids to the acquisition of civic competence, social studies teachers should pragmatically practice those sound educationally conservative techniques that offer the greatest opportunities for civic competence with our young citizens.

The rationale for social studies for civic competence is simple. The quality of our present and future American life are dependent upon every citizen achieving and demonstrating civic competence. To accomplish this goal, teachers from preschool through high school need to grasp, apply, and enliven the ideals of liberal-democracy through meaningful classroom practice.

While the need for liberal-democratic teaching has been merely sketched here, the real challenge is left for teachers, to provide adequate experiences and practice for civic competence. The responsibility is great, the task may be difficult, and the challenges will be many. But, as many people all over the world are discovering, the benefits of liberal-democratic life offer individuals the greatest opportunities for civic growth and maintenance as well as personal well-being.

PART II

Social Issues and the Social Studies Curriculum

CHAPTER FOUR

Social Studies and Feminism[1]

Nel Noddings

Introduction

The first wave of feminist influence on the school curriculum was similar to that of racial and ethnic influence. Curriculum makers responded to the questions, Where are the women? Where are the blacks? by adding women and blacks to the standard story. Now feminist thought challenges the standard curriculum itself—both its form and its content. I want to concentrate mainly on the newer trend, but filling in gaps in the first project may suggest ways to get started on the second.

Gaps in the Standard Curriculum

Standard social studies texts now contain more pictures of women and references to women. In some cases, the increase has a humorous aspect: women just appear in pictures, whether or not their presence is relevant. All female appearances count (Tetreault 1986). In other cases, the addition of women is less amusing. Mentioning females for achievement that would go unrecognized if the subjects were male is demeaning to women and trivializes the history under examination. Teachers can subvert this foolishness by talking about the curriculum-making process itself and encouraging students to reflect on it, but I wonder how many do.

It is clear from what I've said so far that I would not recommend that curriculum-makers dig around in dusty archives to see if there was some female participant in an important political conference whose name can now be included in texts—even though

59

most of the male participants will still be unnamed. The gaps that interest me cannot be closed by raising the count of female names and faces.

Women have done things of great importance that go unrecognized because they were done by women and because the focus of their efforts has not been the focus of political history. Consider the case of Emily Greene Balch. Although she received the Nobel Peace Prize in 1946, her name does not appear in a major encyclopedia published in the fifties. In contrast, Generals Pershing and Patton each have entries of a column or so in length and a picture. Was Balch left out because she was a women or because peace is unimportant compared with war? In the late seventies edition, the same encyclopedia includes Balch in an entry of a few lines. Pershing and Patton still appear prominently—with pictures. My conclusion is that she is now included because she was a woman and important publications today must include women. I do not believe that she is included because historians and curriculum-makers have awakened to the importance of peace studies or because they now recognize the significance of work that women have found central in their lives.

How many students know that women from thirteen countries organized to stop World War I in 1915? That women started the Women's International League for Peace and Freedom (WILPF) in that year and that the organization is still active today? How many know that these women suggested a permanent arbitration body before the League of Nations was established? (see Brock-Utne 1985; Reardon 1985). Although Balch now receives an entry in encyclopedias and texts, we are left ignorant of the content of the WILPF's proposals and totally in the dark about how women organized and what procedures they used. This material—content and process—is more important to education than the mention of Balch's name.

When we begin an exploration of women and peace, we are led quickly beyond the narrower confines of feminism. Reading the autobiography of Dorothy Day (1981/1952), I was struck by the anonymity of most of the men she mentioned. They, too, sacrificed for peace, workers' rights, food for the hungry, medical care for the mentally ill, and a host of causes often identified with women. Only those *inspired* by Day have become well-known—the Berrigans, Michael Harrington, Thoman Merton, and Cesar Chavez, for example. It was a lifelong sorrow for Day that so many who subscribed to the *Catholic Worker* and most of its goals withdrew wholehearted support from its stand on peace. Many were even unaware of its pacifist position until some crisis brought it to their attention. Pacifism, it seems, is respectable for women, but not for men.

A cluster of fascinating issues arises out of this brief discussion, and students might profit from grappling with them: Why are peace and peacemaking so clearly undervalued in traditional historical accounts? Has the association of women with peace aggravated its undervaluation? Or, conversely, has the picture of women as *peaceful* (not an altogether accurate picture [see Elshtain 1987]) contributed to the devaluation of women? On this, students might discuss the possibility that some men submit to conscription and engage in fights because they fear looking "like women." Perhaps women have made a tactical error in organizing all-female institutions for the study and promotion of peace. How often has female authorship been used as a reason for rejecting proposals for peace and social justice? How is this reason disguised, and how can we know that it is operating?

The procedure I'm advocating here is straightforward and commonsensical. As educators, we begin by looking at the present curriculum and speculating on the motives of those who made it and those who use it. Have we, as feminists, made progress? We note the increase in female names and faces, but the maintenance of central male standards. Is this what we want? Some feminists will say "yes" to this; they want full equality in the world as it has been defined by men—even the right to join the military in combat roles. Other feminists say "no" to this. We want recognition of important work that has gone unnoticed precisely because the standard of importance has devalued it. Whichever feminist view we take, we should acknowledge—as educators—that the debate itself is more significant than much of what we teach in standard courses.

Now I want to move on to a discussion of changes that might be considered if we took the latter feminist view. What topics might be included? What questions might be asked?

Challenging the Standard Curriculum

There is considerable debate today in ethics and political philosophy about improving societies. Classical liberals and their descendants still put great emphasis on the power of reason and universal concepts such as "rights" to point the way.

Communitarians, in contrast, locate beginnings and all possibilities for transformation of social thought in tradition. Alasdair MacIntyre goes so far as to call natural rights "fictions"—in the same category with "witches and unicorns" (1984, pp. 69–70). The doctrine of rights, MacIntyre argues, is tradition-bound, not a discovery of something universal.

Both of these perspectives suggest strongly that transformation must emerge from something already present—in one case, a universal insight not yet implemented; in the other, a set of cultural understandings in need of refinement. On one level, one cannot argue against the basic fact: transformation of necessity implies a starting point in what is. But what both perspectives overlook is that there may be traditions unarticulated within traditions, unspoken semiuniversals alongside the highly touted universals identified by philosophers. Thus when philosophers and political theorists insist that we must begin our arguments in a tradition, they miss entirely the possibility of starting with a tradition that is largely unwritten. Let me give an example that illustrates the difficulty:

> Law has long used a "reasonable man" standard to evaluate certain actions. In recent years, bowing to gender sensitivities, the standard has been renamed the "reasonable person" standard. [Noddings 1991/92, p. 65]

Renaming the standard is a move in keeping with the liberal tradition. It supposes universal insight that has fallen short of inclusion in practice. The remedy is inclusion, and that is accomplished by the change in terms.

But the standard itself was developed in a masculine culture, and it reflects male experience. As a result, jurists have encountered difficulty in applying it to women, and considerable controversy has arisen. Consider one example:

> If a man, in the heat of passion, kills his wife or her lover after discovering an adulterous alliance, he is judged guilty of voluntary manslaughter instead of murder. If, however, the killing occurs after a "reasonable person" would have cooled off, a verdict of murder is often found.

> What happens when we try to apply this standard to women? When a women kills an abusive husband, she rarely does it in the heat of the moment. Most women do not have the physical strength

to prevail in such moments. More often the killing occurs in a quiet time—sometimes when the husband is sleeping. The woman reports acting out of fear. Often she has lived in terror for years, and a threat to her children has pushed her to kill her abuser. [Noddings, 1991/92, p. 65]

Many legal theorists recognize that a reasonable woman might behave very differently from a reasonable man, and that the reasonable person standard as it has developed in a masculine culture does not take women's experience into account (Taylor 1986). Changing the name of the standard has not removed its gender bias.

It seems to me, then, that the communitarians are more nearly accurate in their descriptive account than the liberals, and that means that transformation is a very hard project. Communitarians sometimes make it even harder by pushing for identification and conservation of the best in a given tradition. (MacIntyre's return to Aristotle is an example.) Further, the temptation is to identify only one tradition and to suppose that improvement means assimilation and full citizenship in that tradition. It is a line of argument that frustrates some feminist and ethnic theorists enormously.

Consider the area of gender and ethnic studies. Many well-meaning educators want to include topics on race, ethnicity, and gender in the standard curriculum. So far so good. But often recommendations go beyond independent inclusion. Educators also want to phase out separate programs, organized around women, blacks, or Asians. They find these programs divisive and fear the collapse of truly public education. But the danger is that, if the new programs are assimilated, traditions as yet unarticulated or only poorly so will be lost entirely—swallowed up by *the* tradition. I illustrated one facet of this problem in my opening remarks on Emily Greene Balch. She is now included in standard texts, but the power and significance of her work, her point of view, her culture are all still hidden.

Suppose this culture were fully articulated. Suppose the "different voice" identified by Gilligan (1982) were to speak in social studies. What might we hear?

First there might be much more emphasis on what we once called "private" life as contrasted with "public" life. As we know, the sharp separation between the two breaks down under analysis, but the tradition that sustains the separation is still dominant. Surely if we had started with private life, the school curriculum would be very different from the one actually developed.

Instead of the emphasis on citizenship, there might be one on family membership and homemaking. Homemaking! Even feminists tremble at that word! Am I suggesting a return to Catherine Beecher and her *Treatise on Domestic Economy* (1977/1842)? Well, the education described in *A Treatise* is not all bad, but that is not what I am suggesting.

There is nothing inherently antiintellectual in the topic of homemaking. Indeed this is crystal clear in Beecher's work. The topic can include economics, art, nutrition, geography, history, technology, and literature. It can and should be multicultural. Perhaps, most wonderful of all, it can be philosophical. What does it mean to "make a home"? Must a home's occupants be members of a nuclear family? Why is a "home for the aged" not considered a home by many of its occupants? Why is a nation often referred to as a homeland, and how does love for a homeland sometimes induce disagreement and war? Why is exile such a terrible punishment? By emphasizing the intellectual here, I do not mean to denigrate the practical but simply to pique the interest of those who might otherwise be too astonished to listen further.

We should indeed teach the practical elements of homemaking. I'm not sure they were ever well taught in ordinary homes (well-to-do Victorian households were not ordinary homes), and today I'm quite sure they are not. We should teach homemaking in such a way that students become competent homemakers, and also so that they can see both the personal and global tragedies of homelessness whether that homelessness is caused by poverty, psychological neglect, mental illness, or war—whether it is literal absence of shelter or the dreadful alienation of psychological separation.

Citizenship, from this perspective, is not all we have in common as adults. As a woman, I'd like children to be prepared as competent parents, homemakers, mates, neighbors, and friends. I'd like them to be responsible pet owners (if they own pets); to be considerate and appreciative users of the natural and human-made environments; to be intelligent believers or unbelievers in the spiritual realm. Are these not common human endeavors? Are they not as important as citizenship?

One response to my suggestions is to expand the notion of citizenship—to absorb much of what is now considered private life into public life. My preference, for reasons already discussed, would be to start with a different category entirely—perhaps "social" life, and begin where social life actually does begin—in the home and family. I am not suggesting this start as a way of psychologizing the usual subject matter. Such a move would merely recapitulate much that is already common in social studies. The suggestion is to establish a new emphasis.

Another major topic that the different voice might identify is intergenerational life. This would involve a study of life stages as well as of intergenerational responsibility. How do infants grow? When should children be taught to read? What are the special problems of adolescence? Of young adulthood? When does old age begin? Here is a set of fascinating topics for multicultural education. The topics can include demographic and statistical studies, systems of medical care, the history of childhood, attitudes toward death and helplessness, responsibilities of the old for the young, and vice versa. Such study might also include field experience in the form of community service.

Surely another part of social life is the development of a strong sense of self. In traditional psychology the growth of self has involved increasing separation from others and the establishment of firm boundaries between self and not-self (Chodorow 1978). Some thinkers today (including many feminists) define self relationally. In *Caring*, I wrote:

> I am not naturally alone. I am naturally in a relation from which I derive nourishment and guidance. When I am alone, either because I have detached myself or because circumstances have wrenched me free, I seek first and most naturally to reestablish my relatedness. My very individuality is defined in a set of relation. This is my basic reality. [1984, p. 51]

The very fact that we confine a study of self to the discipline of psychology is a manifestation of the tradition against which we are struggling. From our alternative perspective, the study of self should surely be a part of *social* studies. In an important sense, social studies would become the heart of the curriculum, and everything else would spin off from it.

What topics might be introduced in a serious study of self? In *The Challenge to Care in Schools* (1992), I have suggested categories such as physical, spiritual, occupational, and recreational life, but many others might be considered. In an educational plan of this sort, drug and sex education would not be peripheral; driver education and alcohol use would not be add-ons; career education would not be left to spare time in the guidance office; consumer education would not be an elective offered only to those eager to escape the rigors of the disciplines.

These topics are so huge that I can do little more than scratch the surface here, but let's spend some time on spiritual education. This is an area that frightens many educators as well as laypersons. But why? It is no more inevitable that spiritual education should lead to indoctrination than that democratic education should do so. (I grant immediately that, in both cases, it does sometimes do so, but it is a result that can be avoided.)

Not only should children learn something about the history, art, literature, and music of religion. More important, they should have opportunities to explore the questions of spiritual life: Is there a God? Are there perhaps, many gods? Is there life after death? Is this the first life I've lived? What have great mathematicians (scientists, writers, artists, and others) thought about God and religion? Have there been good atheists? Have there been evil Christians?

Consider the fact that in our zeal to protect religious freedom we have deprived many children entirely of an opportunity to engage religious matters. It's no use responding that their families should provide the opportunity. If their families fail to feed them breakfast or lunch, we feed them in school. It's more a matter of what we value and what we have the courage to attempt.

Speaking in the alternative voice, we would not recommend simply adding a course in comparative religion or religious history. Rather we would help teachers to explore spiritual questions whenever opportunities present themselves. Certainly, many such opportunities arise even in conventional classes such as mathematics. When students study rectangular coordinates, they should hear about their inventor, René Descartes, and his attempt to prove God's existence. When probability is studied, they should hear about Pascal's famous wager. When calculus is studied, they should learn that Newton put a higher value on theology than on mathematics and that Leibniz is still as well known for his theodicy as for his calculus. They should also learn what theodicy is and have a chance to consider the ways in which evil has been defined and described.

Working through biography, autobiography, historical anecdotes, fiction, and poetry we can explore many spiritual topics without advocating a religion or transgressing a legal restriction. As the curriculum is organized now, subject matter specialists would have to broaden their knowledge greatly to teach in this way, but it is clearly possible to do so. Organized as the different voice suggests, the curriculum would contain matters of spiritual concern from the start.

Right now, many theme courses or sequences could be constructed around religious topics:

> One might involve conceptions of god and include some of the difficult theological problems that arise when god is defined in particular ways. Another might address religion and politics with sexism and racism as important subtopics. It is particularly important that young women understand the role religion has played in maintaining men's domination over them. If education were to be truly liberal—that is, freeing—the study of religion and politics would be fundamental. [Noddings 1992, p. 83]

Again possibilities for multicultural education abound. For example, students should come to appreciate the spiritual genius of black people who created black Christian churches out of a religion forced on them as slaves. What could have been a slave mentality became instead a wonderful force for solidarity and liberation (Walker 1983). Spirituals, poetry, novels, and biographies that describe black Christianity and its influence are plentiful. Many of the same works also reveal other traditions, and these too should be part of spiritual education (Noddings 1992, p. 83).

Probably many of you are wondering how in the world any of this can be done when religious pressure groups oppose every attempt to introduce any but their own values into the classroom. It is not a small problem. However, I think we educators have brought some of this on ourselves by collapsing easily under every assault—watering down texts, removing books from our library shelves, avoiding controversial issues. None of these concessions has reduced fundamentalist zeal, and, to make matters worse, we have become sophists and hypocrites. We pretend to espouse critical thinking and freedom of thought as primary virtues and aims of education. And then we deny ourselves the opportunity to exercise these virtues and deprive our students of the chance to acquire them.

What am I suggesting? When parents demand that we remove *Huckleberry Finn* from the curriculum, we should refuse to do so. If the concern is that much of the text is racist, we should respond by saying that this "weakness" is a pedagogical strength. It gives us a legitimate reason, within the standard curriculum, to discuss racism past and present. When parents object to the mention of

God in mathematics class, we should respond that biographical and historical materials are part of the standard curriculum and will remain so. Failing to respond this way not only deprives the majority of students of knowledge and discussion to which they should have access, but it also deprives fundamentalist students of the only regulated attempt at critical thinking they are likely to experience.

Let me give a specific example of the kind of thinking that is cramping our style right now. Not long ago two of our teacher education math interns were doing a direct reading with me. They were both teaching geometry, and I suggested that they have their students read Edwin Abbott's *Flatland*. Both agreed that the book was *misogynist*. How could they use a book that so demeaned women? Aha! I responded, that's a great reason in favor of using it! You then have a legitimate reason to discuss sexism in a math class. Similarly, the fact that much of it is a religious allegory counts again in its favor. And the additional fact that it is outrageously classist makes it a triple threat. It can be used in a math class for genuine social education. Math teachers, like social studies teachers, need greater academic freedom and concomitantly greater knowledge and responsibility.

I do not mean to suggest by the foregoing remarks that every curricular demand of parents should be resisted. On the contrary, I believe we should listen respectfully and engage in compromise or negotiation when we are persuaded that the parents' case is legitimate—and, I believe, it often is. For example, I would be quite willing to include both evolution and creation under a general rubric of stories people have told about the origins of the universe and human life. But I would want to include the creation stories of Native Americans, Hindus, Polynesians, and many other peoples as well as the Christian stories. I would include both heterodox and orthodox stories. Approached this way, we need not fight the battle over what is science and what religion. Rather, both scientific and religious version appear as stories in the history of human thought.

Consider one more topic that might properly be part of a social education that begins with and emphasizes private life: love. If visitors from another planet entered our meetings, they would surely be amazed that a topic so central to human life is rarely treated in schools. But what a wonderful school subject it could be! Students could learn something of the history of love: homosexual love in classical Greece, courtly love in the Middle Ages, romantic love in the Victorian era. In addition to reading *Romeo and Juliet*, they might see a film version and listen to the music of both Berlioz and Tchaikovsky. Similarly, they should hear Wagner's "Tristan and Isolde." They might read (and see) *Wuthering Heights*. They might learn something about the history of marriage and how little love has had to do with marriage in most times and cultures. How was marriage bound up in European politics? How, for example, did some of Henry VIII's wives escape the fate of Anne Boleyn? How was the Act of Supremacy related to love and marriage?

More important than all wonderful intellectual topics on love is the fundamental task of learning how to care for intimate others—sexual partner or spouse, close friends, children. In an age when we abuse one another at a disgraceful rate, such learning is crucial. I do not find education for responsible love in the President's agenda for education or any well-known statement of goals by profession. Yet there is obviously much to be learned.

What does it mean to care for another human being? What is commitment? Do females and males look at love differently? How about friendship? Students might appreciate hearing Aristotle's views on friendship—particularly his insistence that friends should help each other to live morally better lives. Friends do not cover for each other's really weak and evil acts; good friends point us upward—toward our better selves, while loving us as we are.

Both girls and boys today need to plan for family life as boys once planned for careers. What skills are needed? How can a true partnership be developed? How should we define success?

Young people today need time to discuss matters of gender. Can we dispense with gender as some feminists suggest? Or are our sexual identities as precarious as our racial and ethnic identities? What does it mean to be a woman in today's world? What does it mean to be a man? Matters of gender are thoroughly intermixed with questions of career and what it means to live a successful life. Many young women today fear that they cannot have both career and family, and many young men doubt that they can achieve the conventional success of their fathers without the full-time support of wives. How well-founded are these beliefs, and what are the alternatives?

In concluding this brief discussion of learning to understand love, I want to reiterate the major points: Nothing is more important to most of us than stable and loving connection; caring for a special person takes precedence over promoting causes and principles; intellectual life is not at all impeded by a concentration on existential concerns; and in intimate life we have an opportunity to learn a fundamental secret of morality—how to promote each other's moral growth.

Conclusion

Feminism's initial effect on social studies changed the surface of the subject to some degree: more female faces and names now appear in standard texts. I have suggested that these effects are not altogether salutary. On the positive side, women have gained access to a world once exclusively maintained for men. On the negative side, social studies as a regular school subject has been flooded with trivia and is threatened by continuing fragmentation. Further, women's genuine contributions have been glossed over because they do not fit the male model of achievement.

The next wave of feminism should be directed toward the articulation of women's culture. It may be prudent for feminists to resist the total assimilation of this material into the mainstream curriculum, because such assimilation could be tantamount to destruction. But, little by little, as the tradition itself becomes stronger and more confident, new curricula should reflect the fundamental interests of private life as well as those of public life, and public life itself should be deeply influenced by the articulation of private life. From this perspective, feminism may really contribute to a revolution in social studies education.

CHAPTER FIVE

Gender in Social Education

Jane Bernard-Powers

In twelve years of school I never studied anything about myself.

Twelfth-grade African-American girl (AAUW 1992)

When Jean Grambs introduced the 1976 publication, *Teaching about Women in the Social Studies,* she entitled her chapter, "What We Must Do" and laid out some clear and seemingly simple ways to include women in the curriculum. Two decades after this important publication, we are still talking about what we must do, curriculum reform is still work in progress, and it seems far more complex than it did in 1976.

We (teachers, professors, and researchers) have only begun to scratch the surface of the complexity of gender dynamics, gendered identities, and gender imprinted knowledge in the social studies classroom and in social education. Moreover, as feminist scholarship in the social sciences has expanded and deepened, so have debates about essential gender identities and gender politics. Are there immutable qualities associated with being male or female in a social/political context? How are those qualities associated with maleness or femaleness mediated by class, race, or ethnic background? Where and when are issues of gender really salient in social education? How can curriculum be transformed and be transformational without being reductionist in content and goals? These questions indicate the complexity of what seemed fairly simple at the beginning of the modern journey—social justice in the curriculum.

This chapter addresses the significance of recent history in gender equity and social studies, perspectives on engendering

71

history, geography, and citizenship education, and some promising directions for the future. The attitude assumed in this writing is modernist rather than postmodernist in that gender equity is still a major concern for young women in education. This is true in a general sense, as the study by Sadker and Sadker (1994) attests to, and in social studies education specifically. Thus I am assuming the familiar tone of advocacy for gender equity in curriculum content and structures that currently exist, while ultimately curriculum transformation is the vision on the horizon.

Historical Framing for Gender Equity in Social Studies

The name of the advisory committee established by the National Council for the Social Studies to address "the woman question" in social studies, "Sexism and Social Justice," reflects what were the major concerns of the 1970s: equity, access, and the absence of discrimination. Sex equity in the social studies curriculum meant identifying and rectifying stereotypes about women and men in textbooks and other curriculum materials, lobbying for the inclusion of women's experiences and histories in textbooks, and providing preservice and inservice education for teachers. Committed social studies educators in all corners of the formal education enterprise have done these things, but the work has been far more difficult and complex than we ever imagined. Advocates needed to develop a better understanding of gender dynamics in the curriculum and in classrooms, and feminist social science had to develop and be disseminated. Moreover substantial resistance to curriculum reform and to feminism developed during the 1980s, short-circuiting the momentum of the seventies.

The 1970s and early eighties were a period of optimism for feminists and sex equity advocates seeking educational change and curriculum reform. Title IX successfully altered the face of high school athletics and promoted a consciousness about gender equity in schooling generally. Legislative successes in the workplace such as Title VII, which prohibited discrimination on the basis of sex, media images that included women working outside the home, the success of *Roe vs. Wade*, the rise of the National Organization for Women (NOW), and the promise of a successful Equal Rights Amendment fueled a spirit of optimism among educators who wanted to change opportunities for girls in schooling. Armed with Women's Educational Equity Act programs and curriculum materials, and supported by the National Endowment for the Humanities and Title IX institutes and workshops, teachers and curriculum developers set out to change the face and the content of curriculum, and ultimately to achieve equality for future female citizens.

By the mid 1980s, the optimistic picture of upward linear progress for America's women—social, political, and economic—was frayed and under siege, as Faludi so carefully documents in her modern history, *Backlash* (1992). The blocked Equal Rights Amendment and attacks on abortion rights coupled with the rise of Reaganism and consequent weakening of support for women in the executive branch contributed to a social and political climate that was sometimes quietly and often vocally hostile to "women's rights."

Moreover, the women's movement in education began to experience growing pains as issues of diversity pushed scholars, teachers, and activists to examine and redefine the meaning of feminism and equity. As a local consultant to the Stanford Summer Institute in Women's History in 1978, I can painfully recall everyone's dismay over the lack of materials available for teachers to pursue their interests in Hispanic and Latina history. They were simply not accessible at that time, and the fact served as profound evidence of the biases that had emerged as women and feminists began to write their histories. Stories and histories of Asian Americans, African-Americans, Hispanic and Latina Americans were waiting to be discovered with the advent and then defense of new methodologies in history—oral history, narratives, and life interviews were in the margins of the field.

While feminist scholars in women's studies programs and in social science disciplines excavated the foundations of knowledge and attempted to build new scaffoldings with women at the center of investigation, the political climate supporting such efforts changed. The Women's Educational Equity Act and feminist educational reforms were targets of the conservative political agenda in the 1980s. Textbooks that included "new" images of women in society and history were singled out for special attention. Faludi describes how one Reagan appointee, who was policy architect for family issues, lamented the loss of women pictured as housewives in school textbooks.

This hostile climate in the federal government, supported by the withdrawal of federal funds, seemed to have a depressing effect on curriculum change and on the structures that supported curriculum change. In the National Council for the Social Studies, for example, the advisory committee on gender and social justice was eliminated in the late eighties. Title IX committees, which were advocates for curriculum, were virtually nonexistent in school districts by the mid-eighties. Whereas the 1970s had generated awareness of discrimination for women and girls in society, and in K-collegiate education, along with the means and some support for change in textbooks and curriculum programs. The eighties witnessed the demise of momentum. The reform literature published between 1983 and 1987 exemplified the nonissue: only one percent of article content dealt with gender in classroom interaction, athletics, or in the curriculum (Sadker, Sadker, and Steindam 1989).

The relationship between the conservative political climate of the 1980s and passionate calls for social studies curriculum reform has had serious implications for consideration of feminism and gender. Critiques of education published in the late eighties called for the restoration of geography and history to the center of social studies curriculum (Ravitch and Finn 1987; Gagnon 1988; National Commission on Social Studies 1989) Resistance to multicultural, gender-sensitive, and feminist curriculum transformation has been a product of the conservative history social science campaign otherwise known as the "Battle over the Canon" (Banks 1994). As Elizabeth Fox-Genovese (1990) observed in her controversial book, *Feminism without Illusions, A Critique of Individualism,* "the apparent goal of conservative educators is to restore the canon of Western Civilization by declaration."

Poor prospects or not, it is evident that the canon controversy came home to roost in the politically charged and manipulated development of the California History Social Science Framework, and in the furor that followed over the Houghton Mifflin textbook adoption (Campbell 1988; Waugh 1991; Ladson-Billings 1993; Cornbleth and Waugh 1995). Defenders of the canon and Eurocentric cultural literacy standards dominated the writing of the framework, influenced textbook adoption procedures, and minimized multiculturalists' and feminist scholars' input (Ladson-Billings 1993).

The allegation that feminists and multiculturalists represent "narrow" special interest groups, and the controversy over the canon has been an issue in the development of national standards for history. Former President Reagan was responsible for conservative education department policy and appointees, including Diane Ravitch, who believed that school curriculum needed to be wrested from the hands of "narrow interest groups," and supported efforts in that direction (McIntosh 1985). Multicultural women's history is minimized in the national history standards, and the history that is represented does not reflect the revisionist, critical, and inclusive historical scholarship developed over the last three decades.

The voices raised in defense of gender-fair, accurate, and inclusive scholarship and classroom practices have been difficult to hear in recent years in national organizations. Social studies teachers and professionals have been on the defensive in the face of attacks from cultural conservatives such as E. D. Hirsch, author of *Cultural Literacy*, and Ravitch and Finn. The social studies reform caravan was hijacked from under the noses of social studies professionals. The last five years have been spent trying to regain some control over the standards controversies and the multicultural special interest debates. Under those circumstances it was apparently difficult for many social studies leaders to see gender as anything but a distraction or a marginal concern.

While advocates for the infusion of gender issues in the social studies curriculum may have struggled for visibility and legitimacy, feminist scholarship in the social sciences reproduced exponentially over the last two decades. The histories, geographies, anthropologies, psychologies, and literatures of women from diverse ethnic backgrounds were researched, written, and debated along with feminist theory. Journals in women's studies flourish, including a journal entitled *Gender and Education*. The myth of a monolithic women's movement was debunked and replaced by conflicts in feminism over questions of class, race, ethnicity, and ultimately essential qualities of women in relation to each other and in relation to men. The politics of identity in all of its complexity unfolded in the field of women's history and essentialism became part of the vocabulary of feminist scholars: Do women have essential qualities beyond biology that would wrap them into one category?

This issue divided historians in the *Sears Roebuck vs. Equal Employment Opportunity Commission* case that was argued by two expert witnesses and prominent historians, Rosalind Rosenberg and Alice Kessler Harris. Women who worked for Sears Roebuck alleged that they had been denied the opportunity to pursue high commission sales jobs. Rosenberg argued that women were indeed less likely to seek jobs because of a preference for stable income and their commitment to family responsibilities. Thus women as a group held special qualities that distinguished them from men. Kessler-Harris argued on the other hand that women, like men, would seek higher income above other considerations (Fox-Genovese 1991). The Sears Roebuck case opened up bitter debate among feminist historians over both feminist tactics as well as essential feminine qualities, and the meaning of feminism. As Marian Hirsch and Evelyn Fox Keller characterized it, "the 'Sears' Case . . . had so intensified already existing divisions that discussion threatened to stall altogether" (Hirsch and Fox-Keller 1990).

The questions and politics of identity and difference have been a central concern of feminism in the last few years. The questions raised in feminist theoretical discussions have implications for the real world, as was very evident in the Sears Roebuck case. Do all women constitute a group sufficiently distinct from men—irrespective of ethnicity, age, language background, and context or life situation—that functions to define them legally, socially, politically, and most relevant to this chapter, in schools and in social education? Or when do women and men, girls and boys, constitute separate groups deserving of distinctive treatment and when is a criterion of equality appropriate to invoke? If all young women or particular groups don't respond to economics, history, geography, and social studies teaching and learning in the same way as young men, how do we define the situation and how do we rectify it?

The importance of theoretical work in feminism is that it can help us understand the complexity of our work for gender equality and sensitivity in schools and curriculum. Barrie Thorne's research in elementary classrooms produced a way of thinking about gender that is very appealing and rings of common sense. She asks, "How is gender more or less salient in different situations?" (Thorne 1990, p. 106). In specific social contexts, how do the organization and meanings of gender take shape in relation to other socially constructed divisions like age, race, and social class? This fluidity is key to appreciating and negotiating the messiness of classrooms and schooling.

Equality of representation and accuracy of scholarship in textbooks seems to be a fundamental right of children. If you never see yourself in a textbook, you will have been denied equal access to education. Equality is most salient under those circumstances. In a discussion of Toni Morrison's *Bluest Eyes*, race and gender may feature prominently in constructions of meaning and student responses. Differences within and between gender groups might be salient under those circumstances. Harassment of young women, in hallways and classrooms, is a generic gender issue—even though the harassment may take on specific racist forms. Referring to "you boys" over in a corner of the classroom invokes a gender system that may be inappropriate. Awareness of the complexity of gender identities and responses in classrooms and in text is critical for social studies educators. With awareness of the pervasive gendered systems, teachers and educators can sort through what is most relevant.

The legacy of the last twenty years—to summarize this historical section—is considerable. Despite the extensive erosion visited by Reagonomics on the hopes and accomplishments of the 1970s, we have learned a great deal about the complexity of gender identities and schooling. There is a renewed sense of direction with the 1990s. Guided by salience as a principle, equality and difference as variables, and caring as goals it seems possible to negotiate gender systems and create learning environments that are more humane for our students.

Texts and Context in Social Studies Curriculum

There are multiple dimensions of the social studies curriculum that could be discussed here. I will focus my attention in this discussion on both the unfinished agendas of the seventies and eighties that are still quite salient, textbooks and social studies content, and some new agendas for the nineties that arise out of recent scholarship and thinking.

As a *New York Times* front-page article proclaimed loudly to the readership on February 12, 1992, "Bias Against Girls is Found Rife in Schools, With Lasting Damage." The researchers in this American Association of University Women study reported that boys still receive more teacher attention than girls do in classrooms—both positive and negative—and that this difference persists across all levels of education (AAUW 1992). What the social education students receive comes from a variety of sources, including books, media programs, pictures, relationships, and utterances of all kinds. Teachers and students construct the gender codes for speech, behavior, and belief, most often in ways that they are not conscious of. The unacknowledged yet powerful gender coding that goes on in classrooms, hallways, lunchrooms, playgrounds, and athletic fields constitutes a social education curriculum that will ultimately carry more power than the knowledge that is generated and considered in more formal learning situations using classroom and text. Teachers who are knowledgeable and comfortable with their own gender identities and biographies will be far better equipped to help students consider gender issues in the classroom, and will be better equipped to deal with gender harassment.

Teacher Education

It is simplistic but important to point out that one significant source of information about gender is the teacher. Thus consciousness about gender attitudes and gender experiences is critical for classroom teachers and preservice teachers. My experience with preservice teachers is that for many their gendered identity is not available to them. For example, in response to an assignment that called for an autobiographical account of schooling and gender, a number of my students had nothing to report or talk about. They didn't have gender in their perspective. Self-knowledge and in particular critical knowledge of one's own school experience can help teachers understand the complex gendered systems of classrooms. As Robert Smith (1995) found in his case studies of preservice teachers, and Ralph Connell (1993) found in his case studies of students, definitions of masculinity are remarkably varied and early school experiences can leave deep impressions, which are not always accessible. "Teachers own character and sexual politics . . . are no less complex than the sexual politics of the pupils" (Connell 1993, p. 204). Moreover, as Evans (1988) found in her research on primary schools in Australia, teacher biographies become part of the negotiated social context of the present. Incorporating critical reflection of self in multicultural gendered terms is an important dimension of teacher education, especially for teachers whose identities are buried.

Curriculum Frameworks and Textbooks

Curriculum frameworks and textbooks are potential sources of curriculum change and transformation. They are rewritten periodically and thus might reflect the watershed of scholarship and research in the social sciences that has been published about women, men, and feminism in the past two decades. But there is considerable evidence to indicate that curriculum documents have not been receptive to the "new" scholarship (Hahn and Bernard-Powers 1985; McKenna 1989). The California History-Social Science Framework is a particularly important case in point. Written by an adjunct professor of history from an out of state institution, a state department employee, and a member of the curriculum commission, without substantive participation by the other members of the framework committee, it was a conservative document that minimized women's history and feminist social science. Feminist groups lobbied to influence the document and the hearings prior to adoption, but were effectively closed out along with other multicultural interests. The standing committee on gender issues of the California Council for the Social Studies was among the groups whose influence over the final document was sharply curtailed. The Western Association of Women Historian's K-12 Committee continues to lobby for change in this document, which may be revised in the next framework cycle. Whereas a framework might serve as a curricula model to move social studies teaching and learning into the next century and prepare the way for our changing clientele, this framework has directed attention to the past.

Curriculum frameworks such as California's can profoundly influence social studies curricula, because they shape textbooks and textbooks are a fundamental source of content knowledge. "About half of all social studies teachers depend upon a single textbook; about 90% use no more than three" (Marker and Mehlinger 1991, p. 849). Textbooks, because of their accessibility, are the most systematically studied data in the field of social studies. Hence content analyses on the inclusion of women in texts are very available.

What do textbook content analyses find? There have been no dramatic increases in either the quality or quantity of content on women in textbooks over the last twenty years. While most texts pay close attention to visuals and language, the figures reported in Tetreault's (1986) study of twelve popular U.S. textbooks are reminiscent of 1975: copy devoted to women did not exceed 8 percent in any text surveyed and was under 5 percent in over half. A Canadian study published in 1989 found similar results. Women were very central in visual representations, but they were marginal to the main text (Light, Staton, and Bourne 1989). All students deserve textbooks that represent current scholarship.

Content Knowledge: Scholarship in the Social Sciences

Topics housed under the umbrella of feminist scholarship in the social sciences are vast. In the following discussion I focus on the three areas that command attention in K-12 social studies curricula: history, geography, and civics.

Historical Scholarship and the Social Studies Curriculum

This discussion of historical content proceeds from the assumption that women of all classes, races, and ethnic groups are left out of the text and that curriculum reform depends on the reeducation of teachers. My own research on Lucy Laney, an African-American educator and social activist from Augusta, Georgia, and the course development work of John C. Walter illustrate this point. Walter (1991) describes his attempts to reshape his teaching the history of the United States between 1875 and 1915 in *Transforming the Curriculum, Ethnic Studies, and Women's Studies*. Standard accounts of that historical period, referred to as the Gilded Age and the Progressive Era, typically include references to Booker T. Washington and W.E.B. DuBois. After participating in a seminar on black history and feminism, however, Walter recast his teaching of the whole period, moving far beyond the typically stereotyped account of race relations of the period. Rather than focusing on the accommodationist stance that Washington is known to have assumed, or the oppositional position adopted by DuBois, Walters chose to focus his teaching on the social and political lives of African-American women of the period. Middle-class African-American women were very involved with the political context of the period, and indeed many were significant political figures who influenced government policy and were far from "accommodationist" in their philosophy (Walter 1991).

For example, Lucy Laney was an outstanding African-American leader of the period who established the Haines Normal and Industrial Institute in Augusta, Georgia. It mentored young women such as Mary Jackson-McCrorey and Mary McLeod Bethune. Laney along with several other African American women also challenged segregationist policies in the YWCA in the early twenties (Bernard-Powers 1994). Walter's new approach to the study of this period led to a transformation of the historical scholarship by challenging some facile stereotypes, by bringing both public and private lives into the center of the story, and by creating an inclusive and more accurate view of what the politics of the period was really like. Starting schools, educating children, and feeding families were significant political acts for African-American women and men in the south (Jones 1985).

There are two major points to be found in the above account. First, this is an example of how history can be transformed. Even if the figures of Washington and DuBois are included, the context of the story changes. Second, this recasting of the story would not have been done without Walter's reeducation. He went "back to school" and participated in a seminar on the African-American history and feminism where he learned about the lives of the African-American women in the context of that historical period. He was thus able to teach a new story. All teachers have to read new sources and new scholarship in the social sciences in order to teach a transformed and multiculturally relevant social education. The rewards of this, as Tracy Robinson and Janie Victoria Ward point out, might be that "African-American adolescent females . . . [will] be empowered through their connection to black women's long history as freedom fighters and social activists" (Robinson and Ward 1991).

Gender and Geography

Geography is a subject that has moved to center stage with the current emphasis on social science disciplines and concerns about students in U.S. public schools who are allegedly geographically illiterate. Along with the general visibility of the subject, interest in gender issues and feminism has grown, especially in university departments. Linda Peake, guest editor of the *Journal of Geography in Higher Education* (1989) brought together a number of women geographers to discuss the status of gendered and feminist geography around the world. In so doing they identified key issues that can apply to other social science disciplines and across the social studies curriculum.

The distinction between gender and feminism was an important point made in the discussion of Australian geography courses (Johnson 1989). Whereas gender-inclusive geography might include information about women who are consumers, migrants, refugees, or paid workers, the norm for geographical understanding would remain male-centered with female added on. A feminist approach to geography would question assumptions of standard geography and pose questions about women's oppression, patriarchal structures, and the use of space both public and private, conceptual and actual. As Johnson states it, "The feminist critique is a total one—it should restructure the assumptions, content, pedagogy and political purpose of any course" (1989, p. 87).

Using geography to question and understand women's positions in economic, political, and social institutions, and using geographic data to inform policy are central to feminist-gendered geographic learning. Peake (1989) points out, in her review of the status of feminist geography in the United Kingdom, that geographers, much like Walter's approach to history, can revisit old questions from new perspectives. Examples of topics cited by Peake are: women and housing in the Third World; processes of gentrification; the position of women in rural societies in the advanced industrial world; women's fear in and use of public space; and the system of child care in the industrialized world.

Reporting on geography teaching and learning in the United States, Eve Grundfest cited evidence that with one exception, "American human geography texts are gender-blind" (1989, p. 109). In precollegiate social studies, gendered feminist geography has not been a central feature in discussions about K–12 curricula revision. Grundfest suggests topics that speak to the possibilities of gendered geography:

- the emerging geography of women's employment
- where women live and work in the United States
- neighborhood planning
- the feminization of poverty and proposals for change
- how Third World urbanization affects women
- child care and public policy
- transportation planning for women

It should also be noted that whenever the category of women is used as an organizing category, it bears some examination to see if distinct within-group patterns emerge.

Joni Seager (1992) identified three general observations that serve as points of departure for feminist geography:

1. Space is gendered and the use of it is determined in part by ideological assumptions about gender roles and relations.
2. Space relations and configurations help to maintain culturally specific notions of gender behavior—for example, suburban women
3. Gender is an interpretive lens that influences relationships with environments.

This rich new area of exploration and understanding holds great promise for K–12 social studies teachers and learners who like myself, may have been looking for new perspectives on gendered human environments—that is, the lived contexts of everyday life where our multicultured, gendered students are found .

Education for Engendered Citizenship Education

The final topic in this discussion of social studies content is the broad arena known as civics or citizenship education—considered by many as the heart of the social studies curriculum. As much as any other subject in social studies education, this area exemplifies the importance of both unfinished gender agendas and transformative *new* agendas. I will consider both in that order.

Good citizenship—that is, behavior and attitudes that promote the community welfare—is taught in primary and elementary education as a function of general socialization. Getting along with others, sharing, and being responsible for the rules of class and school, and cooperating with the teacher, are considered fundamental citizenship behaviors. Embedded in the context of classroom, halls, lunchroom, and playground, relationships are still relatively obscure but powerful understandings about gender and citizenship behavior. As Terry Evans' (1988) extensive case study of primary schools in Australia found, gender-differentiated behavior and norms abound. Corroborating the AAUW study work, Evans found that in general boys received more attention than girls, and dominated classroom interactions. Occasionally girls dominate interactions and shape the agenda of their school lives, but that is often spatially defined. It is particularly significant that on the large playground area—the outside public arena of the school—that both Thorne and Evans found that boys dominate the space and are the rule-makers.

It is also significant that in both elementary schools and secondary schools, female managers and leaders are in the vast minority. Shakeshaft (1985) reported that 80 percent of all elementary teachers and 95 percent of secondary teachers worked under male principals. These figures have not changed significantly in recent years. Both young men and young women are confronted with pervasive examples of men leading and women following.

Gender agendas are well established in primary schools where, in general, men visit and manage. Gender power relations are woven into the fabric of classroom life. Everyday events and citizen roles are shaped in that context. Yet, as Anyon (1983) found in her study of fifth-graders, not all conform. Girls can resist the middle-class, feminine, gender prescriptions by dressing and behaving in ways that teachers find provocative.

By the time that many young women reach high school, however, male dominance in heterosexual relationships is extended and embedded in the trappings of the institution. Lois Weis has written about white male working-class youths in highs schools based on her work in a high school with a large working class population (Weis and Fine 1993). Many of the young white working-class males in the high school Weis studied have a highly protective and dominant posture toward young white women and they aspire to a traditional patriarchal family structure. According to Weis, "the vast majority of boys at Freeway High intend to set up homes in which they exert control over their wives—in which they go out to work and their wives stay home" (Weis 1993, p. 245). The young women at Freeway High School did not hold this same attitude. When asked they would say that they planned on being established in a job or career before getting married, implying control over their own destiny. However, they did not seem to challenge the young men in their attitudes, and this seemed evident in Weis' reports on social studies classes.

Weis (1993, p. 246) describes a social studies class in which the teacher poses the following question: "Women are basically unwilling to assume positions in the business world. Agree or disagree?" One student, Sam, responded in the affirmative, adding that he agreed because "all women want to raise children and get married." When the teacher, followed up, saying, "All women?" Sam said, "No, but most." According to Weis, there was no further discussion of the matter. I would add that the vignette is profound and the silence of "no further discussion" is compelling.

Sexual harassment is another dimension of life in schools that mirrors the asymmetrical power relations of gender and is part of the informal citizenship education. A recent summary of research on sexual harassment in schools found that in studies dating back to 1980, as well as more recent studies, sexual harassment was a serious problem in high schools. In 1986, 133 young women from Minnesota were questioned. Researchers concluded that "depending on the courses in which they were enrolled, 33–60% reported incidents of harassment while only one male out of 130 reported any incident of harassment" (Stein 1993, cited in Sadker and Sadker,

1994, p. 293). Until recently sexual harassment was often dismissed as "just the way people are." However, recent court cases have increased public awareness of the frequency and seriousness of the problem.

The assumption that harassment was not a real problem is similar to how gender issues are perceived generally. For example, an extensive study of the U. S. Ninth Circuit Court identified the perception that gender bias was not a serious problem in this judicial system. The Task Force on Gender Bias found a different reality. According to the task force, gender is a significant factor in the carriage of justice and the workings of Ninth Circuit. "Women bear the brunt of the harms associated with such bias. . . . Gender can have an effect on one as litigant, witness, lawyer, employee, or judge with reference to both process and outcomes"(Ninth Circuit Task Force on Gender Bias 1993, p. 2171).

A key point to be made here is that gender bias is part of the fabric of our society and it is part of the fabric of students lives. As such it is a critical dimension of the citizenship education curriculum and needs to be a subject that is embedded in the K-12 curriculum and developed over the course of students' education. Our students need to be fully aware of the politics of gender, and our teachers need to be educated about it as well. That means providing preservice and inservice teachers with the philosophic and pedagogic tools to both reflect on their own beliefs and behaviors, and to address bias in a meaningful way in the curriculum, the hallways, lunchrooms, and playgrounds.

Another dimension of the unfinished agendas of gender equity in citizenship education is attitudes held by young people about women in the public realm. Documentation of adolescents' attitudes toward women in political office (Are women qualified? Would you vote for a woman?) consistently reveals lack of confidence. For example, research done in the seventies found that young women and girls demonstrate less political knowledge and were less supportive of women as political leaders (Education Commission of the States 1973). A more current study reported that a high percentage of young white and young African-American men, grades 7–12, believed women to be less qualified than men to run a country. Young white and young African-America women, on the other hand, thought that women were just as qualified as men (Gillespie and Spohn 1987).

Regrettably, Harwood and Hahn (1992) turned up evidence in their research on gender in civics that social studies classes in one southeastern community were doing little to challenge the views of male adolescents on gender and public leadership. There were few references ever made to women and women's issues in these classes, and the structured opportunities provided by the textbooks were ignored by the teachers.

Education about women in the public realm and discrimination, and the pathways to public office, is still an important agenda for citizenship education. Role models provided through current events, oral history, literature, and personal contact are a significant source of curriculum change. Molly Ivins (1994), columnist for the Fort Worth Star-Telegram, recently wrote a personal testimonial of the power of personal contact. She supervised a class of junior high school students on a field trip to the Texas state capitol, where they sat in on a session of the legislature. "When Wilhelmina Delco, a black state rep and speaker pro tem of the House, took the chair and started whacking bills through, every black girl in that class went on point. . . . Who's she? . . . Why's she up there?" When Governor Ann Richards came out to talk to them, it gave new meaning to the "role model thing" (*San Francisco Chronicle*, January 28, 1994).

Biography and autobiography are especially important sources for role modeling and for making the critical connections between social science and social studies knowledge, and personal belief and experience. Literature in these forms provide understanding of how bridges can be built between the world that is constructed outside the self and represented in what people say, and what textbooks show, and the inside voice of care, justice seeking, and ego building. Carol Gilligan, Nona Lyons, Lyn Mikel, Joan Pagano, and Helen Buss are among the people whose research on voice, care, justice, and story informs and illuminates issues of gender in social education and social studies. Social studies is *one* critical place in the curricula of public schools where students as young citizens can shape and reflect on their own connections to community.

A story of global history, U. S. history, or local history that omits the multiple and varied voices and experiences of women and many men alienates and burdens students. As Pagano (1991) expresses this idea, "Humans desire to know, to be known, and to find their locations as members of communities." Classroom texts constitute the imaginative field whereby "we acknowledge our identifications and claim our places as member of our communities." Yet for a young woman, becoming an adult in Western culture, presents the "deeply knotted dilemma of how to listen both to herself and to the tradition, how to care for herself as well as for others" (Buss 1991, p. 98). Buss characterizes this connected or disconnected political and emotional terrain as "double discourses." In her article on autobiography she describes the opposing female identities of Maxine Hong Kingston in *The Woman Warrior* (1989), wife, slave, and woman warrior.

Biography and autobiography in social studies curriculum can focus and validate these important tensions that rise up for young women. It can also validate critical feelings of opposition and resistance to silence and invisibility or discrimination. Anne Frank wrote in her wondrous diary, "Why did so many nations in the past, and often still now, treat women as inferior to men? . . . I would like to know the cause of the great injustice. . . . Women are much braver, much more courageous soldiers, struggling and enduring pain for the continuance of humankind" (cited in Gilligan 1993, p. 165). This resistance, remarkable for when it was written in 1944, would probably not have been expressed in a classroom full of her peers. The writing of it has provided many generations of young women the freedom to question and challenge the status quo and to find their place. For young African-American women, biographies such as Septima Clark's *Ready from Within* (Brown, 1990), and Kay Mills' (1993) recent biography of Fannie Lou Hamer, *This Little Light of Mine,* provide important examples of women who claimed their strength, resisted, suffered, and built their own bridges into community.

The citizenship lessons to be learned from the lives of Septima Clark, Fannie Lou Hamer, or Korean feminists Na Hye-Sok and Kim Won-ju speak to the need to redefine civics curriculum. The public domains of power and position are only part of the process of community building and sustenance. While women have been discouraged from the public path that Virginia Woolf (1938) wrote about in "Three Guineas," they have been encouraged in their contribution to elementary schools, family life, churches, caring for elders, and nursing. When they have entered the public realms, it has often been in defense of these family and community issues. This chapter of human experience and citizenship education is often absent from school curriculum—thus validating the double vision of growing up female and denying young men validation of their own personal community experiences.

The citizenship curriculum of which I speak was proposed as part of the school curriculum at the turn of the century when it was slated for home economics. Domestic feminists in the first two decades of the twentieth century lobbied for formal education about environmental issues such as pure air, water, and food, and social issues such as protective labor legislation for women and children (Bernard-Powers 1992). Elizabeth Karmarck Minnich expressed this dimension of community life as follows:

> We did found and run institutions that cared for the sick and old and wounded outside the home. We did found and run schools. . . . We did struggle for goodness in the church, the synagogue, the community and we did so politically. We were active in the abolition movement and the civil rights movement. We outsiders did our work, work of all kind, and whatever we did remained obscured from the light. [Minnich 1982, p. 314]

This curriculum of family, community relation, and social contract was not institutionalized, however, and the central focus of citizenship education in social studies has rested on the public realm and the work of government.

Nel Noddings (chapter four in this volume and 1992) and Jane Roland Martin (1995) are among the feminist scholars who have suggested that there is a woman's culture, and that the ideas and values of woman's culture, especially those domestic issues, belong in the curriculum. Social studies curriculum that weaves together the public and private education for community life, and provides voice for the silences we continue to find, could be transformational. Moreover it seems essential for the next decade as our demography changes.

Resources for Change

The last twenty years has seen the development of a solid network of support for gender-fair and inclusive curriculum change. The National Women's Studies Association has a K-12 network that actively promotes curriculum change. The Canadian Committee on Women's History has supported efforts including the linking of scholars with teachers. The National Women's History Project in Sonoma, California, is a key source of multicultural women's history books, materials, and inservice education. The National Association of Independent Schools, The Upper Midwest Women's History Center, Women in World Area Studies, the Western Association of Women Historians, and the SEED Project of Wellesley have provided support in a variety of forms; books, lobbies, inservice education, and networking.

The American Association of University Women served the United States with a very effective wake-up call when the report, "How Schools Shortchange Girls" was released (AAUW 1992). This report and the passionate responses to conservative curriculum proposals speak to what many of us believe is the mandate and potential of social studies curriculum. The processes and under-standings necessary for citizenship in a representative democracy require texts and teaching that is inclusive of gender, race, class, and ethnicity. Social studies has been and is now vulnerable to the criticism that while professing to represent and teach social justice as a basis for citizenship education, omissions, neglect, and misrep-resentation have served to miseducate.

The time is ripe for curriculum transformation. Our alienated young people in urban areas make that clear. Teen pregnancy is on the rise, adolescents are a significantly growing population of HIV positive people, and death from gunshots is the number one cause of death among young African-American males. These are profound gendered issues that belong in the social studies curriculum. The lives that our young people live is significantly different from the experience of adults who educate them. We cannot afford to ignore the reality of their lives by teaching a curriculum that denies their fundamental and diverse identities.

Each journey must begin with the first step and then the first mile. Carpe Diem.

CHAPTER SIX

Against the Sovereignty of Origins: Contradictions in the Experience of Racial Inequality in Education and Society[1]

Cameron McCarthy

If you want to go with stereotypes, Asians are the smart people, the blacks are great athletes, what is white? We're just here. We're the oppressors of the nation. [student at Berkeley quoted in *The Diversity Project: Final Report to the Chancellor*, 1991, p. 37].

And here we are, at the center of the arc, trapped in the gaudiest, most valuable water wheel the world has ever seen. [James Baldwin, *The Fire Next Time*, 1963, p. 141]

The paradox of race in America is that our common destiny is more pronounced and imperiled precisely when our divisions are deeper. [Cornel West, *Race Matters*, 1993, p. 4]

Introduction

Conflicts in education and society are increasingly taking the form of grand panethnic battles over culture and identity. Riding these developments are acutely localized struggles to territorialize the symbolic and material space of schools and society. The repercussions of these developments are being felt in social and cultural institutions through the length and breadth of the United States. In education, the emergence in the past few years of theorists espousing new paradigms of race relations analysis rooted in Eurocentric and Afrocentric philosophies has contributed to the general hardening of both the popular and the intellectual discourse on inequality in schooling. A particular failing of these emergent theories of racial inequality is their tendency toward essentialist or single-cause explanations of minority disadvantage. That is to say that these educational theorists tend to explain differences in the educational, cultural and political behavior of minority and majority school youth by reference to race pure and simple.

This essay offers a critique of tendencies toward dogmatism and essentialism in current educational theories of racial inequality. I argue that you cannot understand race, paradoxically, by looking at race alone. Different gender, class, and ethnic interests cut at right angles to racial coordination and affiliation. Programmatic reforms that underestimate the powerful role of nuance, contradiction, and heterogeneity within and between racial groups in education are not likely to succeed either in reducing racial antagonism or assuaging educational inequities. Drawing on the qualitative research on race relations in education of Grant (1984, 1985), Omi and Winant (1991), and Spring (1991), I point attention to the contradictory interests, needs, and desires of minority and majority youth and adults. I discuss also the subversive role such competing interests, needs, and desires play in the struggle for race relations reform in education.

The Limits of Ethnic Affiliation

In a recent article, Henry Louis Gates (1991) relates a story that has made its rounds in the jazz world. The story takes the form of an answer to what Gates calls "The perennial question: Can you really tell?" The question is about racial authenticity, racial origins, and their predictive capacity with respect to cultural behavior and meaning of style. Can you really tell who is the black one, who is the white one? Can you really tell? According to Gates:

> The great black jazz trumpeter Roy Elridge once made a wager with the critic Leonard Feather that he could distinguish white musicians from black ones—blindfolded. Mr. Feather duly dropped the needle onto a variety of record albums whose titles and soloists were concealed from the trumpeter. More than half the time, Elridge guessed wrong. [p.1][2]

What Gates fails to mention is the fact that the blindfold test is an institution of the *Down Beat* jazz magazine for well over a quarter-century now and that white jazz musicians presented with the blind-fold test regularly confuse black musicians with whites ones, and vice versa. The problem of racial origins and racial authenticity is a prob-lem all around. The elusiveness of racial identity not only affects blacks, it affects whites. Racial identities can never be gathered up in one place as a final cultural property. And, as we approach the end of the twentieth century, what seemed like stable white ethnicities and heritages in an earlier era are now entering a zone of recoding and redefinition. Omi and Winant (1991) put the problematic of waning white ethnicity in this post–civil rights era in the following terms:

> Most whites do not experience their ethnicity as a definitive as-pect of their social identity. They perceive it dimly and irregularly, picking and choosing among its varied strands to exercise, as Mary Waters (1990) suggests, an "ethnic option." The specifically ethnic components of white identity are fast receding with each generation's additional remove from the old country. Unable to speak the language of their immigrant forbears uncommitted to ethnic endogamy, and unaware of their ancestors' traditions (if in fact they can still identify their ancestors as, say, Polish or Scots, rather than a combination of four or five European—and non-European!—groups) whites undergo a racializing panethnicity as "Euro-Americans." [p.17]

Nowhere is this sense of the "twilight of white ethnicity" felt more deeply than on American college campuses. In these deeply racially balkanized and polarized sites of the American education system we are entering the Brave New World of the post–civil rights era—a new world registered in popular culture by films like *Falling Down* (1993), *White Palace* (1990), and *Dances with Wolves* (1990)—a world in which the proliferation of ethnic diversity has led to a heightened state of race-consciousness on the part of mi-norities and whites. The post–civil rights era is the era of the displaced and decentered whole subject. And white students on college campuses find themselves positioned as the antagonists in an unpredictable racial drama in which middle-class subjects speak in the voice of the new oppressed—a progeny spawned in an era of the discourse of reverse discrimination. For instance, white stu-dents interviewed in a recent study on racial diversity conducted at Berkeley emphasized a sense of racial encirclement, ethnic insta-bility, and the new conflictual nature of identity (Institute for the Study of Social Change, 1991). A few examples of comments made by white students underscore these new dilemmas:

Student #1: Many whites don't feel like they have an ethnic identity at all and I pretty much feel that way too. It's not something that bothers me tremendously but I think that maybe I could be missing something that other people have, that I am not experiencing.

Student #2: Being white means that you're less likely to get financial aid. . . . It means that there are all sorts of tutoring groups and special programs that you can't get into, because you're not a minority.

Student #3: If you want to go with the stereotypes, Asians are the smart people, the Blacks are great athletes, what is white? We're just here. We're the oppressors of the nation. At Berkeley being white is having to constantly be on my toes about offending other races not saying something to be construed as I am continuing to be the oppressor of America. [p.37]

These stories of racial/ethnic instability come at a critical juncture in debates over racial inequality, racial identity, and curriculum reform in the educational field in the United States. They also point to the crisis in the theorization of race and racial logics in education. But it is also, paradoxically, a time in which there is a peculiar language of racial and ethnic certainty, of panethnic camps drawn tightly around specular origins. The world is a vast Lacanian mirror in which theorists of racial purity and racial essence see themselves standing in front of their ancestors. It is the perfect image, the snapshot of history collected in the nuclear family photo album. It is the story of the singular origin, the singular essence, the one, true primary cause. The old Marxists and neo-Marxist orthodoxies of class and economic primacy in education debates are rapidly being replaced by the new panethnic cultural assertions of racial origins.

The proponents of Western civilization and Eurocentrism and their critics, the proponents of Afrocentrism, now argue for the heart and soul of the educational enterprise. (This is not, of course, to suggest that there is an equivalence in the deployment of material and political resources here, for in some way, the playing out of this conflict involves a certain encirclement of black intellectual thinking.)[3] Conservative educators like Diane Ravitch join conservative ideologues such as George Will in insisting for instance, that: "[The United States] is a branch of European civilization . . . 'Eurocentricity' is right, in American curricula and consciousness, because it accords with the facts of our history, and we and Europe are fortunate for that" (Will 1989, p. 3). Europe, through this legerdemain, is collapsed into United States without any difficulty. History and tradition in this country are seen as interchangeable with those of Europe.

On the other hand, Afrocentric theorist Asante (1987) argues for the panethnic unity of all black people of the diaspora, pointing to the origins of African people in the "spatial reality of Africa." We are in the historical moment of what Aronowitz and Giroux (1991) call the "politics of clarity." Of course, it is important to emphasize here that Afrocentrism is a liberatory discourse. When one reads the work of Asante, Jawanza Kunjufu, and others, one recognizes immediately a sustained effort to connect to an intellectual and political history of struggle waged by racially subordinated groups in the United States. But Afrocentrism also contains within its discourse a language that masks issues of contradiction and discontinuity within the diaspora, between the diaspora and Africa, between different economically and socially situated African-Americans and other minority groups, and between differently situated men and women.

Beyond these concerns is the issue of intellectual and cultural workers and their problematic relationships to anything that begins to sound like a singular cultural heritage or cultural stream. It is a necessary condition of dynamic intellectual and cultural work that the specific intellectual worker has the flexibility to draw on the well-ground of history, to draw on the variety of cultural resources that fan out across the myriad groups that make up this society and the world. "Culture," writers such as Coco Fusco, Cornel West, and Stuart Hall suggest, is a hybrid. For that matter, race is a hybridizing process as well—it is the product of encounters between and among differently located human groups.

By hybridity here, I am not referring to a Joseph-coat trope of difference—the proverbial social guilt that happily embraces a cornucopia of differences, laying down these differences, one after the other, side by side. Instead, I am drawing attention to Bhabha's (1986) contention that in any one group or individual there are always competing identities, competing needs, and desires wrestling to the surface. In saying this, I am not denying there is the persistence of what Hall (1989) calls "continuities" between, say, the people of Africa and the people of the Afro-New World diaspora. Neither am I contesting the fact that there are brutal realities associated with the patterns of racial exclusion that affect minorities in the United States. What I am saying is that racial difference is the product of human interests, needs, and desires, human strategy, human capacities, forms of organization, and forms of mobilization; and that these dynamic variables, which articulate themselves in the form of grounded social constructs such as identity, inequality, and so forth, are subject to change, contradiction, variability, and revision within historically specific and determinate contexts. "Race" is a deeply unstable and decentered complex of social meanings constantly begin transformed by cultural and social conflict (Omi and Winant 1991). Racial identities are therefore profoundly social, historical, and variable categories.

Against the grain of this historical and social variability, Afrocentrics and Eurocentrics now argue for school reform based on the narrow limits of ethnic affiliation. For the Afrocentric, the intolerable level of minority failure in schooling has to do with the fact that minority, particularly African-American, cultural heritage is suppressed in the curriculum. Black students fail because schools assault their identities and destabilize their sense of self and agency. (A good example of this these is to be found in Kunjufu, 1990.) For the proponents of Western civilization, Western cultural emphasis in the curriculum is colorblind. Black students fail because of the cultural deprivation that exist in their homes and in their communities. Literacy in Western civilization would be the best antidote for failure among the black poor. E. D. Hirsch (1987) suggests broad cultural literacy would help disadvantaged black youth enter the mainstream.

This essay is written in response to this moment of race- and ethnic-based diagnosis of inequality in education and prescription for change. This is a diagnosis that is driven by a peculiarly recalcitrant concept of race that is discursively based on nineteenth-century biology and naturalization of human distinctions. A nineteenth-century concept of race now inhabits much mainstream and radical thinking about inequality in education.

Race theory is particularly unreflexive about the category of "race" itself. Educational theories of racial inequality are at bottom still informed by notions of "essences," notions of near indelible characteristics in culture, linguistic style, cognitive capacity, family structures, and the like. Neo-Marxist theorists such as Ahmad (1992), Edari (1984), and Jackobowitz (1985) follow the early line of Bowles and Gintis in reducing race to capital labor contradiction. Mainstream and neoconservative theorists such a D'Souza (1911), Orr (1987), Jensen (1984), Bell (1975) and others, pursue one theoretical and programmatic concern: *the issue of the educability of minorities.*

The central task has been to explain perceived differences between black and white students as reflected in differential achievement scores on standardized tests, high school dropout rates, and so forth. As Henriques (1984) has pointed out, one of the unintended effects of these accounts of educational inequality has been the reproduction and consolidation of a powerful pathological discourse on minority cognitive capacities, family structures, linguistic styles, and so forth.[4] Curricular discourses of Afrocentricism tend simply to offer a more positive formulation of race-as-essence in their valorizations of diaspora culture and heritage.

These essentialist or origins-oriented explanations of racial difference do not offer an adequate basis for conceptualizing educational reform. By essentialist, I am referring to the tendency in current mainstream and radical writing on race to treat social groups as stable or homogeneous entities. Racial groups such as Asians, or Latinos, or blacks are therefore discussed as though members of these groups possessed some innate and invariant set of characteristics that set them apart from each other and from whites. Feminist theorists such as Wallace (1990) and de Lauretis (1984) have critiqued dominant tendencies in mainstream research to define differences in terms of transcendental essences. Wallace (1990), for example, maintains that differences in the political and cultural behavior of minority women and men are determined by social and historical contingencies, and not some essentialist check list of innate, biological, or cultural characteristics. Following Wallace, I argue that essentialist thinking about race not only inhibits a dynamic understanding of race relations, but contributes to the ever-increasing balkanization of cultural and public spaces in education and society.

Common to these approaches as well as some of the more recent formulations around multiculturalism is a tendency to undertheorize race (Tiedt and Tiedt 1986). Within these paradigms of educational and social theory, racial antagonism is conceptualized as a kind of deposit or disease that is triggered off into existence by some deeper flaw of character or society. I inflect the discussion of race away from the language of deprivation and cultural and economic essentialism that now dominates the research literature on racial inequality. The fact is that racial differences are produced. Racial relations of domination and subordination are arranged and organized in cultural forms and in the ideological practices of identity formation and representation inside and outside schooling—what Althusser (1971) calls the "mise-en-scène of interpellation." I am therefore interested in the ways in which moral leadership and social power are exercised *in the concrete* and the ways in which regimes of racial domination and subordination are constructed and resisted in education.

The theoretical and methodological issues concerning race are complex. They therefore require a comparative and relational approach to analysis and intervention in unequal relations in schools. Such analysis and intervention must pay special attention to contradiction, discontinuity, and nuance within and between embattled social groups, what I have called elsewhere the process of "nonsynchrony" (McCarthy 1990). By invoking the concepts of contradiction and nonsynchrony, I advance the position that individuals or groups, in their relation to economic, political, and cultural institutions such as schools, do not share identical consciousness and express the same interests, needs, or desires "at the same point in time" (Hicks 1981: p. 221). These discontinuities in the needs and interests of minority and majority groups are expressed in the long history of tension and hostility that has existed between the black and white working class in this country.

Also of crucial importance within this framework are the issues of the "contradictory location" (Wright 1978) of the *new* black middle class within the racial problematic, and the role of neoconservative black and white intellectuals in redefining the terrain of contemporary discourse on racial inequality toward the ideal of a color blind society. Just as important for a relational and nonessentialist approach to race and curriculum is the fact that minority women and girls have radically different experiences of racial inequality than those of their male counterparts, because of the issue of gender. (Wallace [1990] calls these dynamics 'negative variations'.) Examples of the contradictory character of race relations drawn from contemporary developments in the political and educational arenas will be discussed in the next segment of this chapter.

The Contrapuntal Nature of Racial Experiences

As Burawoy (1981) and Nkomo (1984) make clear with respect to South Africa, economic divides that exist between the black underclass from the Bantustan and their more middle-class counterparts working for the South African state (the police, nurses, Bantustan bureaucrats) often serve to undermine black unity in the struggle against racial oppression. Similar examples exist in the United States where some middle-class minority intellectuals such as Shelby Steele and Thomas Sowell have spoken out against affirmative action and minority scholarship programs in higher education. They have suggested that such ameliorative policies discriminate against white males. Another case in point is the 1990 ruling by the U.S. Department of Education's former assistant secretary for civil rights, Michael Williams. He maintained that it was illegal for a college or university to offer a scholarship only to minority students (Jaschik 1990). The irony of this situation is underlined by the fact that the former assistant secretary for civil rights is a black man. The fact is that without these scholarships a number of very talented minorities would not be able to pursue higher education. Here again, the "point man" on a reactionary Republican policy that effectively undermined the material interests of African-Americans and other minority groups was a neoconservative member of the emergent minority middle class.

One should not, however, draw the conclusion that contradictions associated with race and specific social policies such as affirmative action only affect blacks. These dynamics are also reflected in the politics of identity formation among Asian Americans. Let us look at two examples of the contradictory effects of inclusionary and exclusionary ethnic practices among Asian Americans and Pacific Islanders. In order to consolidate and extend their political clout and benefits from land trust arrangements, native Hawaiians voted four-to-one in January 1990 for a highly inclusionary definition of their ethnic identity—one that expanded the definition of their people to anyone with a drop of Hawaiian "blood." According to Omi and Winant, "Previously only those with at least 50 percent Hawaiian 'blood' were eligible for certain benefits" (1991, p. 9).

They also point to a second example, this time of the exclusionary effects of intraethnic contradictions in the politics of Asian American identity formation and affirmative action policy:

> By contrast, in June 1991 in San Francisco, Chinese American architects and engineers protested the inclusion of Asian Indians under the city's minority business enterprise law. Citing a Supreme Court ruling which requires cities to narrowly define which groups had suffered discrimination to justify specific affirmative action programs, Chinese Americans contended that Asian Indians should not be considered "Asian." At stake were obvious economic benefits accruing to designated "minority" business. [1991, p. 9]

The contradictory phenomenon of racial identity formation in this post–civil rights era also manifests itself inside schools. As a case in point, Spring (1991) reports on a longitudinal study of the class dynamics operating within a black suburban community ("Black Suburbia") and the way in which these dynamics get expressed in the relationship of black students and their parents of the school system. Spring's account begins at a point in time when the great momentum of the Civil Rights movement had begun to wane—the late 1960s. It was during this period of the late sixties that the subject of Spring's account, a black professional middle-class (PMC) population, moved into a midwestern suburb, formerly populated predominately by whites. The new residents of Black Suburbia quickly embraced the predominately white-administered school system. As the constituents of the "new" middle class in the district, black PMC parents and their children readily granted legitimacy to the school system in exchange for access to what residents called "quality education." They saw the schools as guarantors of continued upward mobility for their children. According to Spring:

> A study of the community [Black Suburbia] in the late 1960s showed the mobility concerns and educational aspirations of the new African-American population . . . The study found that both the middle-aged and young middle-class African-American residents had high expectations of upward mobility and believed that *quality* schools were a major element in *quality* community. The population group labeled "new, middle-aged, black middle-class residents" were earning more than $10,000 a year and were employed as managers, proprietors, and professionals. This group was found to have an "extraordinarily high degree" of expectations for continuing upward mobility and concern about the quality of schools. [1991, p. 122]

The term "quality school" indeed summarized an ideological and strategic trade-off or "settlement" that was tacitly implicated in the overwhelming black PMC support for the white-administered school system. But this settlement between the school system and its new PMC patrons was soon to be imperiled by a change in the demographic and cultural milieu of the Black Suburbia community and its schools. And both the expectations of upward mobility and the high educational aspirations of the black PMC residents who had arrived in the late 1960s were, by the 1970s, "threatened by the rapid influx of a poor African-American population" (Spring, 1991 p.

123). This influx of low-income blacks dramatically altered the social class composition of Black Suburbia: "Between 1970 and 1973 the percentage of children from welfare families increased . . . from 16 to 51 percent. The migration of upwardly mobile middle-class African-Americans was followed by the rapid migration of African-American welfare families" (Spring 1991 p. 123).

Teachers responded negatively to the entrance of increased numbers of low-income black students into the school system and the "standards of education" in Black Suburbia schools declined:

> One of the first things to happen was that the educational expectations of the mainly white teachers and administrators in the school system began to fall. This seemed to be caused by the assumption of the white school staff that the African Americans moving into the community were not interested in education and would create major problems in the school system. [Spring 1991, p. 123]

The white school staff's negative assumptions about the educational capabilities of their black students was further illustrated when Spring compared the educational expectations of the elementary school principals with those of the members of Black Suburbia's black community:

> In early 1970s, a local government survey of Black Suburbia included a question dealing with the level of educational aspirations. The survey asked parents how far they would like their sons or daughters to progress in school. Seventy-three percent of parents wanted their sons to complete college, and 71 percent had that goal for their daughters. More important, when asked how far they believed their sons or daughters would actually go in school, 60 percent believed their sons would complete college, and 62 percent believed that their daughters would do the same.

> The contrast between the educational aspirations of the parents and the expectations of the elementary school principals illustrates the problems and frustrations encountered by African American residents. When I asked elementary school principals what percentage of the students of their schools they felt would go to college, the response from the three principals were 3 percent, 12 percent, and 10 percent. [1991, pp. 123–24]

The decline in the quality of education in Black Suburbia's schools precipitated a crisis of legitimacy in the school system's relations to its black constituents. However, the racial response of the school system to black students was not met or challenged by a united front among the black residents of Black Suburbia. Indeed, class antagonism between the more affluent blacks and the lower-class black residents intensified both in the schools and in the community. PMC black students blamed the lower-class students for the sharp decline in educational standards in the schools. They complained that the teachers were incapable of controlling the "rowdies"—a code word for low-income black students. This class antagonism spilled over into the community. As class antagonism intensified, the more affluent black parents took the further step of withdrawing their children from the public schools and sending them to private institutions.[5] From the perspectives of these PMC black residents, the Black Suburbia school system had failed to deliver on its side of a social contract. Black students stood to suffer in competitive relations for credentials and long-term futures in the labor market. To say the least, the interests of black PMC residents and their low-income counterparts diverged. Resulting class antagonism undermined racial solidarity among black residents and weakened their collective ability to negotiate with the white-administered school system, or challenge the racial basis of the poor-quality education that the public schools were offering to their children.

Grant (1984) calls attention to another example of discontinuity with respect to minority and majority relationships to schooling—this time with respect to the operation of gender at the classroom level. Based on the findings from a study of "face-to-face interactions" in six desegregated elementary school classrooms in a midwestern industrial city, she concludes that "black females' experiences in desegregated schools . . . differ from those of other race-gender groups and cannot be fully understood by extrapolating from the research on females or research on blacks." Among other things, Grant contends that the teachers (all women, three blacks and three whites) she observed did not relate to their black students and white students in any consistent or monolithic way. Grant places particular emphasis on the way in which black girls were positioned in the language of the classroom and in the informal exchanges between teachers and students. She notes:

> Although generally compliant with teachers' rules, black females were less tied to teaches than white girls were and approached them only when they had a specific need to do so. White girls spent more time with teachers, prolonging questions into chats

about personal issues. Black girls' contacts were briefer, more task related, and often on behalf of a peer rather than self. [1984, p. 107]

Although these teachers tended to avoid contact with black male students, they were still inclined to identify at least one black male student in their individual classroom as a "superstar." In none of the six desegregated classrooms was any of the black girls identified as a high academic achiever. Instead, Grant maintains, black girls were typified as "average achievers" and assigned to average or below-average track placements and ability groups. Gender differences powerfully influenced and modified the racially inflected ways in which teachers evaluated, diagnosed, labeled, and tracked their students. Grant therefore points to a hidden cost of desegregation for black girls:

Although they are usually the top students in all-black classes, they lose this stature to white children in desegregated rooms. Their development seems to become less balanced, with emphasis on social skills. . . . Black girls' everyday schooling experiences seem more likely to nudge them toward stereotypical roles of black women than toward [academic] alternatives. These include serving others and maintaining peaceable ties among diverse persons rather than developing one's own skills. [1984, p. 109][6]

Beyond Dogmatism, Beyond Essentialism

The point I want to make here, then, is that you cannot read off the educational, cultural, or political behavior or minority and majority youth or adults based on assumptions about race, pure and simple. Different gender and class interests and experiences within minority and majority groups often cut at right angles to efforts at racial coordination and affiliation. The findings of researchers such as Grant, Nkomo, Omi and Winant, and Spring help to illustrate and clarify the complex workings of racial logics in the highly differentiated environments that exist in school settings. By drawing attention to contradiction and nonsynchrony in the educational processes of cultural selection, competition, and domination, these critical researchers directly challenge mainstream single-group studies of inequality in schooling that have tended to isolate the variable of race from gender and class. They also challenge radical accounts of inequality that suggest you can read off the cultural behavior of minority groups from economic location or racial origins, pure and simple. Instead, this work underscores the need for comparative analysis and the need to examine the historical specificity and variability of race, and is nonsynchronous interaction with forms of class and gender structuration in education. A nonessentailist approach to the study of inequality in schooling alerts us to the fact that different race-class-gender groups not only have qualitatively different experiences in schools, but actually exist in constitutive tension, often engage in active competition with each other, receive different forms of rewards, sanctions, and evaluations, and are ultimately structured into differential futures. The critical theoretical and methodological task, then, as Hall suggests, is one of "radically decoding and mapping" the specific relations and nuances of particularly historical and institutional contexts:

> One needs to know how different groups were inserted histori-cally, and the relations which have tended to erode and transform, or to preserve these distinctions through time—not simply as residues and traces of previous modes, but as active structuring principles of the present society. Racial categories *alone* will *not* provide or explain this. [Hall 1980a, p. 339]

What is abundantly clear is that monolithic and homogeneous strategies of curriculum reform that attempt to ignore or avoid the contradictions of race at the institutional level will be of limited usefulness to minority youth. New approaches to race relations reform in education must begin with a more sophisticated and robust conceptualization of the dynamic relations between minority and majority actors in the school setting. In this regard, efforts to get beyond the essentialism, reductionism, and dogmatism in current theories would be a very good place to start.

The multifaceted nature of race relations and their operation in education and society requires a many-sided response. I should like, for example, to see multicultural theorists attempt to make connections with analyses of curriculum provided by theorists writing about critical thinking, school effectiveness, and institutional organization. I should also like them to make connections with the urban ethnographic work of researchers such as Fine (1990) and Sullivan (1990) who have begun to look at socio-economic contexts of urban schooling. These dynamics of race, class, and gender are interwoven unevenly into the social fabric of American institutions and structures—in educational system, the economy, and the state.

This uneven interaction of race with other variables, namely class and gender—nonsynchrony—is a practical matter that defines the daily encounter of minority and majority actors in institutional and social settings. Thus, for example, the experience of educational inequality for a black male middle-class youth from a two-parent household is qualitatively different from that of a black working-class female from a single-parent household. As we saw in the case of Spring's report on Black Suburbia, black middle-class youth had more material options than their working class peers when the racially motivated inferior education in Black Suburbia's public schools became intolerable. The parents of these middle-class youth moved them from public to private educational institutions. Black working-class youth did not have this maneuverability—their parents could not afford to pull out of the racist public school system.

However, a nonessentialist theory and practice of race relations in schooling must not merely be negative in its implications. It is not enough to critique existing theoretical and programmatic approaches to race and educational reform. The articulation of a nonessentialist perspective on race and education entails a second, more positive, conceptual and practical task: to stake out a field within contemporary debates on schooling for a more inclusive, affirmative set of practices that take seriously the differential needs, interests, and desires of minority women and men and urban working-class youth. As a matter of first priority, it means that we must seriously insist that urban schools meet their social contract vis-à-vis African-American and Latino students and parents: that is, that much greater effort ought to be placed on equality of access to instructional and learning opportunities, and to equality of educational outcomes.

What is needed is a more dynamic and vigorous approach to school knowledge and curriculum organization that gets us beyond the essentialisms of Eurocentrism and Afrocentrism, and the content addition models of multiculturalism. Such a dynamic approach to school knowledge would emphasize heterogeneity of perspectives, interdisciplinarity, intellectual challenge and debate, and vigorous interrogation of received knowledge and traditions. Curriculum reform should mean students' autonomy with respect to multiple sources of information, not their necessary submission to corrective bits of knowledge that are presented as already settled truth—the good realism of multiculturalism and Afrocentrism versus the bad fiction of stereotypes. Eurocentrism presents us with a similar

unwarranted calcified vision of canonical texts and the history of
the West. Ultimately, there is a desperate need for schools, school
districts, and university teacher education programs to come up
with strategies of interpretation of the urban context as a product
of close collaboration and dialogue with minority parents and communities. These strategies of interpretation and dialogue with urban communities should lead to specific curriculum and instructional initiatives that give priority to the educational needs of
disadvantaged youth.

As a further corollary to this, we should by now be disabused
of the idea that the contradictory politics and practices associated
with racial and identity formation only address the experiences of
minority individuals and groups. At the beginning of this chapter,
I sought to draw attention to the fact that these discontinuities and
contradictions also apply to white. Much work needs to be done to
understand and intervene in the ways in which whites are positioned as "white," in the language, symbolic, and material structures that dominate culture in the West and the United States.
There is a need to move beyond static definitions of whites and
blacks as the currently pervade existing research in education (Fusco
1988; Giroux 1992; McCarthy and Crichlow, in press; Roman, in
press). This means, for example, that we should not continue to
position all whites as the other of multicultural curriculum reform
and other transformative projects in education. It means that in
every local setting, particularly in the urban setting, we must find
the moral, ethical, material, and political resources for generalized
affective investment in schools.

Such an investment must be grounded in a critical reading of
the differential needs of embattled urban communities and the
particular needs of inner-city school youth. Such a "differential
consciousness" (Sandoval 1991) must constantly challenge individual
constituencies to think within but at the same time to think beyond the particularity of their experiences and interests. Schools
cannot continue to function as armies of occupation in the inner-
city setting. They must, instead, become arenas in which diversifying urban communities can participate in building new solidari-
ties for educational access, mobility, and affirmation of minority
youth.

CHAPTER SEVEN

Multicultural Social Studies:
Schools as Places for Examining
and Challenging Inequality

David Hursh

Developing multicultural social studies is doubly burdened by conflicts over whether multicultural education should be implemented and, if it should be implemented, *how* it should be conceptualized. Multicultural social studies, I will argue, is *not* about devoting one month of the year to teaching the contributions of African Americans. Nor is it teaching students the foods, fashions, and festivals of different racial and ethnic groups. Nor is it implementing activities aimed to improve tolerance between diverse groups. Rather, multicultural social studies requires, at minimum, rethinking the social studies curriculum, and, ideally, all of teaching and curriculum.

A central goal of multicultural social studies is to enable students to analyze cultural, political, economic, and historical patterns and structures so that students will not only better understand society, but affect it. Furthermore, because social inequality and diversity is a consequence of not only race and diversity but gender and class, we need to broaden multicultural education to include class and gender. While the social dynamics of class and gender differ from each other and that of race, similarities exist in how women, minorities, and the working class have been marginalized in social studies texts and social analysis.

Furthermore, because I will concur with Hazel Carby, who fears that by focusing on diversity and difference, race (and multicultural education) is "only wheeled in when the subjects are black" (1990, p. 85), I will propose that we examine how we all are racialized, gendered, and classed subjects who, because of who we are and our previous experiences, have come to see the world in particular ways. That is, we should include not only experiences of minorities in our schools, but examine our understanding and experiences as white or minority; as upper, middle, or working class; and as female or male. Additionally, we should not limit ourselves to students' understanding and experience, but include teachers and community members. But in arguing for introducing a wide variety of individual experiences I am not, as Hazel Carby cautions, arguing for pluralism. I am arguing for, in Carby's word's, "revealing the structures of power that are at work in the racialization of the social order" (p. 85).

Lastly, by including the experiences of students and teachers I am not aiming, as in some multicultural proposals, to improve students' self-esteem.[1] Rather, I am recognizing that racism (and other social processes such as sexism) does not take one form but is forever changing, being challenged, and reconstructed in the actual practice in which people engage. Therefore, understanding and changing social practices requires us to situate our own local and specific knowledge and experience within the larger context.

Consequently, multicultural social studies requires rethinking not only how we teach history but the content of the curriculum as a whole, building on the students' and teachers' own experiences. What the curriculum and teaching might look like and the rationales for those changes are the concerns to which I'll now turn.

From "Great Men and Great Wars" to Multicultural and Socially Reconstructive Education

Understanding cultural, political, economic, and historical patterns and structures requires rethinking curriculum content to place less emphasis on "great men and great wars" and more emphasis on analyzing patterns and structures, including social history. History courses would focus less on individual personalities and, instead, promote students questioning "why things are as they are and how they might be different, and to hear and value the voices of those whose life histories have been different from theirs" (Sleeter 1991, p. 20).

Herb Kohl (1991) provides examples of how children's books about Rosa Parks and the Montgomery bus boycott typically misportray the boycott and the civil rights movement as the result of spontaneous individual action rather than the collective activity of a group or organization. The former approach, he argues, besides being historically inaccurate, promotes social passivity in students

by presenting social change as the consequence of individual heroism rather than "a community effort to overthrow injustice" (p. 13).
While not every child, writes Kohl, can imagine her or himself to
be a Rosa Parks, "everyone can imagine her or himself as a participant in a boycott" (p. 13) And every child can imagine her or himself as part of a community working for social change.[2]

The need to look at history in a way that includes the view of
those normally mis- or unrepresented is reflected in Bill Bigelow's
proposal that teachers and students analyze biographies of Christopher Columbus for how the authors portray Columbus, the different motivations for his voyages, and his treatment of the Native
Americans. Bigelow provides his own analysis of texts on Columbus to reveal how they perpetuate racism and colonialism, and
"inhibit children in developing democratic, multicultural and non-
racist attitudes." He gives suggestions for how teachers might provide a more balanced view of Columbus and locate the discussion
in issues of justice and equality (p. 1).[3]

Bigelow encourages teachers and students to examine history
as reflected in textual presentations. Teachers and students can
expand their field of study to examine how race, class, and gender
are represented not only historically but in past and contemporary
media, including books, advertisements, film, and television.[4]

In undertaking such examinations it becomes apparent that
students and teachers bring different experiences and knowledge
to the task and would, therefore, offer different interpretations and
conclusions. How I as a white male would interpret Alice Walker's
The Color Purple is likely to differ from that of an African American female. We simply bring different lives to the text. One of the
aims of multicultural education is not only to present different
material and make different analyses, but to realize and build on
our different interpretations. Multicultural education offers the
opportunity for educators to see themselves and students as learning from one another.

By realizing that we bring different experiences and knowledge to the classroom, we inevitably recognize that our knowledge
and experience reflects our lives as racialized, gendered, and classed
subjects. For example, as a white male who grew up working class,
I experienced pressure to excel in sports rather than academics,
and initially had difficulty maneuvering through college because of
a lack of cultural preparation for higher education. Tensions of my
race, gender, and class background continue. On the one hand, I
still feel estranged from academia wondering how I can be teaching

students in a university that would not have accepted me as a student, and fear that my inadequacies must be transparent. On the other hand, as someone who had been involved in organized struggles to reduce class, race, and gender inequalities, fret that my attempts to forge alliances across different social groups may be interpreted as either liberal guilt or opportunism rather than to seek common ground across our differences. As a teacher, and teacher educator, I desire to learn from students their perspectives of the world, both so that I might learn and have something to offer. I want to understand how my students evaluate curriculum and perceive their students, how they understand the causes of social inequality, and their perceptions of race, gender, and class.

Multicultural education, then, requires rethinking and reforming what and how we teach in ways that are neither easy nor predictable. It requires teachers and students to raise questions of whose knowledge is in the curriculum, and how power and inequality are maintained. It requires teachers and students to give voice to their own experiences and for social studies to become, as Michelle Fine suggests in *Framing Dropouts* (1991), a crucible within which students give voice to their own concerns and lives, and connect with others. Because the assumptions of this approach are similar to those behind Christine Sleeter's (1991) "education that is multicultural and socially reconstructive," I will use the same identifying phrase.

Because a variety of approaches to multicultural education have developed over the last twenty years, approaches that differ in their assumptions about the nature of society and the purposes of school, I will contrast the approach offered here with the prevalent human relations approach.

The Human Relations Approach to Multicultural Education

This approach developed in the late 1960s in reaction to deteriorating race relations and feminist concerns with sex role stereotyping. Sleeter depicts the human relations approach as aiming:

> Towards sensitivity training and teaching that we are all the same because we are different. Human relations advocates talk of the power of love, unity, and harmony, and of the need for individuals to try to change the attitudes and behavior of other individuals who thwart loving, harmonious relationships. [1991, p. 11]

The primary aim of the human relations approach to multiculturalism is to educate students about the culture of different racial and ethnic groups in the belief that such knowledge will foster cultural understanding and harmony. For example, educators often include activities describing the foods, festivals, and fashions of racial minorities or ethnic groups such as the Italians or Irish. Such activities aim to teach students that while groups may have specific cultural differences, they have similar human needs.

In the same way that the human relations approach to multicultural education has aimed to improve relations among racial and ethnic groups, those concerned with sexism have aimed to improve relationships between the sexes. Nonsexist educators have focused on reducing teachers' and students' stereotypes that are particularly harmful to the academic and vocational prospects of females. For example, specific efforts have been made to analyze and change the ways in which females have been portrayed in science and math textbooks, and to ensure that females receive in the classroom encouragement equal that of males.

While the above goals of developing cultural understanding and reducing stereotyping are also part of an education that is multicultural and socially reconstructive, such goals are placed within a larger social and political context. That is, it is not assumed that equality can come about simply by informing teachers and students of racial and gender biases, but that equality requires an analysis of how such biases are a consequence of the economic and political structure. The human relations approach, in its emphasis on developing cultural appreciation, trivializes the issue of inequality between groups, and how that inequality is maintained by unequal economic and political power. The human relations approach may ask how the culture of blacks, Hispanics, and whites are different and similar, but it is not likely to ask, for example, why is it that people of color in the United States have had less wealth and power than whites, and have had to continually struggle for equality. Nor is the human relations approach likely to situate Rosa Parks within an examination of political and economic inequality. Instead, is likely to present Rosa Parks as a black heroine so that students can appreciate that all groups have courageous individuals.

Furthermore, the human relations approach differs from that offered here in that it tends to emphasize the knowledge of the expert over that of teachers, students, and community members. In the human relations approach it is assumed that the expert in multicultural or nonsexist education knows what the educational goals should be, what the desirable student behaviors and attitudes are, and what "treatment" should be given to achieve the desired change. Such reliance on the expertise of one or a few individuals who identify the "symptoms" and then "treat" the problem, has been labeled the medical model of helping relationships (Brickman et al. 1982). Embedded in such a hierarchical approach is the assumption that teachers should merely transmit to students the knowledge developed by the educational expert. Consequently, teachers do not use their skills or knowledge, resulting, over time, in a diminishing of those skills.

Lastly, the students' own culture and knowledge, as well as that of the parents', is excluded from the classroom, effectively "silencing" the student (Fine 1991). The possible negative consequences of silencing students and how they might be overcome will be the focus of a later section describing an African-American student's alienation from school, and a suburban white student's animosity toward African Americans.

In contrast, education that is multicultural and socially reconstructive has very different goals. First, this approach encourages raising questions of how not only individual attitudes but also how social structures foster inequality. Education is not viewed as separate and detached from politics and economics but, rather, as embedded in the larger social context. Second, the student is not viewed as merely a receiver of knowledge transmitted by the teacher, but as someone who uses their own knowledge and culture to "enter into the conversation" with educators (Rose 1989). Finally, race and gender are part of a larger analysis, which also includes class and disabling conditions.

While it is not possible to do more than hint at the recent social and educational theories and research that support an antiracist, antisexist, socially reconstructive approach, the pedagogical implications of these three goals will be briefly situated within supporting theories and research.

From Changing Individual Attitudes to Understanding Education as Part of a Larger Social Structure

Beginning in the 1970s, a shift occurred in how social and educational theorists understood social inequality. Rather than focusing on how individual differences led to inequality, questions began to be raised about how the structure of school and society perpetuated inequality. An influential yet unrefined study was economists Samuel Bowles and Herbert Gintis's *Schooling in Capitalist America* (1976). Because Bowles and Gintis were particularly interested in the relationship between an individual's social class and economic success, they examined the statistical relationship between intelligence, educational achievement, and economic success. While critics are correct to contend that Bowles and Gintis tended to overemphasize the effect of economic background, Bowles and Gintis maintained that, contrary to what one would expect of a society where economic success is hypothetically an outcome of intelligence and effort, economic success was most closely connected to the economic class into which one was born.

Contrary to the assumption of the human relations approach that if educators promoted better academic performance on the part of minority and female students, the students would achieve improved economic outcomes, Bowles and Gintis argued that inequality would persist, because schools prepared students to fit into the capitalist hierarchical social structure. Bowles and Gintis helped spark a renewed concern with class and race inequalities, and an increased skepticism regarding the ease with which equal opportunity can be achieved in a capitalist society.

Subsequently, some educational theorists, such as Michael Apple and Jean Anyon, began to examine the role schools played in perpetuating or reproducing economic inequality. Michael Apple, in *Ideology and Curriculum* (1979), examined what messages students were likely to receive about society and knowledge. Through examination of what and how teachers taught and how these were connected to the dominant knowledge and assumptions of the social sciences, Apple argued that the most significant lesson students learned in school was to passively accept what they were taught as true. This lesson was not so much overtly taught but implied by presenting knowledge as unproblematic and emphasizing conforming and following directions.

A study by Jean Anyon (1980) examined the degree to which students' class background was related to the presentation of knowledge as unproblematic. While questions have been raised regarding Anyon's research methodology, my own experience observing in inner-city minority and working-class schools and affluent private schools, confirms that schools make different assumptions, depending on the overall economic status of the students, about the student's relationship to and use of knowledge. Like Anyon, I have observed in urban classrooms where the most expected of students is that they copy notes off the chalkboard and are examined via a multiple choice test on how well they have memorized those notes.

I have also observed schools in which upper-class students were using the available social studies resources and a variety of media— including film and television—to present unique historical and social analyses. Apple and Anyon raise the question of whether it is not just changing teachers' and students' attitudes so that minorities are viewed as similar to the majority population, but whether the problem is of how in a capitalist society the middle and working classes, which includes most minorities, are educated to memorize information and follow directions rather than actively produce knowledge.

These initial studies not only introduced class as a category, but demonstrated that economic and educational inequality was at least partially an outcome of the lack of control the middle and working classes had over the goals, methods, and content of education. More recent studies and proposals have focused on developing a more sophisticated understanding of the role of economics and knowledge in the relationship between race, class, and gender. For example, Cameron McCarthy, in *Race and Curriculum* (1990), presents a nonsynchronous theory of race relations in which neither individual attitudes nor explanations emphasizing class, such as those of Bowles, Gintis, Apple, and Anyon, have priority. Rather than thinking of minority groups as homogenous entities, McCarthy emphasizes the diverse interests and needs of minorities. The human relations approach, he argues, tends to "overemphasize the difference among ethnic groups, neglecting the differences within any one group" (p. 46). As an example, McCarthy summarizes the research revealing how the culture and politics of middle-class blacks differs from working-class blacks.

McCarthy also cites Linda Grant's research in elementary schools, which concludes that the experience of black females in desegregated schools differs "from those of other race-gender groups and cannot be fully understood . . . by extrapolating from the research on females or on blacks" (Grant 1984, p. 99). Grant's research revealed that elementary school teachers assumed that black females are more socially mature, but only average achievers compared to both black males and white students, and black males are assumed to be socially and academically immature compared to all other groups. Therefore, we cannot simply assume homogeneity in minority groups or even, as in the case of black females, that the assumed characteristics are wholly positive or negative.

The current concern over societal difficulties black males face and the debate over separate schools for them, indicates the gender and class heterogeneity of minority cultures. Correspondingly, the majority white population also differs by gender and class. It is required, therefore, that educators not create a curricular and teaching approach intended to fit everyone, but should aim to develop classrooms that help students make sense of their own lives within a larger context. The need to do so seems especially crucial given the current problems students face. As bell hooks writes:

> If we are to live in a less violent and more just society,then we must engage in anti-sexist and anti-racist work. We desperately need to explore and understand the connections between racism and sexism. And we need to teach everyone about the connections so that they can be critically aware and socially active. [1991, p. 63]

A central concern of the critical theorists, such as Bowles, Gintis, Apple, Anyon, and McCarthy, is the way in which students—other than those at elite institutions—have been taught to passively accept as truth what they are taught, and to assume that they have no part in either assessing or creating knowledge. Students are silenced; their voices stifled. The following pedagogical proposals are intended, in the words of James Banks:

> To help students to reconceptualize and rethink the experience of humans in both the U.S. and the world, to view the human experience from the perspectives of a range of cultural, ethnic, and social-class groups, and to construct their own versions of the past, present and future. In the transformative curriculum multiple voices are heard and legitimized: the voices of textbooks, literary, and historical writers, the voices of teachers, and the voices of other students. [Banks 1991, p. 131]

From Making Knowledge Inaccessible to Engaging Students in Historical and Social Analysis

In an ethnographic study of social studies teachers and classrooms, Linda McNeil (1986) reveals how the method of social studies teaching—a method that heavily relies on teachers lecturing and students copying teacher-prepared outlines and being tested on the same—makes history and social processes obscure to the students. Teachers, writes McNeil, "make knowledge inaccessible."

Yet, if as stated at the outset, students are to make sense of their own lives and the lives of others, they must, to again quote from Sleeter, engage in a process whereby they "analyze events and structures" and "question why things are as they are and how they might be different." The goal of analyzing events and structures requires rethinking how curriculum might concentrate less on the great men, wars, and political events of history, and concentrate more on examining the lives and social conditions of those excluded from the headlines; from focusing on a history from above to developing a history from below. The debate would shift from deciding which minorities deserve equal billing on the historical stage with great white men, to focusing on the political and social struggles of minorities, women, and the middle and working classes.

Such a shift is supported by fundamental changes over the last twenty years in the social sciences, changes that include but extend beyond contributions minorities have made to Western culture. Many social scientists—including historians—have become aware of how traditional social sciences have taken for granted the current structure of society in terms of race, class, and gender, and have begun to raise different questions in their research.

The kinds of questions that historians have asked about women and the construction of gender is outlined by Mary Kay Thompson Tetrault, in her article "Rethinking Women, Gender, and the Social Studies" (1987). At its earliest stages, women's history aimed to uncover the contributions that women have made to mainstream male-centered culture, such as women who were "significant rulers or contributors to wars or reform movements" (p. 171). But such an approach only includes women who have contributed to the public sphere, and excludes the bulk of women's lives, which occur in the private sphere. We have more recently shifted, according to Tetrault, to "histories of women" and "histories of gender." Histories of women are characterized by first, "A pluralistic conception of women . . . that acknowledges diversity and recognizes that variables other than gender shape women's lives—for example, race, ethnicity, and social class." Second, "history is rooted in the personal and the specific." Third, "the public and the private are seen as a continuum in women's experiences." Histories of gender add to the histories of women the aim of developing "multifocal, relational, gender-balanced perspectives . . . that weave together women's and men's experiences into multilayered composites of human experience" (p. 173).

Tetrault's analysis lends credence to an approach to social studies that includes, but encompasses more than, focusing on the contributions of women and minorities to mainstream culture. While such contributions should not be ignored, it is more important to assist students in developing a diverse analysis of society, one that includes the personal as well as the public, the local as well as the general, female as well as male, and minority as well as majority. Consequently, as teachers we can begin to call forth, as Sleeter writes, the voices of those different from ourselves and our own voices.

Examples of the kinds of history suggested by Tretrault and Sleeter were provided by Bigelow and Kohl at the outset of this paper. Bigelow suggests we analyze Columbus not only in terms of the voyage's impact on Europe but also its impact on Native Americans. Furthermore, we would need to question what racial assumptions permitted the enslavement and murder of thousands of Awarak Indians. Kohl urges us not to simply add Rosa Parks to the pantheon of American heroes, but to situate her heroism within the civil rights struggle in Montgomery and the nation.

Engaging in the Students' Own Histories

While some of the current proposals for multicultural education focus on improving self-esteem by teaching about minority contributions, Michelle Fine questions the adequacy of such an approach as long as students remain silenced in school—that is, when there is:

> A systematic commitment *to not name* those aspects of social life or of schooling that activate school anxieties. With important exceptions, school based silencing precludes official conversation about controversy, inequity and critiques. [Fine 1991; p. 33, emphasis in original]

While multicultural education has existed in schools for two decades, it is rare that teachers and students confront issues of inequality, race, class, or gender. What passes for multicultural education may well be similar to an observation I made in an eleventh-grade noncollege-bound class in a suburban high school. At the end of a three-day unit on the civil rights movement, the teacher was preparing students for the test by reviewing names and vocabulary words. During the lesson, one of the students, a white student—as were all the students in the class—complained that blacks now "had more" than whites. The teacher ignored the comment and continued reviewing words. But the student names what he perceived as a problem and voiced his view—a view that probably reflects conservative views regarding affirmative action and social welfare.

While I disagree with the student's view, it is of little value to teach about the civil rights movement if we ignore students' beliefs that the movement has adversely affected their lives. As Simon and Dippo write, teachers need to "acknowledge student experience as a legitimate aspect of school while being able to challenge both its content and its form during the educational process" (1987, p. 106). Rather then ignoring the comment, we might ask the student to elaborate: What evidence does he have for his view? What is his understanding of either the past or present economic conditions for minorities? The incident offers the possibility of a lesson that begins with the student's experience and expands to an analysis of the civil rights movement within an economic and historical context.

But silencing more commonly occurs not through ignoring students, but through the persistence of an environment where students would never voice their beliefs and ideas. For example, while playing tag with a group of young boys on a school playground one evening several years ago, John, a black nine-year old inquired of me regarding my then nine-year old son: "How come your son is so smart?" As we decided who was "it" this time, I replied "He's not so smart; he just likes to learn. Don't you like to learn?" John yelled: "You're it" and as he ran off to escape my tag added: "I'm smart; I just don't like to learn."

Because the game continued and I did not have an opportunity to ask John more questions, I was left wondering whether by third grade John was already alienated from school. And given that John lives in the working-class neighborhood surrounding the school, what role does growing up black, male, and working-class play in his feelings regarding school? Finally, has John voiced in school his feelings and how did the teachers respond? Did the teachers assist John in recovering his own voice, "to fashion meanings and standpoints, and negotiate with others" (Britzman 1991), to incorporate "a more critical understanding of experience" (Giroux 1987), and "to raise fundamental questions regarding the nature of school knowledge" (Crichlow 1990)? If educators perceive the goal of multicultural education as entering in discussion with students regarding their understanding of society—an

understanding influenced by a student's race, gender and class—
then a new way of interacting in the classroom and a new curriculum can emerge.

Fusing Content and Process

A curriculum that is multicultural and socially reconstructive transforms the classroom so that the curriculum is created, in part, out of an ongoing dialogue between the teachers, students, and the wider community. The aim is not simply to expand the "great men and great wars" curriculum to include "great" women and minorities, nor to show that while racial and ethnic groups may have different customs, they are more similar than different. Rather, the aim is to recognize, draw out, and analyze with students, the diversity of their own lives and society. The school becomes a public arena where teachers, students, and others use history, political science, and other social sciences to make sense of their lives.

Ideas for how such a public arena could be created in school are provided by Michelle Fine. She writes that for part of each semester a "school could be organized around a series of community issues: infant mortality, lead poisoning, local politics, the history of the area" (1991, p. 217). Oral history projects, such as those described by Cynthia Stokes Brown, in *Like It Was: A Complete Guide to Writing Oral History* (1990), might be part of such projects.

If we encourage students to give voice to their own experiences in and conceptions of the world, the personal becomes public. In making the personal public, we also begin to make the personal political. For example, asking John to say more about why he "doesn't like to learn" would probably lead to discussing the relationship between schooling and economic success, and between the school curriculum and personal knowledge. It is only through engaging in such discussions—discussions that encourage teachers and students to analyze the relationship between race, gender, class, knowledge, and power—that we might connect with students and develop a curriculum that is not static but reflects the diversity of school and society.[5]

PART III

The Social Studies Curriculum in Practice

CHAPTER EIGHT

Crafting a Culturally Relevant
Social Studies Approach

Gloria Ladson-Billings

Introduction

Over the past decade scholars have attempted to look at ways to make the schooling experience of students more compatible with their home and cultural experiences. The focus of this research has been on students who have been, heretofore, underserved by traditional schooling. Most of this research in this area has been done by anthropologists (specifically socio-linguists) who have tried to examine communication patterns that might ease the transition from students' home language to school language. A variety of terms have been used to describe this literature. Among the terms are *culturally appropriate* (Au and Jordan 1981), *culturally congruent* (Mohatt and Erickson 1981), *culturally responsive* (Cazden and Legett 1981; Erickson and Mohatt 1982), and *culturally compatible* (Jordan 1985; Vogt, Jordan, and Tharp 1987).

Many of these studies have been conducted in small-scale community cultures. However, more recently scholars have begun to examine the issue of school and cultural match in more complex, urban settings. Both Irvine (1990) and Ladson-Billings (1990a, 1990b, 1991, 1992a, 1992b, 1992c) have examined the relationship between student culture and school instruction in classrooms of African American students.

Irvine developed the notion of *cultural synchronization* to describe the necessary interpersonal context that must exist between the teacher and African American students to maximize learning. Ladson-Billings uses the term *culturally relevant* to describe the kind of teaching that is designed not merely to *fit* the school culture to the students' culture, but also to *use* student culture as a basis for helping students understand themselves and others, structure social interactions, and conceptualize knowledge.

Juxtaposed to *assimilationist* teaching, designed to help students fit into the existing social order, culturally relevant teaching is a pedagogy of opposition that recognizes and celebrates student culture (in this case African American culture). Culturally relevant pedagogy shares many similarities with critical pedagogy, which according to Giroux and Simon (1989):

> Refers to a deliberate attempt to influence how and what knowledge and identities are produced within and among particular sets of social relations. It can be understood as a practice through which people are incited to acquire a particular "moral character." As both a political and practical activity, it attempts to influence the occurrence and qualities of experiences. [p. 239]

Both critical pedagogy and culturally relevant pedagogy "strive to incorporate student experience as 'official' content" (Giroux and Simon, p. 250). However, while critical pedagogy seeks to help the *individual* critique and change the social environment, culturally relevant pedagogy urges *collective* action grounded in cultural understandings, experiences, and ways of knowing the world.

The primary goal of culturally relevant teaching is to empower students to critically examine the society in which they live and to work for social change. In order to do this, students must possess a variety of literacies: language-based, mathematical, scientific, artistic, musical, historical, cultural, economic, social, civic, and political.

The second wave of school reform (the first being ushered in by the Commission on Excellence in Education's report *A Nation at Risk*) suggested that much of the problem with American education lay at the feet of teachers and teaching practice. Shulman (1987) identified three aspects of pedagogy—content knowledge, pedagogical knowledge, and pedagogical content knowledge—that need to be considered in the analysis of pedagogy. Thus, teachers need to know their subject matter. They need to know how to teach, *and* they need to know how to teach their subject matter. In the case of social studies, this means that teachers need to be well-grounded in history and the social sciences. They need to know and be able to use a variety of instructional techniques. They need to know and be able to use the kinds of instructional techniques that are appropriate for the teaching of social studies.

Other aspects of Shulman's (1987) work that failed to garner the same level of attention as the three previously mentioned elements were "the classroom context, the physical and psychological characteristics of the students, [and] the accomplishment of purposes not readily assessed on standardized tests" (p. 6). Does it matter whether or not the students are of color, from a variety of social-class backgrounds? Does it matter whether or not teaching is taking place in a suburban, upper middle-income community, or a large urban, inner-city, lower, and working-class community?

The premise of this chapter is that these factors (and many more) that constitute the *context* of teaching are critical to pedagogy. They influence the content or knowledge, they influence the instruction, and they influence the ways in which teachers think about how to teach particular knowledge/content.

Why Culturally Relevant Social Studies?

Previous investigations of culturally relevant teaching (see Ladson-Billings 1992b, 1992c) have looked at ways in which teachers have used culturally relevant approaches to teach language-based literacy. More recently, investigations of culturally relevant mathematics teaching have been discussed (Ladson-Billings 1993). What precipitates the need for a culturally relevant approach to social studies?

There is evidence to suggest that social studies is among the least liked school subjects (Goodlad 1984). Even during the era when students demonstrated for a more "relevant" curriculum, there was a concern that changes in course content were not accompanied by concomitant changes in instructional techniques (Cuban 1973). Thus, the same students who were failing "white" history were also failing African American, Chicano, and Native American history. If schools are to serve all students, social studies programs must be more accessible to all students.

The content-rich nature of social studies means that it relies heavily on text material. Thus, students who are facile readers tend to enjoy more success in social studies than those who are not. The task of the social studies is to help create active, participatory citizens who are capable of high-level functioning in a democratic, multicultural society. This means, regardless of students' functioning in reading, they are entitled to high-quality social studies experiences.

In the next section I suggest that culturally relevant teaching can provide a way to engage students in social studies learning regardless of their academic ability. The evidence for this assertion is the real-life classroom practice of two culturally relevant teachers.

Brief Background of the Study

The search for culturally relevant teachers began with a process called *community nomination* (Foster 1989). By talking with African American parents in a low-income, largely African-American community, I was able to identify eight elementary teachers who were successful teachers of African American students (for a fuller discussion of the methodology of the study, see Ladson-Billings 1990b). After two-hour ethnographic interviews (Spradley 1979), each teacher agreed to be observed teaching and later videotaped. The teachers' videotapes were analyzed and interpreted by the entire group of teachers who had become a research collaborative. Through their collective discussions and analyses, the teachers constructed a profile of culturally relevant teaching.

For the purpose of this discussion, I will focus on the social studies teaching of two of the teachers, Gertrude Winston and Ann Lewis (pseudonyms).

Gertrude Winston and Ann Lewis:
Culturally Relevant Teachers at Work

Gertrude Winston has taught elementary school for forty years. She began her teaching career in a one-room school in rural Michigan. After teaching twelve years her school district consolidated with another, and Gertrude decided to join the Peace Corps. As a white, single female she was a novelty in Liberia where she taught for two years. However, according to Gertrude, teaching in this all black setting was the beginning of an important personal transformation:

> I had never been in a place where I was in the minority. I came to see how ridiculous it is to place oneself in the center of the world without ever considering that others placed themselves and their perspectives in the center of the world.

When Gertrude returned to the United States, she took a teaching position in East Los Angeles and later moved to the San Francisco Bay area where she taught in a low-income, predominantly African American community. At the beginning of this study, Gertrude was a year away from retirement. Most of her teaching experience was at the fifth- and sixth-grade level. My year-long observation was in her fifth-grade classroom. Gertrude started her school year in August (on her own initiative) by preparing materials for her class. In her home office she duplicated materials, made folders, and organized instructional aides and other materials. From the first day that students enter Gertrude's classroom, they are aware that this is a classroom in which they will *all* have an opportunity to learn because they will all be equipped with the necessary materials.

Gertrude believes in creating a sense of community in the class, and helping the students develop both a personal and collective sense of empowerment. Her classroom is the center of activity. Some students, because of their parents early-morning schedules, arrive at school before 8:00 A.M. Rather than require that students stay home until the playground is supervised (as is the school rule), Gertrude allows students to come early and play board games, finish school projects, and socialize.

Social studies in Gertrude Winston's classroom is United States history from the culture of the indigenous peoples to 1865. Gertrude begins by asking "What does any of this (U.S. history) have to do with you and your life?" After a series of shoulder shrugs and "I don't knows, " Gertrude proceeds to show students the relationship between them and U.S. history. "How long has your family been in California? How long have they been in the Bay Area?" are two of the opening questions. Students take a few minutes to document their family's arrival to California and the San Francisco Bay area. "How do we know what you have written is accurate?" asks Winston. "How can we verify your information?" Students suggest that they can interview their parents and relatives to document the accuracy. "But what if you *lie* to prove yourself right?" comments Winston. This provokes a spirited student discussion about the ways in which lies are eventually uncovered.

Winston talks to students about ways in which historians and other social scientists construct and interpret knowledge. "Well, what else could we do?" asks one student. "What do *you* think?" asks Winston. The students decide that they could pair up and interview each others' parents and relatives. The quest for a voice without a vested interest has begun.

The students set out with tape recorders, note pads, and cameras to get the story of how their classmates' families came to

California. Within a week students are buzzing about their information. The students work together to create a "migration map" complete with colored strings, pins, and name and date tabs. Gertrude talks to the students about history as a way of uncovering truths. She explains to her students that they cannot afford to let others misinterpret, lie, or forget about the truths of their lives, and this is why history should matter to them.

"Now," asks Gertrude, "How do we find out how Indians came to the Americas?" The process of uncovering information begins anew. The textbook is but one source the students decide is worthy of consulting. Before their knowledge quest is over, they have talked with an American Indian, a scholar in American Indian studies, viewed several films, and read some American Indian literature.

Gertrude Winston teaches United States history by framing (and helping students to frame) critical questions about the past. The process is long, arduous, and filled with fits and starts. She does not expect to "cover" the material (Newmann 1988). Instead, she hopes that her students will come to "see themselves" (Asante 1991) in history, and challenge the ways in which their stories are told (and not told). Gertrude puts it this way:

> We can't rely on the textbooks to tell the story. I have to help the students understand that they are history makers—that they, and their ancestors, have contributed magnificently to the broad sweep of human accomplishment. They have to see that in their past so that they can continue this tradition in their present and future.

Ann Lewis teaches in the same school district as Gertrude Winston. Their schools serve largely African-American and Latino student populations. Standardized test scores in the district are among the lowest in the state. The high school dropout rate hovers near 70 percent. Ann has been offered any number of opportunities to work in districts where students are performing at or above grade level. She consistently rejects these offers.

Ann Lewis is a white woman in her mid-40s. Her tie to this school community is emotional and physical. This is the community in which she grew up and continues to live. She is teaching in the same district in which she attended school. This community, this district, these people, all have special meaning for her. Ann says:

> I love teaching here. I think I understand the students here because I was one of them. I was a pretty tough kid, always getting

into trouble for little stuff. . . not particularly motivated. But I had teachers here who gave me a chance. That's the least I can do for the community . . . give its children a chance.

One of the things that strikes a person initially upon meeting Ann Lewis is her close identification with African American life and culture. From the register of her voice to the idioms, expressions, grammar, and syntax, Ann's speech is the speech of African Americans. These speech patterns are not affected; this is the language Ann has grown up speaking. Away from school, Ann's social contacts are almost exclusively African American. Formerly married to an African American, Ann has two young adult children who identify themselves as African American rather than biracial.

Ann is passionate about many things, among them teaching, learning, and fighting racism. She has developed a strong whole language (Goodman 1989) program in her classroom. Through the use of both literature and critical social issues, Ann and her students build meaningful learning activities.

During one of my series of observations in Ann's classroom, she and her students were using the book *Charlie Pippin* by Candy Dawson Boyd. This story is about an African American girl in the sixth grade who seems to have trouble getting along with her dad. One of the sources of their friction is Charlie's father's refusal to talk about his time in Vietnam. During the course of the story, Charlie and two classmates begin a project to protest nuclear proliferation.

One of the more interesting aspects of using this particular piece of literature in Ann's class is the fact that a member of the class was Vietnamese, several students had parents and other relatives who had served in Vietnam, and this study was taking place after the United States had issued an ultimatum to Iraq. Without directing students to either support or condemn the impending war, Ann helped students to explore a variety of issues surrounding the war. The students read Eleanor Coerr's *Sadako and the Thousand Cranes*, after which they began making origami cranes as a gesture of peace. They viewed the feature-length film *Amazing Grace,* which is about a boy's refusal to play Little League baseball until some missiles are removed from his community. They staged a debate around the question, "Is violence ever justified?" Class members brought in parents and relatives to talk about their war time experiences. Several talked about Vietnam. One, a refugee from Nicaragua, talked about the day-to-day fear and brutality. At one point, a speaker brought up the notion of "post-traumatic stress." After explaining that some people continue to experience physical and psychological symptoms well after experiencing war, one of Ann's students, Jerry, raised his hand and asked, "who cares about our posttraumatic stress?" Able to read the puzzled look on the speaker's face, Jerry continued, "We live in a neighborhood that's like a war zone. People are driving by and killing innocent by-standers. Everyday people we know are dying."

Ann posed the question, "What do you want to do about this situation?" The students agreed that they wanted it to stop, but seemed at a loss to suggest how to make that happen. One student suggested that they also needed to know more about how it all began. Somewhere in the discussion they agreed that they needed a better understanding of their community. Rather than learning about "community helpers," the students insisted on trying to understand how the community works and what opportunities for change were available to them.

By January 15, when the United States engaged in war against Iraq, Ann's students had successfully completed 1,039 paper cranes as a testimony to their commitment to peace. As they watched the televised reports of the war in their classroom, their classroom front window, covered with paper cranes, belied the anguish they felt. Many eyes were filled with tears. They had spent four and a half months understanding that war was a serious undertaking, not a video game. Although they seemed defeated, they had developed a deeper sense of what it means to be at war.

Ann used the students' concern about war to direct their attention to the war that was being waged in their own community. Mindful of Jerry's earlier question about the "post-traumatic stress" he and other students suffered in their own community, she posed some questions about the community to get the students focused on a community investigation:

Ann:	How do you feel about this community?
Student:	I hate this place. I can't wait till I grow up. I'm moving away from here and never coming back.
Ann:	Do you hate your parents and family?
Student:	No!
Ann:	Do you hate Mt. Moriah Baptist Church?
Student:	No!
Ann:	Do you hate me?
Student:	NO!!
Ann:	Then what exactly do you hate?

Student: Well, you know, the drugs, the gang banging, crime. . . .

Ann: I hate that stuff too. But I don't think of that as a part of the community. I think of it as things that have *invaded* our community. I've lived here all my life and I know how much this community has to offer. I'll bet you'd be surprised to learn about the pivotal role this community played in the developmeznt of the entire area.

This discussion led to an in-depth exploration of the community. Particularly interesting was the fact that Ann linked the "excavation" of the community's history and culture with that of ancient Egypt, which was a part of the mandated curriculum for sixth graders in this district. Having "witnessed" multiple "excavations of ancient Egypt" over many years of social studies supervision, I devoted much of my classroom observation time to the community exploration.

Ann begged, pleaded, and cajoled a historical society curator to allow her and a few of the students into a special collection to take notes and make copies of documents never before shown to the public. Another group of students began interviewing long-time residents of the community. A third group of students conducted a survey about what changes people would like to have happen in the community.

Within a few weeks, Ann's classroom was a beehive of activity with people moving in and out to rediscover their community. One of the major projects the students settled on (which came from the data gathered in the survey) was addressing a concern about a burned out strip mall that was a gathering spot for drug dealers, users, alcoholics, prostitutes, and other indigents. Located in a central spot in the community, many residents complained that it was both dangerous and an eyesore.

The students who worked on the historical data presented information about the various changes the property had gone through. Students learned that the area dated back to the Coastanoan Indians. When white settlers took over the land, it became a poultry farm. Later it was zoned for residential use and later rezoned commercial. A small shopping center was built, but a weak economy and rising rents caused its demise. A series of arson fires destroyed the buildings and left charred shells where bustling stores once stood.

When it was thriving, the shopping mall was the center of the community and the library, a post office, and city service building were built nearby. Now, these services remained while in their midst sat the crumbling mall. To use these services, community residents were forced to pass the antisocial and criminal activity that was housed in the burned out center.

Ann's students spoke with an architect and a city planner, and developed a plan for renovating the mall. Their new plans called for the creation of a much needed day-care center, a few stores, an emergency clinic, a bank, and a small park. They wrote their ideas up in the form of a proposal (after having seen some formal proposals) and Ann arranged to have the students placed on the agenda of a city council meeting where three of the students made the presentation.

Because of tremendous budget constraints, the city council could only listen to the proposal without acting on it. However, Ann's students came away from the experience with a different perspective on ways that the community functions and ways in which they could function within it. My own assessment of their work is that its benefits will outlast those of a more traditional reading and class discussion format.

What Social Studies Teachers Learn from Culturally Relevant Teaching

The space constraints of this chapter make the discussions about Gertrude Winston's and Ann Lewis's classrooms truncated. My limited ability to accurately convey what transpired in those classrooms is another constraint. However, despite those constraints, I believe it is possible to cull some important tenets from Gertrude and Ann's teaching to make social studies teaching more culturally relevant.

I have previously described three major categories of culturally relevant teaching: (1) conceptions of self and others; (2) conceptions of social relations and; (3) conceptions of knowledge (see Ladson-Billings 1990a, 1990b, 1991a). Because these are categories that serve as heuristics for explaining and understanding teacher practice, readers must be aware of their limitations. First, they represent ideals and do not function as absolutes. The teachers displayed these behaviors to varying degrees. If we think of teaching practice along a continuum extending from assimilationist to culturally relevant, these teachers' practice more closely resembles the culturally relevant end of the continuum.

Although the larger study includes data about eight teachers across all three of these dimensions, for the purpose of this chapter,

I will restrict the discussion about Ann and Gertrude to the third dimension—their conceptions of knowledge.

1. *Culturally relevant teachers believe that knowledge is continuously re-created, recycled, and shared by teachers and students.* Gertrude Winston and Ann Lewis believe that their students come to them with knowledge. Rather than seeing the students as empty vessels, the students' knowledge is used as a foundation on which to build social/historical knowledge. Thus, their teaching rarely involves mere imparting of information from the teacher to the students. Instead, students and teachers together sort through what knowledge they have and what additional knowledge they need to acquire.

2. *Culturally relevant teachers view knowledge (course content) critically.* For both Gertrude and Ann a necessary part of social studies learning was learning to challenge the content. Their insistence that student knowledge was to be seen as "official knowledge" (Apple and Christian-Smith 1991) meant that students' real life experiences had currency. The students from Gertrude's class who interviewed their parents and others to help create personal histories were challenged to look at ways in which histories are constructed and to begin to develop some ownership for the "American story."

The boy in Ann's class who raised the question about *his* post-traumatic stress was engaged critically with social studies content that is rarely discussed. The issues of social inequity, drugs, and gangs are not merely textbook topics for him. In Ann's class the topic could be aired and investigated freely.

3. *Culturally relevant teachers are passionate about content.* Gertrude and Ann were both excited about the subject matter they teach. They were teaching students things about which they themselves cared. Their own level of enthusiasm and genuine interest was contagious. If teachers are unable to demonstrate that the subject matter has interest and meaning for them, how can we expect students to develop interest in the subject matter? Unfortunately, too many social studies teachers either (at the secondary level) teach social studies by default (as a space holder for their coaching or other extracurricular activities), or (at the elementary level) fail to teach it at all. In both instances, the lack of interest is readily apparent to students.

4. *Culturally relevant teachers help students develop prerequisite knowledge and skills (build bridges or scaffolding).* Neither Gertrude nor Ann penalized students for not knowing information

that should have been a part of their previous years' social studies experiences. As fifth graders, Gertrude's students (according to the state curriculum framework) should have had some exposure to the history of California and the early Indian settlement there. This knowledge would have provided them with ample background information with which to answer Gertrude's questions about origins and inhabitants of the early Americas. Either they had not had exposure to that information or the way in which it was presented did not allow them to connect it with their fifth-grade curriculum. It was not "knowledge-in-use."

Similarly, in Ann's sixth-grade class, the students should have had some exposure to the notion of community in earlier grades (third grade, according to the state framework). One can speculate that even if they did have exposure to the notion of community, it was an idealized representation that was foreign to the students real lives. Ann worked with students to reconstruct a notion (and feeling) of community that would have lasting value for them all.

5. Finally, culturally relevant teachers see excellence as a complex standard that may involve some postulates but takes student diversity and individual differences into account. The nature of social studies and the dispositions social studies educators seek to develop in students, makes authentic assessment (Gomez, Graue, and Bloch 1991) complex, but necessary. Thus, culturally relevant teachers' ability to see excellence along multiple dimensions means that students are more likely to participate in a variety of experiences and activities that demonstrate their competence in social studies.

For Gertrude Winston's students, excellence was demonstrated via the ability to communicate across generations, to make connections from concrete to abstract, and to understand something about the structure of history. For Ann Lewis's students excellence was seen as a benefit to the learning community. Students were reinforced for what they contributed to the entire classroom community. In her classroom I often heard the words, *we* and *us*. "Look how well *we* worked together to do this proposal to the city council!" "What do *we* need to know to be able to find out about. . . ." In both classrooms students' personal reflections about what and how they learned was a part of individual assessment.

Both Gertrude and Ann recognize that the true tests of the students social studies learnings would be in how they felt about themselves, how they treated each other, and how they approached knowledge.

Conclusion

My primary motivation for writing this chapter is to address what I believe is missing in the social studies dialogue—the importance of instruction. So much of the current debate has centered on the "what students don't know" (Ravitch and Finn 1987; Hirsch 1987) and the weakness of social studies content (Ravitch 1988) that many have forgotten that regardless of the quality of the curriculum, it cannot teach itself.

This chapter also is an invitation to social studies educators to consider the "wisdom of practice" (Shulman 1987) of those teachers who are successful teachers of students who traditionally have not performed well in school. It is time to think about ways that teacher preparation can become more responsive to the desires of preservice (and inservice) teachers to become more effective pedagogues with students who, heretofore, have not benefited from schooling. If social studies is to realize its true mission—to prepare students to be active, responsible participants in a democratic and multicultural society—then social studies teachers will need to develop more culturally relevant teaching approaches.

CHAPTER NINE

Social Studies and the Arts

Terrie L. Epstein

Imagine, if you will, the following scene: a class of twenty twentieth-century middle-class European American high school students living in the metropolitan area of a large northeastern city have spent two weeks learning about nineteenth-century enslaved African Americans living in the southern regions of the United States. They have done so by interpreting nineteenth-century African American spirituals, work songs, and game songs about life and death in heaven and on earth, and ancient African folk tales about tricksters and hustlers in animal guises. They also interpreted twentieth-century African Americans' oral histories, paintings, and sculptures related to nineteenth-century themes of slavery and freedom. During the final two days of the two-week unit, each student represented something he or she had learned about African American life during the great enslavement by writing a poem or story, painting or drawing a picture or writing or performing a song.

As a former classroom teacher and researcher, I routinely have used "artlike" primary sources like oral histories, poems, paintings, and songs to teach about the past, and have had students represent history through stories, poems, paintings, and songs. What I have found is that rather than represent a descent into frill or fantasy, students' interpretations and creations of the arts in historical contexts represent intellectually complex understandings. Similarly, by learning to interpret artlike primary sources from the perspectives of the African Americans who created them, students recognize and reconstruct multicultural perspectives on history. Equally significant, certain students are more successful at achieving educational experiences and outcomes when they interpret and create artlike forms than when they work with traditional textbooks or tests.

In the following pages, I begin with a review of the literature on the significance of learning in and through the arts. I then present examples of work from a study I have conducted, which illustrates the kinds of educational experiences and outcomes students can achieve when working with the arts in historical contexts. I end with suggestions for using the arts to teach history. My purpose is to illustrate that by integrating the arts into the social studies curriculum, teachers can enable students to broaden and deepen the historical knowledge they are capable of constructing when they work solely or primarily with traditional history textbooks, texts, or tests.

The Arts as Forms for Constructing Complex Understandings

It is well established in philosophical, psychological, and pedagogical literatures that to interpret or create artlike forms constitutes intelligent or thoughtful activity. Dewey (1934) describes the intellectual processes practiced by artists and audiences alike as conceptually complex activities:

> The artist selected, simplified, clarified, abridged and condensed according to his interests. The beholder must go through these operations according to his point of view and interest. In both, an act of abstraction, that is of extraction of what is significant, takes place. In both, there is comprehension . . . that is, a gathering together of details and particulars physically scattered into an experienced whole. [p. 54]

Similarly, interpreting or producing an object of art is no less rigorous intellectually than figuring out or fashioning discursive texts or mathematical problems. What does differ, Dewey and others claim, is the *nature* of knowledge constructed from or through different representative forms. Jerome Bruner (1985, 1986), for example, describes the differences in form and function between the knowledge represented by two types of written texts, themselves the products of two distinct modes of thought. The purpose of knowledge presented in logically constructed texts, like persuasive essays or scientific treatises, is to tell the truth or prove a point. The author constructs truth by making an assertion and constructing reasoned arguments based on facts and evidence. The knowledge or interpretation is judged to be true if expert readers are persuaded or convinced of the argument the author has put forth.

The purpose of knowledge depicted in narrative texts, on the other hand, is not to tell truth or prove a point, but to reveal "human or humanlike intention and action and the vicissitudes and consequences which mark their course" (Bruner 1986, p. 13). An author constructs knowledge in narrative texts not through maintaining assertions or arguments, but by creating characters, plots, settings, and scenes that depict the variability of human intentions and interactions. The successful or effective narrative text, Bruner claims, doesn't so much convince expert readers of its truth or validity. Rather, narrative power resides in its capacity to carry readers vicariously into the "compelling human plights" of others, from which readers come away with a knowledge of human consciousness and action.

Similarly, poems, paintings, music, and the like convey knowledge and conceptions of experience that cannot be conveyed through literal or logical language. In analyzing musical forms, for example, Suzanne Langer (1942) has written "the tonal structures we call 'music' bear a close logical similarity to forms of human feeling— forms of growth and attenuation, flowing and slowing, conflict and resolution, speed, arrest, terrific excitement . . . that greatness and brevity and eternal passing of everything vitally felt" (p. 27). Langer, like Bruner, notes the form and function of music enables humans to grasp or generate unique understandings. "Because the forms of human feeling are much more congruent with musical forms than with forms of language," Langer writes, "music can reveal the nature of feelings with a detail and truth that language can not approach" (1942, p. 235). By interpreting or arranging the temporal and tonal qualities of music, educated listeners or composers can construct the kind of understanding that yields insight into conceptions of human emotion.

Historians (Craig 1989; Handlin 1979), too, write about the complex and unique understandings they construct from their interpretations of historical stories, songs, paintings, and poems. The interpretations of such sources require a great degree of historical empathy, the ability of the historian to "reach across time and somehow penetrate the hearts and minds" of historical actors or groups (Handlin 1979, p. 142). Historians invoke historical empathy to construct the perspectives and consciousness that motivated past people's actions in ways that make sense to contemporary readers. The historian Oscar Handlin (1979) has written historical interpretation constructed from the analysis of artlike primary sources does "not overturn that from paper, but amplifies and deepens its meaning" (p. 245). Such amplification of meaning results from, and reinforces, historical empathy.

Similarly, individuals can convey through stories, songs, or paintings empathic conceptions of historical experience. By shaping or manipulating an art work's structural elements, like imagery and mood in story, poetry, or painting, an individual can represent lifelike conceptions of human thought and emotion. The expressive qualities of paintings or poems also enable educated others to take a leap of imagination into another time and place, and gain insight into historical actors' or groups' intentions and interactions. By depicting history through the arts, students can represent historical events or experiences with an empathy they cannot communicate through essay form.

Equity in Educational Experiences and Outcomes

Recent research on the concept of multiple human intelligences has significant implications for the integration of the arts into the social studies curriculum. The psychologist Howard Gardner (1993) has posited a theory that humans possess seven distinct intelligences, including logical-mathematical, linguistic, musical, and spatial, among others. By intelligence, Gardner means the ability "to solve problems or to create products" (p. x). All humans possess different "profiles of intelligence" or different capacities to solve problems or create products within each of the seven intelligences. And any individual's ability to use one intelligence well (for example, the use of musical intelligence to critique or create musical scores) is independent from her or his ability to use other intelligences well (the use of logical-mathematical intelligence to read or write discursive language).

Traditionally, American schools have emphasized logical-mathematical intelligence because, as Gardner maintains, nineteenth- and twentieth-century Western cultures privilege this form of understanding over others. And at best, in social studies classrooms, logical intelligence holds sway. Because social studies teachers most often rely upon textbooks or lectures to convey information, and students write short or long explanatory or logically structured sentences or essays to demonstrate what they have learned, teaching and learning in social studies is dominated by explanatory or logically structured language, representing lower or higher levels of thinking (Goodlad 1984; Ravitch and Finn 1987). Students who have talent or training in the use of logical intelligence have an advantage in learning social studies over students whose talents or abilities lie in other domains of intelligence.

As students in the study presented in these pages worked with curricular forms comprehensible to linguistic, spatial, and musical intelligences, they had opportunities to employ a multiplicity of intelligences to construct understanding. Students who could not or would not read the textbook or write an essay, for example, proved quite capable of interpreting oral histories or creating historical stories. Other students who had demonstrated average ability in interpreting or synthesizing discursive texts seemed to have an "eye" for interpreting or creating paintings, or an "ear" for interpreting or creating songs, as evidenced by the richness and complexity of their interpretations or creations of paintings or songs (Epstein 1990, 1994).

By providing access to a range of curricular forms and by instructing students to interpret them, a teacher can provide equity in the intellectual experiences students undergo, as students no longer are constrained by constructing understanding primarily from a textbook or text. Similarly, by permitting students to represent historical knowledge through various forms, a teacher provides equity in outcomes, as certain students represent what they have come to learn through a form they have the talent to manipulate well. By integrating the arts into the social studies curriculum, teachers can open up the range of intelligences students develop and employ to construct historical knowledge. By doing so, teachers are increasing opportunities for students to comprehend or create historical knowledge.

The Arts and Multicultural Perspectives on the Past

A multicultural approach to teaching social studies has taken on multiple, and often incompatible, meanings. Most agree the inclusion of people of color in social studies textbooks has grown over the years (Garcia 1993; Nash 1992; Ravitch 1990), but questions still arise about the nature of inclusion. Is it accurate or useful to discuss African American history within a traditional historical framework about the growth of American power and democracy? And how does a topic like slavery play itself out within the contexts of traditional historical themes? Most contemporary textbooks treat slavery as a tragic aberration in the history of national development, most often characterized by slow but steady upward mobility of waves of successive immigrant groups. Yet, some historians—and particularly many African American historians of African American history—(Holt 1990; Huggins 1990), perceive slavery as part of a historical pattern based on the institutionalization of racist policies and practices, as much a part of the American fabric as stories of pirates and pioneers.

For those who conceive of a multicultural approach to social studies as one that emphasizes the significant contributions people of color have made to historical events or experiences, the concept of cultural crossings or the hybridization of cultures often defines the character of inclusion (Ravitch 1990). In the case of nineteenth-century African American enslavement, primary sources from the period created by African Americans demonstrate not only the ways African American and mainstream cultures influenced each other during and after the period, but they also illuminate the enduring contributions enslaved African Americans have made to the cultural history and heritage of the United States.

For example, students in the study were surprised to discover the Br'er Rabbit folktales they had heard as children originated in Africa and were handed down through the generations first by African Americans and then by European Americans. Students also studied how the structure of African music and the traditions of African and European American religions shaped nineteenth-century African American songs, which in turn influenced mainstream forms of American music over the last century and a half (Southern 1983). Overall, artlike primary sources created by African Americans proved to be a powerful tool for illustrating the profound effects African cultural forms have had on African American culture and mainstream American culture. Artlike primary sources also illustrate how the interactions between Africans and African Americans, on the one hand, and European Americans, on the other, intertwined with and enriched the others' culture.

The primary sources used in the study also responded to concepts of multiculturalism that place African American historical actors and perspectives at the center of the historical stage (Asante 1991; Holt 1990). Rather than interpreting the African American experience during enslavement primarily from the perspectives of European Americans, as older historical studies have done, students studied the topic from the perspectives of African Americans. They thereby learned about a distinct and largely separate African American culture and community shaped by individual and group efforts to resist oppression and dehumanization. In this context, the arts-based curriculum encouraged students to challenge and complicate textbook images of African Americans simply as historical victims or victors (Garcia 1993). It also enabled students to recognize that when race is used as a lens to analyze the past, traditional interpretations about the meaning or significance of historical events or experiences need to be reevaluated from the multiple perspectives of all groups of people who participated in their making or were affected by their results (New York State Review and Development Committee 1991).

The Classroom and the Curriculum

During the 1990–91 academic year, I worked for ten weeks with an eleventh-grade class in a suburban high school in the northeastern section of the United States. The community's 80,000 residents include skilled blue-collar workers, middle-class white-collar professionals, and affluent professionals. The community has two high schools; I taught in the one that draws students from the less affluent sections of town. Sixty-eight percent of the 1991 graduating class attended four-year colleges or universities, while another 10 percent enrolled in two-year postsecondary schools.

The twenty students in the class with which I worked had enrolled themselves in the middle track of a three-tiered system, lodged between honors and general social studies classes. All of the students were Caucasian; seven were first- or second-generation Americans whose families had emigrated from Ireland, Spain, eastern and southern Europe, the Soviet Union, Lebanon, and India. Students' academic abilities ranged from those who graduated in the top 10 percent of the eleventh-grade class to those who fell into the bottom quartile.

The teacher who allowed me to work with her class taught social studies traditionally. Most nights, she assigned five to ten pages of textbook reading and completion of questions at the end of the section or chapter. Classroom activities most often involved teacher-led recitations based on the reading and lectures in which the teacher elaborated on textbook topics. Students also completed map assignments, vocabulary, and short-answer essay sheets. On occasion, students read and discussed an excerpt from a general or college-level history textbook that explained a historical topic in greater detail.

The ten-week arts-based curriculum I developed consisted of five two-week units centered on major historical periods or themes. The first unit was comprised of African Americans' oral histories, paintings, sculptures, songs, and folktales related to enslavement. After having read the section in the textbook on enslavement, students worked as a whole class during the first two days of the unit to interpret four or five oral histories each day. On the third and fourth days, they interpreted twelve to fifteen slides of twentieth-century African Americans' paintings and sculptures related to themes of slavery and freedom. On the fifth and sixth days, students interpreted four to seven songs originally sung by nineteenth-century enslaved African Americans. On the seventh and eighth days, students interpreted three nineteenth-century African American folktales. At the end of each day, students synthesized their interpretations of individual primary sources to answer two broad questions:

1. How did African Americans interpret their experiences as enslaved people?
2. What role did culture and community play in the lives of enslaved African Americans?

The excerpts from class discussions cited below illustrate how students' historical knowledge is shaped by their interpretations of narrative text and musical form created by the historical actors they sought to comprehend. The final example depicts the relationship between access to the arts and equity in intellectual experience, as one student constructed historical knowledge by interpreting narratives and folktales.

Students' Interpretations of the Arts in Historical Contexts

Sound and Sensitive Multicultural Understandings

During the first two days of the unit, students read and discussed African Americans' oral histories related to four important themes: labor, learning, leisure, and loving. On the second day of the unit, students read and discussed the following excerpt:

First thing I remember was us brought by Massa Colonel Pratt Washington from Massa Lank Miner... [Massa Washington was pretty good man.] He boys, George and John Henry, was the only overseers. Them boys treat us nice. Massa always rid up on he hoss after dinnertime. He hoss was a bay, call Sank. The fields was in the bottoms of the Colorado River. The big house was on the hill, and us could see him coming. He weared a tall beaver hat always.

The reason us always watch for him am that he boy, George, try larn us our ABC's in the field. The workers watch for Massa, and when they seed him a-riding down the hill they starts singing out, "Old hog round the bench! Old hog round the bench!"

That the signal and then everybody starts working like they have something after them. But I's too young to larn much in the field, and I can't read today and have to make the cross when I signs my name. [Botkin 1945, p. 140]

Teacher:	What's the man's view towards learning?
Craig:	He wanted to learn but he wasn't allowed to, so they snuck books and stuff.
Mary:	The white people didn't want blacks to learn to read or be as smart as they were.
Hannah:	Maybe they [whites] thought if they [blacks] could learn to read or write they would rebel or something, so they wouldn't let them read books.
Karen:	This went along with white people's view that blacks were lower. As long as blacks couldn't read, whites could think blacks were inferior.
Reika:	It showed how important learning was. He remembered this because it was important to him.
Teacher:	What was important to him?
Michelle:	That blacks learned to read.
Peter:	That way they could read the Bible.

*****

Donald:	Or maybe he remembered it because it shows blacks outsmarted whites. This was a way to go against whites. And the master didn't know it. And his son even helped them.
Sam:	The narrator seems disappointed that he didn't learn to read and write. In the other story, the man was proud he could read and write.

*****

Students' interpretations, constructed from the multiple perspectives of nineteenth-century African Americans and European Americans, are couched in the language of human intentions and experiences. Craig and Mary begin the conversation by recognizing African Americans and European Americans perceived African American literacy quite differently. Hannah and Karen note that for whites, African American literacy raised fears of rebellion and belied beliefs of white racial superiority (Douglass 1982; Gates 1988). Reika, Michelle, Peter, Donald, and Sam commented on the multidimensional personal, political, and religious meanings reading and writing held for African Americans (Blassingame 1979; Levine 1978). By reading the historical narrative from the perspectives of multiple historical actors and by reading *into* the narrative plausible intentions, feelings, or attitudes of the narrator, students endowed a seemingly simple historical story with rich and complex meanings.

A little later in the conversation, I asked students to comment on the significance of African American literacy:

Teacher: What does this tell us about the meaning of reading or writing to blacks?

Mary: It was a source of pride ... they could learn to do it even if they weren't supposed to. It showed they were really equal to the white man.

Teacher: In whose eyes? Did whites think blacks were equal?

Craig: No, they [European Americans] thought they were less 'cause they [African Americans] couldn't read, but blacks did [think they were equal to whites], even if whites didn't think so.

Donald: It showed they could outsmart the white man, maybe they thought they were better than whites.

Teacher: How?

Donald: Because whites didn't want them to read and they did it anyway.

*****

In the excerpt, students recognized that African Americans considered reading and writing to be acts of resistance against a racist society premised on European Americans' beliefs about Africans' and African Americans' racial inferiority. Rather than defining historical significance in terms of the causes or consequences of wars, mass migrations, or institutional origins or development, students constructed historical understanding based in the intricacies and intimacies of human relations. By reconstructing the historical record from narrative form, students broadened their understanding of the significance of nineteenth-century African American literacy beyond the simple mastery of reading or writing (Douglass 1982; Gates 1988).

On the fourth day of the unit, students again constructed rich and complex historical knowledge when interpreting a nineteenth-century African American work song. Students heard a recording of the song, "You Gonna Reap," which has a slow rhythmic quality, similar in tempo and tone to traditional renditions of "Swing Low, Sweet Chariot." The singers follow the African "call and response" pattern, where a singer chants the verses and a group of singers repeats the chorus:

> You Gonna Reap
> You gonna reap
> what you sow
> You gonna reap
> what you sow
>
> CHORUS
>
> Tell it on the mountain
> tell it in the valley
> You gonna reap
> what you sow
> Tell my father
> to keep on working
> Tell my brother
> keep on working
>
> CHORUS

Teacher: What's this song about?

Judy: Harvesting and planting—the kind of work slaves did in the fields picking cotton or tobacco.

Teacher: So this is a work song? Why would they sing while working?

Dan: Keep their spirits up.

Craig: So they wouldn't be bored.

*****

Karen: I think they're talking about they'll be justified one day because it says from all the planting one day they are going to reap it or harvest it. Maybe it means for all their hard times being slaves, one day they'll be freed, you know, get what they deserve.

Teacher: How will they get free?
Karen: Like they'll be freed when they go to heaven.
Teacher: Very interesting.
Peter: Or maybe on earth. Maybe whites will let them go free.
Sam: Or maybe they're planning to run away. Tell your father and brother, if you run away, maybe you'll make it to the north.

*****

Teacher: How would you describe the tone or mood of the song?
Reika: Hopeful. I think it's like they're saying to each other, "Don't give up on life. We're going to be freed soon." So, like, "hang in there."
Karen: Solemn or spiritual-like, not as if they're praying exactly, but they want God to hear them, to know how they have suffered.
Tony: Maybe the slaves are referring to their masters. That all the time they're treating blacks poorly and it's going to come around to them in the end. What goes around, comes around.
Teacher: What do you mean by "what goes around, comes around"?
Tony: They've [European Americans] spent all this time making blacks slaves, and sooner or later they're gonna have to pay the price. . . . Like one of those songs with a double meaning . . . a way to make fun of white people or threaten them and they [whites] don't even know it.
Teacher: How would you describe the tone or mood?
Tony: As kind of sarcastic or threatening.

*****

In the first section of the excerpt, Judy, Dan, and Craig noted African Americans sang songs to denote or take note of activity, relieve boredom, and offset downheartedness. In the second section, Karen, Peter, and Sam each construct several shades of meaning about the role of historical agency in obtaining freedom on heaven and earth. Reika's remarks, in the third section, are informed by her interpretation of the song' hopefulness, while Karen rendered a somber spiritual interpretation, based in part on her interpretation of the song's "solemn or spiritual-like" tone. And Tony constructed an entirely different interpretation, couched in a sarcastic reading of the lyrics and mood (Levine 1978; Southern 1983). The range of interpretations reveals how students mixed in their minds musical tones and written words to make the kinds of complex and lifelike historical meanings they could not have constructed from their readings of, and renderings of meanings from, lyrics alone.

At the end of the fourth day, after having listened to nine African American spirituals, work songs, and game songs, students constructed the broader historical contexts in which the songs made sense:

Teacher: So what? What do these songs mean to the people who sang them? What do they tell us about their community, their culture, their lives?

Reika: It was their way of communicating with each other. It was one of the things whites let them do and they took advantage of it to express their feelings.

Karen: The spirituals were their way of talking to God, to be close to him, to practice their religion, even when they're working.

Peter: It helped the time go quicker when they're working or just to relax and have fun.

Tony: The songs were a way to get back at whites . . . like the songs that had a double message, where they would pass messages or just say one thing and mean another. You know, get one over on the white people, know that they were smarter than the whites.

Reika: It was their way of life, a way to keep themselves going. It was their heritage, what they brought with them from Africa . . . something they could hold onto that was their own.

*****

Students noted African Americans sang songs for multiple purposes: to communicate religious faith and feeling, to facilitate rest or relaxation, to resist oppression and sustain pride in their African heritage. By speculating on the significance of songs in historical context, students constructed conceptions of a vital and vibrant African American culture and community, simultaneously separate from and intertwined with the mainstream culture's conditions and concerns. Overall, students constructed from their engagement with African American music insights into historical actors' consciousness and experiences rarely or barely imaginable from their reading of textbooks or analytic texts.

Equity in Educational Experiences

Throughout the year, two students' classroom participation and performance changed markedly when the class worked with artlike primary sources. When the class worked with the traditional curriculum, Craig never spoke in class. He failed or only marginally passed most of the tests throughout the year and completed a term paper that reflected the analytic and writing ability of a seventh- or eighth-grade student. In contrast, Craig became engaged intellectually when working with the primary sources, and ventured sound and sensitive interpretations of primary sources in class discussions. In the literacy excerpt cited above, for example, Craig commented that European Americans resisted African American literacy as African Americans struggled to achieve it. Similarly, when interpreting "You Gonna Reap," Craig's comment on the song's purpose extended beyond the literal or obvious.

Craig also demonstrated he could "think historically" when the class first heard and wrote an interpretation of the African American spiritual, "When the Saints Go Marching In." The version played in class consisted of verses beginning with the following lyrics:

> When the sun refuse to shine,
> When the moon goes down in blood,
> When the stars have disappeared,
> When they crown Him Lord of all,
> When the day of judgment comes

In his written work, Craig offered the following explanation:

> It shows their faith in God, they believe that He watched over them, that in the end, they'll go to heaven. It could mean when they die, they want to be with God. They sound happy when they're singing; like, they feel close to God. They're not afraid of him, they placed their trust in him. They're not afraid to tell him how they feel, like about their hope for a better life in the future.

Craig's interpretation displays his abilities to synthesize previously acquired knowledge from class discussion and to employ interpretive skills to construct a credible and complex interpretation. He has synthesized evidence from other primary sources and class discussions to construct an image of the personal and intimate nature of the nineteenth-century African American religious experience (Southern 1983). And his knowledge possesses a richness and humanity he could not have captured by reading a textbook or dissecting an analytic text, were he willing or capable of doing so. By diversifying the curricular materials and instructional strategies to which students came into contact, the arts-based social studies curriculum provided equity in the educational experiences that Craig and others were able to achieve.

The Teachers' Role

Creating the Curriculum

To create an arts-based social studies curriculum, I use the following three criteria to select primary sources: (1) cognitive and conceptual appropriateness, (2) historically significant themes, and (3) structural and expressive qualities. Each are briefly discussed below.

1. *Cognitive and Contextual Appropriateness*—When working with an arts-based curriculum, I select primary sources many or most of the students can interpret when given some instruction. Sources include those in which the level of difficulty or complexity are not beyond students' comprehension levels. Many textbooks or teachers' guides, for example, include photographs, paintings, and excerpts from speeches geared toward the levels of students. I also include sources that twentieth-century adolescents can interpret credibly from the perspective of an eighteenth- or nineteenth-century historical actor. That is, I don't include sources where the meaning of language has changed so considerably or the referents in the text or painting are so obscure that only historians who specialize in the field can interpret their meaning accurately.

Students also need to acquire a context for interpreting one or more primary sources by reading background information from the textbook or other source, and by relating their interpretations to the major questions framing the unit. In the study discussed here, students received a two-page handout on the African origins and structure of nineteenth-century African American music. They then related the information and evidence they constructed from the primary source or sources to the unit's major questions. Students acquired a preliminary context for interpreting the primary sources from the background information in the textbook and handouts, and built upon the context by interpreting the sources and their significance in relation to the major questions.

2. *Historically Significant Themes*—The questions historians pose about the past direct their examination of the evidence. The two questions framing the unit in the study discussed earlier—African Americans' interpretations of their experience and creations of a culture and community—encompass a major theme historians have examined over the past twenty years. The questions then shape the selection process of primary sources, as I choose sources that answer the questions, highlight major themes, and lend breadth or depth or complexity to the information students acquire from background readings.

In the study described here, I selected excerpts from the thousands of pages of African American oral histories by creating the categories of labor, leisure, learning, and loving as a means to name and order the diversity of the African American experience during enslavement. In selecting songs, I chose those from among well-recognized categories of spirituals, work songs, and game songs and those that ranged in theme and tone. For example, a song like "When the Saints Go Marching In," sounds joyous or uplifting, and creates the possibility and hope of rejoicing and redemption. A more serious-sounding song, like "Certainly, Lord," illuminates more somber sentiments, like endurance and redemption through suffering and sacrifice.

3. *Structural/Expressive Qualities*—The third criterion I use for selecting sources relates to their expressive or structural qualities. Unlike history textbooks or analytic texts like the Articles of Confederation or the Constitution, primary sources like stories or songs contain themes and tones capable of evoking in the educated reader images of and empathy for the historical actors or events portrayed. In literature, writers have written about the differences in meaning that readers render when reading poetic or literary texts versus expository or informational texts (Rosenblatt 1978). Similarly, when working with historical texts like poetry or narratives and songs and paintings, students construe less literal and more figurative or symbolic meanings from their interpretations of phrases in poems or objects in paintings.

In the study, I chose historical narratives not only in terms of the amount of information they contain, but also for their unusually visual or graphic descriptions or depictions of people or events or for the subtle or ambiguous voice or tone of the narrator. Such sources oftentimes are open to a greater range of interpretations and historical meaning, making than discursive texts. Similarly, students can and did interpret the lyrics and mood of the song "You Gonna Reap," from multiple perspectives and thereby construct complex historical messages and moods from a simple set of lyrical and sounds. By focusing on and interpreting the expressive or structural qualities of the arts, students add human and humane dimensions to their construction of historical knowledge.

Instruction

Before introducing primary sources, I explained to students that history is constructed from evidence culled from primary sources. Primary sources like oral histories, songs, paintings, and poems are unique in their capacities to reflect the varieties and vicissitudes of cultural and social life. I then instructed students to interpret each source by asking the following questions:

1. What is the author's/creator's purpose in telling a folktale or singing a song?
2. What is the narrative's or song's theme?
3. What is its mood?

At the end of each day, I asked students to synthesize their interpretations of several primary sources to construct the broad contexts in which African Americans lived their lives by answering the following questions:

4. What is the significance of the songs or folktales to the people who created or heard them?
5. What do the narratives or songs reflect about nineteenth-century African American community and culture during enslavement?

The Classroom Conversation

Research has shown what experience suggests: most social studies classrooms consist of conversations where teachers or students reiterate information from the textbook (Goodlad 1984, Ravitch and Finn 1987). In this study, students who had no experience interpreting primary sources at first needed encouragement to suggest anything other than a literal or obvious interpretation. When interpreting the first two narratives on the first day of class, for example, students were especially hesitant to discuss the authors' moods or to speculate on the narrators' purposes or subtle meanings. As the first few students ventured literal or conventional comments, I encouraged others to contribute to the conversation by asking, "What else?" By the second day, students began to read meaning and significance into narrative form. In interviews conducted at the end of the unit, fourteen students commented that as I, the teacher, accepted a range of interpretations, rather than confirming a one-right answer, and as they listened to and built upon the comments of their classmates, they became bolder in venturing forth multiple meanings.

Is any interpretation of a historical narrative or poem acceptable? What distinguishes historical fact or interpretation from fabrication or fantasy? In teaching history, I take my cues from professional historians, maintaining a standard of "historical plausibility" (Handlin 1979, Holt 1990). Students construct historically plausible interpretations by examining "the evidence as a thing in itself and in its social context." An interpretation must not violate or contradict any aspects of the primary source itself. If, for example, a student had interpreted the narrative on literacy as demonstrating unmitigated hatred between African Americans and European Americans, she or he would have contradicted the narrator's own declaration that his master's sons were "nice boys."

Similarly, an interpretation must make sense within the historical context in which the primary source originated. If a student had interpreted the lyrics to the song "You Gonna Reap" literally, as evidence that African Americans reaped the benefits of their work in the fields, she or he would have rendered a historically inaccurate interpretation, one that did not fit the historical context of nineteenth-century African American enslavement.

In reviewing the transcripts of students' classroom conversations over the year, I found, for the most part, students who participated in the conversation rendered historically plausible or possible interpretations, although with varying degrees of sophistication or subtlety. In those instances when a student constructed an interpretation I thought implausible, improbable, or impossible, I either asked the student to elaborate upon the interpretation or I presented my reasons for doubting its plausibility. If neither of us was convinced of the other's perspective, we then entered into a conversation where we continued to examine critically the arguments for and against its plausibility. In most cases, one of us came to see the validity of the other's perspective or assertions.

Examples of Students' Historical Art Work

After working with the historical arts for eight days, students spent the ninth day devising and revising a rough draft of a historical poem, painting, story, or song. Neither the classroom teacher nor I spent time in class teaching students to create artlike forms. The quality of students' art work varied according to the level of skills they already possessed. Nonetheless, I encouraged students to exploit or take advantage of the expressive and structural characteristics of art forms': to use vivid, rhythmic, and emotion-laden words and phrases when writing poems or stories, or to use colors and shapes in paintings with sentient, as well as symbolic, import. Six of the seventeen students who completed projects had the knowledge and skills to produce good or excellent examples of historical art work. The four examples presented below illustrate the unique understandings students can represent in and through artlike forms.

Lifelike and Empathic Representations of History

As the classroom teacher described her, Hannah was the brightest student in the class. Analytically quick and verbally articulate, Hannah also excelled on multiple choice tests and in writing analytic essays. When asked why she decided to write a poem, she said she liked writing poetry and thought she could best represent through a poem the hardships of the African American experience during enslavement. Equally interesting is how Hannah's poem presents meanings she did not intend to represent, as reflected in a classmate's careful and considerate reading:

SLAVERY

My rich chocolate skin scorches in the sweltering sun
Deep in the midst of Virginia, we work
The Richmond cotton plantation, forty-five slaves
Work day in and day out
We are rewarded
With beatings, the thrashing of the master's rawhide whip
It echoes in all of our minds
We work, we work, we work
We suffer, we bleed and we pray
God, dear God, He knows it ain't right
He knows

And He's gonna change it one day.
We've got our bible
God's word, it's all we've got
No books, no words
Our hymns and ourselves, we survive.
Through the summer, we haul cotton
We haul till we bleed
Then we bleed alone
A bad look, a mumbled word, no reason at all
My skin tears and blood runs
With each stinging thrash
The salt and pepper stings, for extra pain
Sick pleasure for my Master.
We endure, we pray, we sing
We survive
We believe, our day will come.

Hannah has written realistically of the place of labor and religion in African American life and of the harshness and cruelty of race relations. By fashioning the poem's content or themes from the oral histories she read in class, Hannah reveals in descriptive detail the physical fatigue and intellectual monotony of labor, the cruelty of punishment, and the spiritual hope in salvation. By employing graphic and vivid language in poetic form, Hannah constructs a personal and empathic conception of enslavement.

When asked what she wanted to convey by writing the poem, Hannah commented:

> I wanted to explore their life and basically most of their life was their work, so I wanted to put that in. And then I wanted to put in their meetings, and I didn't want to make it "Our life is so hard." I wanted to make it "Our life is so hard yet we go on" because you gave us songs that showed they had hope. I was trying not to make it very morbid. I didn't want to make it "this is horrible." I wanted to get reality, as close as what I know of their reality, like "this is our everyday life and this is how we handle it."

When asked if she believed the poem effectively represented the reality of slavery, Hannah said she was happy with it, even though the tone belied feelings of helplessness or, as Hannah expressed it, "it might sound a little lame."

When she shared her poem with the class, Hannah provided an opportunity for others to bend and extend the poem's meanings in historical context. Tony read into its lines themes of resistance and tones of defiance. Focusing on the last two lines of the first and last verses, Tony commented, "It's like God is going to punish the white people for what they've done to blacks.... It sounds like they're being like slaves, like, 'we're just praying to God,' but they want to get even with whites ... when they say, 'our day will come,' they're standing up to the whites." Hannah's poetic representation enabled Tony to contribute by constructing a slightly different, yet plausible, interpretation.

A second student named Ben wrote and recorded a blues song. Ben occasionally spoke in class and received Bs in most of his work in class. In his spare time, Ben played guitar in a rock and roll band, and spent many hours writing and performing songs. He said he decided to write a song because the ones he heard in class reminded him of Leadbelly's songs, which had influenced his own writing and playing:

> Goin' down to the river
> tryin' to get to the other side
> Goin' down to the river
> tryin' to get to the other side
> Been put down and beaten up
> ain't no place left to hide.
>
> Lord, I'm runnin' on empty
> dogs at my heels
> Lord, I'm runnin' on empty
> dogs at my heels
> Gotta know how freedom feels
>
> If I drown in the river
> might not be so bad
> If I drown in the river
> might not be so bad
> Got them workin' blues,
> worse than I ever had.

In a simple set of lyrics, Ben has captured recurring and relevant themes and tones in African American history and culture. When asked about the song, Ben said he wanted to write an escape song. He built its theme around the phrase "going down the river," a familiar motif in blues music. The song, he said, was about African Americans' desire for freedom, a desire so strong that to some African Americans, Ben commented, death was more desirable than slavery. He also commented that he used the phrase "dog at my heels" literally to refer to European Americans' use of dogs to pursue

African Americans who escaped from slavery and figuratively to con-
note "dogs were the white man, always on the black man's case."

Ben also noted a blues song was a good way to convey the
contradictory moods of defiance and depression. "The man took the
first step and ran away," he said, but "he was down because his life
was hard and running away was dangerous." "The blues," Ben
commented, "are about feeling the blues."

Public Representations of Private Conceptualizations

Donald, a good student who received As and Bs on multiple
choice and essay tests, painted the following picture. The painting
(Figure 1) and Donald's comments demonstrate he had a solid understanding of the roles of labor and music in African American life
and the significance of African American labor in the development
of American economic life.

Figure 1.

This is a painting of blacks working, building a railroad track. I wanted to show a powerful black man working—that although to the white man he had no power, he really had power—*this* was his power, his strength, his labor was his power. He's working with other blacks and probably someone is singing so they could take turns and not get in each other's way.

When asked about the painting's form, and specifically about why he painted figures without faces, Donald said:

Well, I did that because I'm not good at drawing faces. But also, that way the whites couldn't see their faces, their feelings or what they really thought, like they're hiding themselves from whites. Like the songs with hidden meanings; if whites heard them, they might think they were singing about religion or just work, but they really were singing about getting free.

Donald also commented on how he conceptualized the idea for the painting. As he interpreted the narratives, songs, and paintings in class, Donald said he formed "pictures" or visual images of enslavement in his mind (Eisner 1982). Two primary sources in particular stuck in his mind. Donald borrowed conceptually from the song "Hammer Ring," a work song sung by groups of three or four men to establish a rhythm for successive turn-taking in hammering railroad spokes into the ground. Donald also borrowed visually from a Jacob Lawrence's painting he had seen in class. Like Lawrence's painting, Donald's work is dominated by big, boldly colored human figures devoid of facial features.

Through painting, Donald represented publicly what he imagined privately: a visual conceptualization of African American labor and song, and its significance to African American and national life. Donald's construction of historical knowledge developed as he interpreted a range of artlike primary sources and his exposure to a range of sources influenced the shape and meaning of his understanding. If Donald had not engaged with narrative, song, and painting, he would not have constructed the visual conceptualization that provided the basis for his painting. And even if Donald had interpreted historical narratives and songs, but had been asked to write an essay, the historical understanding he had conceptualized *visually* in his mind would have been lost or changed in the process of translating his vision into literal or logical language.

Equity in Educational Outcomes

Craig completed the final piece of work presented (Figure 2) and explained the historical context in which he set the work:

Figure 2.

> All the stuff we talked about in class gave me a picture of how together the slaves were with each other. They had a lot of love. They had a lot of faith in God. Everything was so bad for them but they still sometimes were happy and had fun together.
>
> This is how I picture them—just dancing. These graceful people. The hands represent God and how close they are with him. How He's always there with him. They probably had great respect for the earth . . . for all the trees and everything.

By juxtaposing Craig's verbal explanation and visual conceptualization, the complexity of his thought takes on greater form. His painting and comments reveal a knowledge of the context of African American song and dance, and the significance of African American religious faith, represented through joyous and communal expression. Craig's skillfulness and care as an artist especially is evident in the lifelike and loving qualities of the large hands, and the detailed and animated drawings of human figures (Dewey 1934). By keeping Craig's comments in mind and engaging intellectually with the drawing, an educated viewer is capable of constructing a conception of historical experience Craig meant to represent.

By examining Craig's work throughout the year, his drawing takes on greater meaning. As mentioned earlier, by traditional measures, Craig was a failing student. He became more engaged and occasionally participated in the classroom conversation when working with the primary sources. The difference in his written work and the drawing shown above is remarkable, however. When asked about the incongruity, Craig commented:

> I don't really understand the textbook. This stuff [the primary sources] is easier to understand. You have something you're listening to or looking at and it helps your figure it out. . . . We learn about their ways of living—it's more interesting than facts. . . . I can draw pretty good and I like it, but I can't write essays or research papers, at least not like Mrs. Jones [the classroom teacher] wants them.

Craig's comments reveal that an arts-based social studies curriculum not only enabled him to engage intellectually in ways he did not or could not when working with the textbook, it also provided an opportunity to represent the historical knowledge he had mastered through a form he had the talent to manipulate well. Because Craig's ability to draw far outstrips his ability to write analytically, he demonstrated through drawing his ability to construct historically rich thoughts and understandings. Although it is not clear what role motivation played in the development or exhibition of Craig's skills, his drawing represents anything but a failure to comprehend and communicate sound historical knowledge.

The Production and Evaluation of Historical Artwork

Like Craig and Donald, many students in the study noted the paintings or poems they created were influenced by the content and form of the primary sources they learned to interpret in class. Part of the student's task in interpreting historical paintings or poems is to analyze its form—how words or phrases in poetry or narrative create or contribute to a particular mood or theme. The analysis directs students' attention toward an art form's form—the ways words and phrases in songs and stories create messages and moods—and can contribute to students' understanding of song or story writing. In addition, a social studies teacher can explicitly teach about the structure or elements of poetry or story writing, just as some teach about the mechanics of writing a research paper or five-paragraph persuasive essay. Or colleagues from the English, art, music, or drama department can work with students individually or as a group in teaching students skills in poetry or story writing, painting, or performing.

As alternative forms of assessment, poetry or painting enable the skillful student to represent the kinds of empathic and lifelike historical understandings they cannot convey through an expository or persuasive essay. By allowing students to determine the form through which they represent what they have learned about a topic, a history teacher provides opportunities for one or more students to communicate how or what they have come to know through a form they are interested in completing, or in one they have the talent to manipulate well.

Evaluation

In this study, I judged each example of students' historical art work along three dimensions. First, I assessed each work in terms of the representativeness of its themes. By representativeness, I employed a standard of historical accuracy, probability, or plausibility. That is, did the student's work represent either a relatively historically accurate or realistic conception of the historical experiences depicted or a relatively historically possible, probable, or plausible conception? Hannah's poem, for example, represents a realistic and representative conceptualization of the African American experience during enslavement. Similarly, Donald's painting, along with his explanation, represent actual themes or experiences typical of African American life of the period.

Ben's song, however, represents a conceptual leap thematically. While related to themes of religious faith and escape, Ben's explanation of the song reveals a musical representation rooted in a historically probable or possible or plausible perspective or context. Craig's painting, too, although not a realistic conception of the experience of enslavement, represents a solid knowledge of the reality of the experience and more significantly, of the significant themes and influences shaping African American life. All four examples of students' historical art work represent imaginative renditions of the historical themes and perspectives that characterize African American life of the period.

The second set of criteria for assessing students' art work included judgments about the quality or skillfulness of form. Obviously a student who has gained a great understanding of the African American experience in slavery but is a poor painter will not be able to represent ideas effectively or even adequately through painting. Because we did not take time in class to teach students poetry writing or painting, the classroom teacher and I did not use formal criteria or a scale to assess students' work. We assessed a student's skill more generally, determining whether or not the skill or craftsmanship was inadequate, adequate, or exceptional in communicating the content or themes he or she meant to portray. [Another way to assess skill would be to use the formal criteria, appropriate for secondary students, for story writing, poetry, or painting (Bishop 1990; Michael 1983).]

The third criterion employed in the study involves the expressive or aesthetic qualities of historical art work. A primary purpose for representing historical understanding through poetry or painting is that art forms enable students to communicate an empathic, rather than a literal or logical, understanding of the past. A student conveys this by shaping or exploiting the sensory and expressive elements of painting or song in ways that enable him or her to represent an empathic or lifelike understanding. Expressive qualities also enable a knowledgeable percipient—that is, a teacher or classmates—to grasp a human or empathic conception of the historical experiences depicted. Thus, an effective or successful piece of historical artwork conveys to others an empathy for the historical experiences represented.

Like the criterion of representativeness, the teacher and I characterized a work's expressiveness in simple terms of adequacy or inadequacy. We each asked ourselves if during our engagement with the work and with the student's explanation of it, if it evoked "forms of imagination and forms of feeling, inseparably" (Langer 1953, p. 397). That is, were we able to construct or conjure up in our minds some image of or feeling for the African American experience as the student portrayed it? Were we able to construe or come away with an empathic understanding of the historical experiences portrayed? Or, upon our best efforts, were we incapable of constructing from our engagement with the work any increase in "the acuity of insight" (Goodman 1978) into the topics or themes delineated?

By integrating the arts into the social studies curriculum, teachers can accomplish a number of goals that enhance the educational experiences and outcomes of the students with whom they work. Besides the cognitive benefits, teachers also can make the experience of learning social studies far more interesting and enjoyable than it is commonly considered to be, by students and teachers alike.

CHAPTER TEN

Science in Social Studies: Reclaiming Science for Social Knowledge

Stephen C. Fleury

Science-Technology-Society (STS) is a science curriculum reform that has surfaced in the social studies within the past decade.
A corps of social educators who envision the potential for STS as
an alternative to traditional social studies topics have garnered
professional organizational support and recognition. Both the National Council for the Social Studies (NCSS) and the Social Science
Education Consortium have supported educational publications,
provided journal space, and published manuscripts on STS. By
1991, STS was included as part of the NCSS curriculum guidelines.
Remy (1990) asserts that STS can contribute to the "core mission
of social studies—the preparation of citizens." Yet Heath's (1988)
claim that a "trend" exists may be more hopeful than descriptive of
the actual status of STS in the social studies curriculum. An overall paucity of science-related social studies materials exists, as does
an ominous silence among teachers, most of whom are busily working to meet the renewed historical objectives of local, state, and
national social studies frameworks.

In this chapter I critically examine the role of science in social
studies and the STS curriculum movement for its potential as an
alternative framework. My concern, in particular, is with the meaning that studies of science and technology can have for the further-
ance of an education for democratic citizenship. It is perhaps the
neglect of science in the social studies curriculum that is most
striking. Science as an epistemological development is usually given
only cursory attention as a historical event—that is, the "scientific
revolution." Rarely do social studies students understand tensions
in the contemporary world as manifestations of this continuing

revolution, or how the appropriation of different types of knowledge through social practices and institutions influences economic, political, and ultimately social behavior. The objective of this chapter are to argue that:

1. School science and social studies function to separate facts and values, subsequently preventing student awareness of relationships between knowledge and power. The difficulties for integrating STS are compounded by the positivistic underpinnings of school science and social studies curricula.
2. Although espousing participatory rhetoric, STS programs are prone to the promotion of technical understandings rather than the democratization of knowledge.
3. Social educators might counter the narrowing of democratic practices and redefining of citizenship, which has resulted from the traditional structuring of science and social studies curricula, by looking to the tenets of the new philosophy of science and cognitive sciences.

Social Education's Omission

In 1971, President Nixon pledged to reduce cancer rates by 20 percent within the next twenty years. His pledge evoked the same fundamental faith in science and technology as President Kennedy's earlier vow to put an American on the moon by the end of the 1960s. In 1969 Neil Armstrong walked on the moon, quietly affirming Americans' faith in science and technology. Yet in 1995, and with 25 billion research dollars invested in a "war on cancer," the rates for the major cancer killers—lung, colon, testicular, brain, prostrate, and breast cancers—remain the same and, in some cases, increased dramatically (Greene 1995).

Are scientific accomplishments this random? Why has this problem remained unassailable? Why a major human success in one area, and the lack of progress in another?

Public policies have directed tremendous human effort and financial resources toward AIDS research, but education continues to be promoted as the best preventive cure for this dreaded disease. All segments of the population are affected, but none more so than gay men. Yet AIDS education seems not to be working. The meaning of life and death has changed for gay men, 50 percent of whom are now infected, and of whom 45 years is the mean life expectancy (Odets 1995).

Are there fundamental flaws in our assumption that providing people with knowledge will bring about desired social behaviors? Are there problems with the way knowledge is provided? Is there more to "correct" knowledge than merely correct information?

These situations provoke questions about what scientific knowledge is, how it relates to personal and social behavior, how it is mediated by educational institutions, and most fundamentally, how it relates to power in the broadest sense—political, economic, social, individual, and otherwise. These are basic social studies questions, but one is probably safe in alleging these questions are rarely, if ever, voiced in social studies classrooms. Although some educators will argue that elementary and secondary students lack the academic sophistication to handle such questions, it may be safe to say these kinds of issues are rarely more than peripherally considered in most college curricula.

The traditional history-orientation of the school subject called social studies may be offered as a reason why science and science-related issues have not found their into the school curriculum. Yet the point is even more poignant. Why, in a nation like the United States with devotion to the values of science and democracy, are the historical as well as present dynamics between science and social goals omitted in the basic education of youth? Why are these issues not a working part of a social studies curriculum framework, especially one that is structured historically?

School Science and Social Studies

When discussing the implementation of STS in the schools, promoters speak in cautionary terms about the need to overcome difficulties relating to its interdisciplinary nature. Although some proponents provide extensive advice about including STS in the social studies curriculum through "infusing" topics, units, or creating distinct social studies courses (Heath 1988; Marker 1992; Remy 1990), no one has proposed replacing either science or social studies with STS. Remy (1990) relates a perplexing problem for curriculum writers:

> There is no broad theory of knowledge that incorporates the sciences and the social studies. There is no universal framework which could be the foundation for a comprehensive interdisciplinary curriculum. [p. 206]

It seems odd that no theory of knowledge unifies these two school subjects. School science and social studies share a historical background. They are both outgrowths of twentieth-century educational reforms. As part of the common educational system, their ends are ultimately justified on citizenship grounds. Within the enlightenment tradition, their promotion (at least rhetorically) of sound reasoning through disciplinary study is deemed essential for the maintenance and promotion of a republican democracy.

Theories of knowledge, much like foundational curriculum frameworks and knowledge disciplines, are social constructions. They are influenced by historical, social, political, economic, and a host of other institutional forces. The social construction of social studies and school science began in the early part of the twentieth century with the formation of mass public education to address the particular social and economic problems of the modern industrializing United States. In *A Political Sociology of Educational Reform*, Popkewitz (1991) states:

> The significance of modern pedagogy is its tie to problems of social regulation; pedagogy links the administrative concerns of the state with the self-governance of the subject. The forms of knowledge in schooling frame and classify the world and the nature of work, which, in turn, have the potential to organize and shape individual identity. [p. 14]

One might properly deduce from Popkewitz's statement that the structures of the school subjects of science and social studies *organize* and *shape* a particular kind of individual identity. In other words, the disciplinary organization of these two subjects—their content and rules for learning—have a socialization function as well as a cognitive one. Popkewitz explains that "the 'rules' of science embody visions of the social order as well as conceptual distinctions that define power relations." (p. 15). These rules are translated in public schooling as school disciplinary subjects.

I am proposing that school science and social studies are complimentary disciplinary partners that "frame" and "classify" the world for students in such a way as to prevent them from becoming aware that issues of individual and social power relate to issues of individual and social knowledge. For example, the authority of scientific knowledge, who can share it, and toward what purposes are both attitudes and understandings about the nature of knowledge and the role of citizens that are learned through school science and social studies. A positivistic theory of knowledge—in which facts are separated from values and objectivity from subjectivity—undergirds these school subjects, allowing them to appear like separate realms of knowing. This positivistic underpinning is not merely conceptual, but political as well, in promoting a theory of knowledge that actively conserves the prevailing social order by preventing most students from creating, examining (testing), or understanding the tenuous basis of social knowledge.

Positivism and Science Education

The philosophical position of positivism holds that scientific knowledge is objective, certain, and a mirror of absolute reality. Tracing its philosophical roots from Bacon, Berkeley, and Hume, the term itself was coined by Comte, whose ideas influenced work in the nineteenth and twentieth centuries. Positivism assumes that the knower and the known are clearly separated, an assumption reflected in the belief that theories (beliefs) are sharply distinct from facts, and facts from values. Most importantly, positivism holds that subjectivity plays no role in the gathering of objective knowledge. *Logical positivism,* also called *scientific empiricism,* emerged in Europe within the Vienna Circle in the 1920s around issues about the idea that natural laws can be inferred from experiences.

Duschl (1988) convincingly argues that the authoritarian demeanor of present science education—its factual orientation, textbook dependency, and lack of inquiry—is directly related to the prevailing positivistic view of teachers about knowledge in general, and science in particular. Describing it as an "ideology of scientism," he implies that the positivistic assumptions of education are inextricably related to the larger social and political context. For example, teaching practices and materials often communicate positivistic ideas that science research methods are objective, or that proof is obtained from such methods. Faulty reasoning is fostered via teaching practices and instructional materials when the logic of scientific confirmation, which involves a logical fallacy, is taught as though valid. Since few teachers are aware of the assumptions underlying scientific methods, such instruction is most likely an unintentional and unrecognized part of the hidden curriculum.

How common is such instruction? An examination of science textbooks provides evidence of the entrenchment of positivism. Science textbooks are, after all, the chief source of the curriculum in most schools (Stake and Easley 1978). Usually, the positivistic orientation of a textbook is explicit in the first chapter or two which describes the nature of science. Textbook authors often present the scientific method as a series of logical steps, beginning with observations or questions, proceeding to the formation of hypotheses and tests, and ending in conclusions (Appenbrink and Hounshell 1981; Moyer and Bishop 1986).

Although scientific research is often presented in this logical form, the work itself proceeded along multiple paths. Kaplan (1964) first pointed out the distinction between the logic of *doing* science with the logic of *reporting* scientific findings, calling the former *logic-in-use* and the latter *re-constituted logic* (p. 3). Through pedagogical practices and selected content, school science is presented as reconstituted knowledge, an image that camaflouges its tentative nature and presents it as a technical and mechanical process for solving problems. School textbooks rarely clarify the "scientific method." A few authors note the tentativeness of scientific knowledge, but fail to explain it. Usually a reader is told that particular scientific data have been "discovered" or "proven."

The typical pattern of student activities and experiments in science classes and textbooks leads to confirmation bias. "Confirmation bias" is the tendency to only consider evidence that will support a particular idea, while ignoring everything else. We often accept predictions on the basis of incomplete evidence, while discrediting and reinterpreting evidence that does not support our hypothesis (Ross and Lepper 1980). We also tend to neglect to conduct tests that truly expose our ideas to a genuine risk of being disconfirmed (Snyder and Swann 1978; Snyder and White 1981).

Textbooks are a major source of this *inductivist fallacy*. As an example, in a study of science materials, nine elementary school science textbooks series were examined and found to contain "cookbook-style hands-on activities with predetermined results" (p. 9). Typically, a problem or question is presented first. Then the aim(s) or purpose(s) or objective(s) of the study are stated. Third, materials and procedures are listed. And finally, questions about the results or intended conclusions are provided. The hidden lesson of the cookbook format is that "right" answers are possible through a linear induction process.

Citizenship and Social Studies

When asked to describe how science and social studies are alike or different, high school and college students respond that science is more objective and factual, while social studies deals more with opinions and personal values (Fleury and Bentley 1991). I have discussed above how the objective and factual impression of science emanates from its positivist philosophical background and school instruction. There is no epistemological equivalent to the scientific method in social studies education; instead, there is the recurring theme of citizenship.

Anecdotal evidence, personal experiences, and research investigations support the claim that social studies, as it is taught and learned, feed what Parenti (1983) calls a *social orthodoxy*. This is not news. In an address to the National Council for the Social Studies in 1967, former NCSS president Wesley criticized the mythologizing function of teaching students selected historical and geographic events that de facto supported a romanticized image of the United States and its role in the world.

Wesley lamented the truncated values, glorified images, and misconceptions of the world and the United States that are passed from one generation to the next through the content and teaching of social studies. This traditional approach to social studies predominates despite the efforts of Dewey, Griffin, Metcalf, Engle, and a host of other historic and contemporary social educators (Barr, Barth, and Shermis 1977).

Shaver, Davis and Helburn's evaluation of the New Social Studies projects in 1979 found the vast majority of social studies teachers continued to believe their main responsibility was to socialize students into the status quo. Leming (1989) defensively implied that socializing students into the status quo may be the most credible social studies approach because of the existence of a culture of schooling. The traditional organization of social studies has incredible staying power. The recent work of the Heritage Foundation, the Bradley Commission, and others in the 1980s and 1990s has reaffirmed the historic and geographic framing of the social studies curriculum.

How does such an orthodoxy retain hold in the face of changing social, political, and epistemological institutions? C. W. Mills (1959), no admirer of social studies, explained that the use of selective historical events is understandably seductive, since there are so many wonderful stories in America's past. There is no absence of historical approaches that could promote a more critically oriented understanding of the complex development of human societies and of American culture. But the organization of social studies knowledge has been shaped by the identity and the role that historical knowledge has assumed because of the influence of positivism. The mission orientation of positivistic knowledge influences school science and social studies alike.

History, originally a literary and moralizing subject, has been riddled with an identity crisis since the transformation of speculative to scientific philosophy at the end of the nineteenth century (Handlin 1979; Reichenbach 1951). This epistemological transformation marked a splintering of the discipline of history into several spheres of social scientific inquiry. The professionalization of *historical* and *social science* knowledge through the formation of professional organizations, standards, and college departments has added to the politicization of social knowledge. Although history itself, as a discipline, has proceeded from primarily a literary endeavor to an increasingly scientific-epistemological one, history in the schools has retained its moralizing import.

Freedman (1989) is cited by Popkewitz in explaining that teachers during the development of mass public education assumed a wider mantel of moral authority and political stewardship over social goals. Such political stewardship was enacted through "pedagogical strategies designed to encourage children to develop individual discipline." Through such strategies, an individual's goals became "tied . . . to useful social and economic practices" (Popkewitz, p. 57).

How strategies are tied to useful social and economic practices has been the subject of studies by critical curriculum theorists in the past few years. In *Contradictions of Control,* McNeil (1986) finds that social studies practices and strategies reflect the teachers' need to maintain classroom control. Classroom control, conceptual as well as organizational, is maintained through the manipulation of the subject matter content. Disruptions to both a teacher's conceptual and organizational control are avoided through the omission of certain topics. Another strategy is to "fragment" social knowledge by treating complex topics superficially and by presenting outlines and lists of phenomena to convey the appearance that social knowledge is obtuse, isolated, and unrelated. Another technique is to "mystify" knowledge by alluding to students that a certain piece of information is important to know, but failing to explain its significance or how it relates. All of these techniques are used without providing students the means for examining or challenging this knowledge.

McNeil's study is illustrative of how the historical structuring of social studies contributes to the socialization of social control. Historical knowledge tends to be presented to students as a mirror image of what really happened in reality. The chronological structuring of social studies suffers little because of selected omissions, mystifications, and fragmentations, which portray certain social images of social authority, order, and control. The particular content of social studies is imbued with the need for social control in the classroom. It may be easy to see how similar views of good citizenship can be generalized and acted upon as the primary moral responsibility of social studies teachers.

Summary

Those involved in teacher education understand how the nature of subject matter influences its teaching methodologies. The individual discipline that children are encouraged to internalize from school science and social studies reinforces a positivist sense of their social world. Science education promotes a sense of the physical world as nonproblematic, objective, and knowable through sophisticated methods by highly sophisticated experts. Emphasis is placed on the scientific method, but little room is made for considerations that scientific knowledge is human knowledge, created for subjective purposes, and riddled with limitations and human values.

The structures of school science and social studies seem to function inversely in developing students' understanding of knowledge. Science education presents an epistemological method but few opportunities for interpretations. Social studies is conducive for interpretations of its "truths," but fails to provide students with the methods and skills for examining and evaluating knowledge.

In the social studies, little attention is provided for how its "facts" are derived. A challenge to any of social studies knowledge tends to be explained as a different value position. Students are bereft of opportunities, however, to explore why some value positions attain higher status than others, disempowering their ability to reason and judge knowledge about their social worlds.

The Technocratization of Knowledge

STS proponents advocate its ability to promote active citizenship participation (Patrick and Remy 1985; Remy 1990, Wraga and Hlebowitsh 1990). It is unclear, however, if active citizenship has ever been more than a rhetorical goal of either science or social studies education. Leming (1989), for example, challenges whether a critical orientation or active citizen participation *ought* to be social studies goals, contending that these social ideals are merely vestiges of reconstructionist educational ideologies of the 1930s.

It is true that the 1930s were a time when social studies and science education experimented with problem-centered rather than discipline-centered approaches. Hurd (1991) explains that uncertain economic and social conditions were accompanied by a social disenchantment with science and technology because of their association with automation. The Progressive Education Association called for a socially based approach to school science, including personal, social, civic, and economic goals. In addition, progressive educators called for a critical thinking that was a "more flexible cognitive concept" (Hurd, p. 255) than the mechanistic, technical version of scientific problem-solving that had prevailed previously in the curriculum.

John Dewey's educational philosophy was influential on much of what was called progressive education. Dewey linked a problem-centered scientific epistemology with the development of democratic values:

> The only freedom that is of enduring importance is the freedom of intelligence, that is to say, freedom of observation and judgement exercised in behalf of purposes that are intrinsically worthwhile. [Dewey 1939, p. 69, in Splittgerber 1991]

While some schools during the progressive education movement went from subject-centered to problem-centered curricula, the onset of the World War II brought a renewed patriotism to the content of social studies. For science education, the social relevancy of the problem-centered approach was soon overshadowed by the technological demands of World War II, fostering an upsurge of interest in technology-related science education.

The evolution of social studies from the school history of the nineteenth century transpired amid the series of educational policy-making committees between 1893 and 1916. Social studies included the newer social sciences to assist in studying how society was organized. Its founders were influenced by Dewey's philosophy, but it was in the progressive educational era of the 1930s that problem-centered approaches became popular in social studies.

The onset of the "big science" era after World War II has had, perhaps, the most profound impact leading to the development of the present status of science and social studies education, and ultimately to views of citizenship. Two reports commissioned by the federal government after World War II have been foundational for linking technological development with science education, and eventually social studies education. The Bush Report:

> Defined a policy that American's peacetime future in health, economy, and military security required the continuous deployment of new scientific knowledge to assure social progress. [cited from Hurd 1991, p. 256]

The report called for a complete revamping of science teaching and content. The implication of this report was that a specific type of social knowledge—science—was politically identified and socially sanctioned as the *most* valuable kind of knowledge for maintaining and promoting national interests.

Subsequently, the Steelman Report defined the social crisis that justified forming the National Science Foundation in 1950. Produced by the President's Scientific Research Board and the American Association for the Advancement of Science Cooperative Committee, this report warned that the United States faced a serious shortage of science researchers, science workers, and science teachers (Steelman 1947, cited from Hurd, p. 256). Sound familiar? As a result of this impending national crisis in knowledge, the National Science Foundation was created to "improve the quality and quantity of science education in schools, colleges, and universities" (England 1982, p. 228, cited from Hurd, p. 256). The epistemological and social effect of the NSF on science and social studies education should not be underestimated.

The broad directive of NSF educational projects was to engage students in "real science" with chances to "think like scientists" (England 1982, p. 228). Although the role of science in schools has been debated since the 1600s (Hurd 1991), the historical tendency has been for school science to mirror the research disciplines of universities—in effect, preventing the masses from the "cultivation of science." One very real effect of NSF influence was that the disciplinary grip on science teaching and learning was increasingly institutionalized.

The relation of science to society was seldom mentioned, and science itself was presented as predominantly quantitative inquiry, laboratory work, and discipline-specific. Since goals and objectives were defined in terms of the structure of a particular discipline, few places were left to consider "integrative concepts of science and technology or those of science, technology, and society" (Hurd 1991, p. 256).

Social studies was not part of early NSF initiatives—that is, it received no grant money. But the NCSS yearbook *Science and the Social Studies* (1957) was an overture to lucrative times to come. The yearbook promoted the interdependence of science and social studies, and invoked that science was an "irreducible minimum of education" for responsible citizenship (Cummings 1957, p. 27, cited in Splittgerber 1991).

Social studies teachers were instructed in how to help their students develop scientific understandings. The yearbook provided guidelines for:

> (a) Integrating science into American culture, (b) understanding how scientists have contributed to discoveries and formulation of new knowledge, (c) studying the role of science and technology as one of the important aspects of modern citizenship, and (d) reducing delays in taking action on dangerous scientific and technological problems. [Splittgerber 1991, p. 244]

By 1963, the NSF provided major funding for what came to be called the new social studies. The intention was to reform social studies by utilizing the best scientific understanding of both subject matter content and learning theories. By combining Joseph Schwab's ideas about the structure of scientific disciplines with Bruner's theories about the structure of learning, the epistemological intent of these projects encouraged student inquiry about their world by equipping them with the intellectual tools of the social science disciplines.

Such an intent met with successes and failures. In an evaluation of NSF projects in 1978, Shaver found that few materials were used, that traditional textbooks provided the structure of social studies teaching and content, and that most social studies teachers still perceived that their function was to socialize students into the status quo of American society. There was an inclusion of social science vocabulary, but little understanding of how to engage students in building or examining social science generalizations. Shaver called the new social studies a nonevent.

The fate of *Man: A Course of Study* (MACOS) by Bruner should be instructive to social studies educators who mix the scientific study of society with the socialization goals of social studies education. This fifth- and sixth-grade curriculum raised empirical and ethical questions about humans and their world. It sought to have students examine these questions through studying the life cycles of different types of animals and of Netsilik Eskimos.

By 1975, MACOS was used in over 1700 schools, but its funding was cut because of a controversy that erupted when NSF requested congressional funds to support teacher training. Similar to the way in which Harold Rugg's textbooks were eliminated from schools in the 1940s, conservative groups launched media campaigns and school board attacks against MACOS with charges of cultural relativism and environmental determinism. A politically powerful portion of the public was unwilling to involve scientific knowledge in social studies.

Social studies educators seemed reluctant to embark on new science-related projects after the MACOS controversy. The curriculum became increasingly pressured by a back-to-basics environment throughout the 1980s, culminating in a plethora of history and geography frameworks on the local, state, and national level. The frequently reported results of the National Assessment of Educational Progress (NAEP) serve to continually remind the American public that school social studies inadequately prepares the majority of students about history.

In the late 1970s, because of the work of the NCSS committee on science and society, STS began to appear as a social studies topic. A special section of *Social Education* was devoted to science and technology. An NCSS bulletin, *Science and Society: Knowing, Teaching, and Learning* (Charles and Samples 1978) was published. Sporadic articles appeared throughout the 1980s. By the 1990s, STS was the theme of an issue of *Social Education* and included in the NCSS curriculum guidelines.

Social studies arguments for STS generally begin with serious warnings about impending social consequences of recent scientific and technological developments. Too many citizens are "uninformed" and "irrational" (Remy 1990). Social educators have "no choice" (Marker 1992) but to adopt STS to responsibly develop civic decision-makers—citizens—who will understand the risks, probabilities, tradeoffs, and uncertainties involved with scientific applications. Social studies educators are reinforced for the contribution that the "ethical" way of thinking of social studies can make to the "factual" way of thinking in science. In addition, social educators are warned that an attitude of anti-science is growing in the United States, an attitude which is directly threatening to the western tradition of which the development of science is at the center (Heath 1988; Marker 1992; Remy 1990; Tanner 1990).

Cautions are provided about introducing the STS interdisciplinary approach to the traditional curriculum of social studies (Remy

1990; Wraga and Hlebowitsh 1990; Wraga 1993). Suggested implementation strategies include infusing special STS topics, lessons, and units in the social studies curriculum, or offering separate elective courses (Heath 1988, 1992; Marker 1992; Remy 1990).

The persistent efforts of these social educators to draw attention to a severely ignored aspect of social knowledge is a valuable contribution to social education. The work, however, is rife with problematic issues involving both the epistemological and citizenship assumptions of science and social studies education, and related to a complex web of social, economic, and political factors.

May (1992) identifies a number of issues that riddle the modernist-type (positivistic) thinking of most STS proposals and curricula. She observes that STS educators seem to have a low tolerance for ambiguity, and by implication, a need for certainty. Ironically, this is contrary to effectively helping students understand the tentativeness of scientific knowledge.

Secondly, STS approaches tend to reinforce the belief that school subjects are similar, but simpler, forms of university research disciplines. The entrenched beliefs among educators and students about the immutability of scientific knowledge prevent students from becoming aware of the complexities and creativeness involved in doing science.

Another, and perhaps more serious issue, is that STS topics tend to be presented in a way that prevents students from being the "subjects of study." Scientific knowledge continues to be viewed as acontextual and unrelated to cultural values. Problems are presented for technical policy solutions, but examinations of the relationships between scientific knowledge and technical solutions to race, class, gender, and other social variables are avoided.

May points out that no social educator has yet proposed the "radical restructuring" of social studies:

> It is difficult for science, technology and social studies teachers not to perpetuate a modern, western world-view in post-modern times. In our traditional separations and interests, we have been guilty of rationalizing and simplifying the most intriguing and complex human endeavors and problems. [p. 81]

Arguing that "reflection and critical dialogue" are necessary to work across the artificially constructed boundaries of school subject disciplines, she asserts that:

It is naive to claim that we lack a universal theory in education because we disagree on goals and definitions or are "immature" compared to science. Disagreement is the catalyst of all fields; it requires diverse interests, a shared understanding (agreement) about what we disagree on, dialogue, and critique, all of which maintain and transform fields. [p. 73]

May calls for a postmodern approach to STS to "promote an ecological, moral, cultural, pluralistic, and spiritual perspective, an 'ethic of caring' and a critical pragmatism"(p. 73). With a transformation to a postmodern approach, science, scientists, and the effects of their work could be involved in moral considerations, technological applications could be critically analyzed in terms of human intentions and social consequences, and social studies would not be the mere transmission of facts, values, and patriotic images.

Reclaiming Science for Social Knowledge

Rosenthal's (1989, cited in Carter 1991) distinction between two different perspectives of STS clarifies May's position. The "social issues" approach has been imported from science education (Yeager 1990). Carter (1992) argues that its problem-solving epistemology assumes a "fix" exists. This is the technical, modernist approach May refers to. Carter warns that STS issues too easily become one-sided and fail to examine prevailing political, economic, and social assumptions.

On the other hand, the social studies of science approach involves educators in examining the assumptions, beliefs, values, and methods of doing science and their relationship to society and technology. Its attention to the doing of science is ultimately more democratic. When hidden assumptions and values, which relate science and social dynamics, are brought to the surface, students become aware that science is accessible to them. Carter draws attention to the similarity of this type of empowering education and the problem-posing education of Freire (1989):

In problem-posing education, [people] develop their power to perceive critically *the way they exist* in the world *with which* and *in which* they find themselves; they come to see the world not as a static reality but as reality in process, in transformation (pp. 70–71, cited in Carter, p. 278).

What types of questions could social studies educators begin to ask about science in social studies education? An analysis of STS itself serves as a starting point. Educational reform proposals concerning science education have warned of an impending shortage of scientists since the Steelman Report in the 1940s. Yet these shortages really have not existed (Cheek 1992). The present "crisis" is also nonexistent. What social forces are responsible for the definition and promotion of this mythological educational and political claim?

Why is scientific knowledge considered high-status knowledge? What is the role of schooling in perpetuating this status? How are institutionalized economic interests served by the manner in which school science and social studies are offered?

What is the relationship of scientific "literacy" to citizenship? How is literacy determined? By whom? To what degree might the promotion of STS be a means to ameliorate public resistance to technological changes that have far-reaching effects on political and economic power?

What type of knowledge is needed for individuals to participate in decision-making about scientific and technological matters. For example, our assumptions about causation influence both policies and research on cancer. Governmental policies in the 1980s have redefined cancer "causes" as individual choices—that is, lifestyles—while more productive research might focus on social factors such as toxic fumes, radiation, and food additives.

Lastly, how is scientific thinking different from historical thinking, and how might this influence social knowledge? Philosophically, historical knowledge is concerned with particular, time-bound ideas and phenomenan, while scientific knowledge is patterned knowledge—that is, it involves the construction and examination of relationships among and between particular "historical" information (Freese 1980).

Research on the bicameralization of the brain provides interesting support. Sagan (1977) calls science "paranoid thinking applied to nature." He refers to the hemispheric function of the brain to connect disparate information, to visualize patterns, to search for connections. The analytical function of the left side of the brain compliments thinking by examining if patterns "fit reality" or not. The ability to construct patterns, and the need to examine these "conspiracies," are necessary functions of scientific thinking.

Sagan argues that the human condition would greatly improve if we applied this thinking socially, politically, economically, religiously, and culturally. It is fitting to argue that in traditional approaches to social studies, we too often provide students with grand patterns, but fail to provide them with the information and the guidance for examining if these patterns make sense. We too often foster, perhaps, the grandest of teaching and learning disabilities.

The present understanding that students seem to have about relationships among economic, political, and social conditions serves as an example. In an issue-oriented social studies class, students may debate and discuss current problems. The predominate narrative is that the American work force has become too expensive because of higher wages. Companies are unable to find workers who are sufficiently trained. To achieve efficiencies, companies are "understandably" forced to downsize or move to more receptive labor markets, laying off thousands of American workers in some cases. Joblessness, poverty, higher local, state, and federal taxes are all viewed as an inevitable result of economic laws. All these factors have brought American society to a time when we need to curtail social spending to ensure the viability and survival of our economic system.

Provided a small amount of data (Barnet 1994), students might begin some paranoid thinking. They might notice that as many companies downsize, they also merge with other businesses, creating even larger ones. They might notice that in the name of efficiency, banks are growing ever-larger, and hold more money nationally and internationally. Students might observe that the media are concentrated in fewer hands; global corporations are chartered in the United States, but disavow any national connection or social responsibility; one-fourth of the world's economic activity occurs by the two hundred largest corporations; and one-third of world trade is within a single global economy. Provided with more social data, students might construct and examine a cognitive pattern of thinking that points to an increasing globalization and centralization of economic power, one that could appear to be the largest economic transformation of the world's distribution of resources since the "Age of Exploration."

How might an examination of technology be involved? The advances in labor-saving devices have contributed to the automation of labor. Corporations now control the technology to place their operations anywhere in the world. Students might observe labor unions in the United States have weakened to less than 12 percent of the work force. The driving motivation for school reform, that students need to be prepared for a high-tech society, might be viewed as a winner-take-all proposition. Once graduated, there are not enough jobs, and many that exist are low-paying and require a lower level of education.

Political apathy or discontent might be visioned differently by students involved in paranoid thinking. In three years, five companies laid off 324,650 workers. Job slashers are well rewarded. The CEOs of 23 of 27 companies that reduced labor received an average 30 percent wage increase. In a 1993 GAO study, 40 percent of the corporations that earned 250 million dollars paid no tax, or less than 100 thousand dollars. Students might compare the 23 percent of income tax paid by corporations in 1950 to the 9.2 percent paid in 1991. Provided with these particular pieces of data, students might notice that the media seem to focus on individualistic traits of politicians, rather than patterns of relationships between political and economic institutions (Barnet 1994).

Conclusion

The most recent appeals for courses and programs on Science-Technology-and Society are well-intentioned and important. Helping students to understand the importance and social ramifications of modern scientific development—that is, technological changes possible by the utilization of scientific knowledge—and to examine the value issues seems to be a refreshingly bold educational strike for citizenship education. Yet the type of citizenship resulting from STS may be little different from what we already have, unless traditional categories of how we think about science and social studies are also critically examined. Neglecting to critique traditional categories of how we think about science and of how we think about social studies allows the school curriculum to resist significant changes, ensuring these subjects continue to contribute to a social orthodoxy of cosmetic democracy. Consequently the populace is deprived of educative experiences that would purposefully develop a broader social knowledge to engage in discussions and decision-making on a more equal basis with individuals and corporations whose economic prowess and interests supersede social concerns.

CHAPTER ELEVEN

Infusing Global Perspectives into the Social Studies Curriculum

Merry M. Merryfield

It was only twenty years ago that Chadwick Alger introduced "Columbus and the World, the World in Columbus." It
was a new approach to world studies that focused on the increasing interconnections between that Ohio city and people,
organizations, products, and ideas around the world. Through
research in their community, students in central Ohio learned
how they, their families, and neighbors were linked through
goods and services, technology, politics, religion, the arts, and
other ties to people in every part of the globe. Alger's new
curriculum became a benchmark in the American movement to
teach students about their world from a global perspective,
rather than the traditional nation-centric approach of international relations or the conventional culture-centric approaches
of world history or geography.

Today global education is an integral part of the K-12 social
studies curriculum in many states and school districts across the
United States. In a 1982 position paper the National Council for
the Social Studies (NCSS) defined global education as "the efforts
to cultivate in young people a perspective of the world which emphasizes the interconnections among cultures, species, and the
planet." The NCSS paper goes on to recommend that social studies
curricula should teach that:

1. Globalization of the human experience has led to a
   world in which we all are constantly being influenced
   by transnational, cross-cultural, and multicultural
   interactions.

2. Individuals, nonstate groups such as multinational corporations, churches, and scientific organizations, as well as local governments and national leaders are all actors shaping the world today.

3. People and the environment make up a single interdependent system with finite resources.

4. There are linkages between past and present social, political, economic, and ecological realities and alternative futures.

5. All people make choices in the ways they participate in world affairs. [NCSS 1982]

In order to understand the curricular dimensions of global education, we will examine the rationale for this innovation, explore some of its characteristics, and finally learn about the practice of global education in actual social studies classrooms.

Why Global Education?

The movement for global perspectives in education is a response to the profound changes that have shaped our world in the late twentieth century. Although we can trace incidents of increasing interconnections and growing interdependence between peoples back hundreds of years, recent breakthroughs in technology and emerging global issues have thrust us all into an age where we can no longer separate our interests, concerns, and everyday lives from those of people around the world. The content of the social science disciplines demonstrates these changes and forms much of the basic knowledge young people need to be prepared for their global age.

There was a time when it made sense to study the economy of one's town or state or nation. In today's world it is impossible to separate the economy of Seattle or Washington state from trade and foreign investment in the Pacific Rim. We cannot understand the success of the American computer industry without learning about operations in Asia or competition with the Japanese. Americans who are ignorant of Europe's moves toward economic integration will probably not be prepared to trade successfully with one of the world's largest markets.

Although it may be easy to recognize our dependence upon products from all around the world (all we have to do is inventory our homes), most Americans are only vaguely aware of how their local multinational company, neighborhood bank or stockbroker influences the employment of women in the Philippines, loans to Taiwanese entrepreneurs, or the prices Sierra Leonean farmers receive for their cocoa. More and more American jobs are dependent upon world markets and the ability to compete globally. Our economic future is tied to people and organizations around the world, and their future is linked to ours.

The United States is also centered in a global political system dependent upon the cooperation and negotiation of many nations, organizations, and individuals. Whether it be concerns over acid rain, the flight of refugees, decisions over nuclear wastes, aggression in the Balkans, or the conservation of tropical forests, today's global issues require nations to come together to find political solutions. Yet in this global age it is not only governments that make foreign policy or interact with the global political system. Church groups in our communities and global organizations such as Amnesty International work for improvement of human rights and the release of political prisoners around the world. Cultural or religious organizations send money and support political action in countries as different as Israel and Northern Ireland. Environmental groups such as Greenpeace cross national borders to influence fishing in international waters or the dumping of toxic wastes. American governors lead delegations to other countries to compete for foreign investment or set up trade missions abroad. Mayors and chambers of commerce work out sister city agreements with people around the world, and lure international art exhibits or sports events, such as the Olympics, to their cities.

Borders are becoming less relevant to global political movements as ideas and news of current events are spread instantly through new technologies. New nonstate actors from terrorists to multinational companies to immigrants are influencing political decisions of people and political parties. New types of interactions through electronic networks and teleconferencing are changing the dimensions of human relationships around the world.

Geography plays a new role in our shrinking world of the late twentieth century. Once mountains, oceans, vegetation, or severe climates effectively isolated people, events, ideas, even diseases. Today's transportation and communication systems bring us together at the speed of jet engines and fiber optics. Mapping the spread and increase of cases of AIDS demonstrates what a small planet we have become. Technological breakthroughs in communications through satellites, computers, electronic mail, and facsimile machines have increased the flow of information around the world so that more and more people have access to world news tonight. We are a global village when people on every continent can gather at their radios and televisions in the evening to listen to the Berlin Wall coming down, to witness a failed coup in the Soviet Union, to hear the words of Nelson Mandela as he walked out of prison in South Africa, or watch a Chinese student face down a tank in Tiananmen Square.

Culture plays a critical role in our interpretation and reaction to the phenomena of globalization. As the world grows smaller, a global culture is developing that transcends nation states and ethnic enclaves. This global culture of international business, science and technology, fashion, music and the media overlaps with and at times conflicts with myriads of other cultures related to geographic regions, linguistic differences, lifestyles, ethnicities, and religions.

There are other dimensions to human identity in the late twentieth century. Differences in gender, age, social class, race, and sexual preference create subcultures within cultures. Cultural diffusion accelerates change and conflict as movies, television, and print media forward new ideas, information and misinformation around the world. Changing demographics have led to a world that has fewer homogeneous nations and more cross-cultural interactions. Economic and political refugees have influenced the demography, politics, economies, and cultures of many countries since World War II. These changes are particularly evident in the United States, a nation where minorities are growing much faster in number than the so-called majority.

All these changes and global systems are incredibly complex and continually evolving. How can we prepare young people to understand these changes and succeed in a global age? Global education has developed as a response to that challenge. Although it has its roots in the traditions of international relations, cultural anthropology, and world history, global education takes advantage of the information age to develop a new perspective—a global perspective from which we can see ourselves, our community, and our world in a new way.

What is Global Education?

Many people have written about what global education is or should be. Historians, anthropologists, political scientists, and geographers have made major contributions to discussion and debate. Other conceptualizations have been developed by educators, professional organizations, and curriculum specialists in home economics, science, and the arts. Although the literature on global education is replete with controversy and ambiguity, there is growing consensus on several characteristics of global education that are grounded in the conceptual work of Chadwick Alger, Charlotte and Lee Anderson, James Becker, Roland Case, Robert Hanvey, Willard Kniep, Steven Lamy, Richard Remy, and Robert Woyach, and the research of Giselle Martin-Kniep, Merry Merryfield, Judith Torney-Purta, Jan Tucker, Barbara and Kenneth Tye, and Angene Wilson. The resource list at the end of this chapter includes references about curriculum and instruction in global education.

When educators infuse global perspectives into curricula, there is usually attention to human values and multiple perspectives, the interconnectedness of global systems and global issues, the historical antecedents of today's globalization and increasing global interdependence, cross-cultural understanding, recognition of human choices, and an emphasis on higher-level thinking skills and experiential learning. Table 1 outlines social studies topics that are particularly relevant to these aspects of global education. Although teachers may choose to focus on some topics more than others, because of the nature of their courses, their grade level, or other characteristics of their students, a global education includes the following eight elements:

Understanding of Human Values

Global education focuses on both universal and diverse human values. In the global classroom, students learn to seek out multiple perspectives on events and issues. They develop perspective consciousness through studied examination of different points of view and the practice of putting oneself in another person's shoes. Students analyze the relationships between people's values and their interpretation of history and current events. In the process of studying human values, students recognize and clarify their own perspectives and worldviews.

Understanding of Global Systems

Students understand that in the world today there is a vast network of overlapping systems. Our global economic system includes the trade and pricing of goods and services, the global assembly line of workers and managers, world markets, organizations (multinational corporations) and institutions (the International Monetary Fund) and agreements (the General Agreement on Tariffs and Trade) that reach into the lives of people around the world. Political systems include the intricate webs of interactions, conflicts, diplomacy, treaties, and negotiated settlements that characterize international relationships today. The United Nations, the World Court, and other global organizations often provide an arena for international political debate and conflict resolution.

Our planet is a complex ecological system in which humans play a powerful role in effecting change. Few ecological problems today are isolated to one country or region. We have only to examine major environmental or natural resource concerns to recognize how the planet's closed ecosystem calls for collaborative problem-solving. New technologies overlap with the economic, political, and ecological systems as the global community witnesses breakthroughs in agriculture, transportation, health, medicine, communications, and weapons systems.

All these systems are interrelated, and they interact and evolve in complex ways. As students develop an understanding of the evolution of global systems and the procedures, mechanisms, and transactions of persons within these systems, they begin to understand global dynamics and the state of the planet.

Examination of Global Issues and Problems

Students learn that most of the world's major issues and problems cross borders and need to be addressed through multilateral negotiation. Peace and security, development, human rights, self-determination, and energy are some of many issues that confront people around the world. See Table 1 for a more extensive list of global issues pertinent to social studies.

Making Connections across Global History

Unlike state-centric history, global history focuses on the development, diffusion, and borrowing among cultures across time and space. Students look across civilizations and time periods to analyze the acceleration of interdependence over time, evaluate antecedents to current issues, and assess changes in cultures and global systems.

Attention to Cross-Cultural Awareness

A major part of global education revolves around experiences in learning about other cultures and the world from the other cultures, beliefs, values, and worldviews. By exploring the role of their own culture in the world system, students come to recognize the complexity of cultural diversity. They develop skills and experiences in cross-cultural understanding.

Building Awareness of Human Choices

In a global age, individuals, organizations, institutions, local communities, and nations make choices that affect the planet. Regional economic or political alliances create new relationships and opportunities. In global education students learn how past and present actions lead to alternative futures. They come to recognize the complexity of human behavior and the interaction between human choices and life in their community and the world.

Development of Analytical and Evaluative Skills

The major rationale for global education is application of knowledge about the world in one's local community. The slogan "think globally and act locally" means that we learn about diverse cultures, global systems and issues, in order to make better decisions in our daily lives. Students must be able to collect, analyze, and use information about their world. Critical thinking skills, such as the ability to detect bias, or identify underlying assumptions, are essential if students are to evaluate information instead of accepting as truth any printed page or media story. Part of the development of these thinking skills includes the recognition of the role that values and context play in the writing of history, literature, and the reporting of current events.

Strategies for Participation and Involvement

Finally global educators provide their students with opportunities for making and implementing decisions, addressing real-life problems, and learning from experience. Global education is not an esoteric study of people and issues far away. It is involvement with global issues and diverse peoples who are interconnected with one's community and life.

How Does One Infuse Global Education into the Social Studies Curriculum?

Over the last twenty years, teachers have found many ways to teach global education within the social studies. Here we will examine five frequently used approaches developed by classroom teachers. The discussion of these approaches is followed by examples of actual practice of several outstanding teachers. Their exemplars illustrate the integration of global education and social studies.

Comparisons across Cultures

One of the most common strategies for infusing global perspectives into ongoing courses is through comparisons across cultures, civilizations, nations, or world areas. In a comparative approach, teachers bring in ideas and events from other cultures to teach cultural universals and cultural diversity. For example, in teaching about the development of the U.S. Constitution, a teacher has students compare it with the constitutions of France and Nigeria to look for commonalities as well as differences. Such comparisons help students recognize the universality of certain rights and responsibilities of citizens and governments, as well as particular ideas that may be distinctly "American." Students can also appreciate the influence that the American constitution has had on peoples around the world.

> *Exemplar:* Patricia Bosh, a sixth-grade teacher at Mifflin International Middle School in Columbus, Ohio, has her students research literature about diverse cultures (such as Bedouin, Japanese, and American) to analyze the concept of "nation." Her goal is student understanding of different perspectives on the relationship between culture and nationhood. Because of their work in global education, Patricia's sixth-graders find commonalities as well as differences in how these people conceptualize a nation. They also demonstrate tolerance of cultural diversity and do not perceive cultural differences as negative.

Multiple Perspectives

Another popular strategy is to focus on developing perspective consciousness through the study of multiple viewpoints on social studies concepts (for example, self-determination), events (the Holocaust), issues (protectionism), people (Gandhi), or personal experiences (of slaves). In recent years many social studies teachers have incorporated multiple perspectives in their teaching of Columbus' voyages to the Americas by adding viewpoints of Native American peoples to European perspectives. Multiple perspectives are often a part of the discussion of current events in the community (for example, issues related to new immigrants) or abroad (understanding conflicts in the Middle East). Resources for multiple perspectives usually include primary sources (especially literature), guest speakers from the community, electronic mail hookups with people in other countries, and news articles, cartoons, or media coverage from other parts of the world.

> *Exemplar*: Connie White, a social studies teacher at Linden-McKinley High School in Columbus, Ohio, has her students share their views about education, conflict, and other global issues with high school students in Geneva, Switzerland, via Compu-Serve technology that uses telephone networks and computers. As Swiss students type in their questions about recent news of stabbings and murder in American daily life, Linden students use information on their community to counteract international media reports and stereotypes of violence in America. In turn the Linden students query their Swiss counterparts about what actions Swiss schools and communities are taking to promote multiculturalism in Switzerland.

Connections to Students' Lives

A third approach focuses on connecting global content to the lives of students. Teachers use their knowledge of their students—backgrounds, experiences, abilities, and interests—to motivate and teach them about local-global connections and their place in the world. Some teachers see global connections as a way to increase students' self-esteem as they learn that they are a part of history and actors in the world community. Connecting global content to students' lives may be as simple as tracing the ingredients of a favorite candy bar to imports from Brazil, Cote D'Ivoire, and Haiti, or examining the cultural diffusion of African rhythms into American jazz, rock music, and rap. Or connections can be a complex study of the outcomes of a local power company's burning of high-sulphur coal on acid rain in Canada, or the potential effects of the North American Free Trade Agreement on local businesses.

> *Exemplar*: In their team-teaching of a mixed fourth/fifth-grade class-room at Fifth Avenue International Elementary School in Columbus, Ohio, John Fischer and Bruce Stassfurth have students trace movements in their families' histories across several generations. The students then connect their "family maps" and their class statistics of immigration with global migrations of the same time period, in order to see how they and their classmates fit into the large global movements of peoples in the last hundred years.

Linking Knowledge over Time and Space

Teaching about interconnectedness between history and the contemporary world is another popular approach to globalizing social studies. Teachers may emphasize global connections across time periods or across world regions. In the study of the geography of Asia, the social studies teacher helps students connect both past and present with other cultures and world regions. Students learn about how peoples of China, Korea, and Japan have interacted with peoples of Europe, the Middle East, and the United States. They understand how Japan and the United States have influenced each other's history. They learn to relate problems of religious conflict in India to that region's historical connections with the Middle East and British colonization. Unlike the conventional world cultures course that separates cultures, a global geography or history course emphasizes how cultures are continually shaped and influenced by contacts with others.

> *Exemplar*: Shirley Hoover, a social studies teacher at Upper Arlington High School, Upper Arlington, Ohio, requires her ninth- and tenth-grade global history students to make connections between their study of history/geography and their world today. As a regular part of class, students present their research and analyses of how events and themes in history are related to contemporary events and issues. For example, her students noted how economics, politics, and religion are often interconnected as they compared Philip II's religious intolerance and political economics with the role of religion, economics, and politics in the contemporary Middle East.

Development of New Global Courses

A fourth approach goes beyond modifying an existing course to the development of new units or courses designed around global issues, global studies, or global history. These courses often are organized by themes (for example, conflict, cooperation, cultures, interdependence) or issues (hunger, population, security, environmental concerns). They bring together several disciplines to provide a more holistic examination of the world.

> *Exemplar*: At Reynoldsburg High School in Reynoldsburg, Ohio, Steve Shapiro teams with four other teachers to integrate social studies, math, science, art, and language arts into "Global Connections." As part of the overall restructuring of the school's curriculum to meet the needs of a changing world, Steve's team provides ninety tenth-graders with an interdisciplinary and in-depth study of global issues related to the environment and themes such as culture, conflict, and historical connections. (See Levak, Merryfield, and Wilson 1993 for more on "Global Connections.")

Teachers may use a variety of these approaches within a school year to meet the needs of their students, local or state curricular mandates, or special circumstances in their local community. Often dramatic events, such as the Gulf War, lead to teachable moments where student interest provides the impetus for an examination of historical antecedents, multiple perspectives, or global interconnections (see Merryfield 1993).

In many ways global education is different from the traditional ways social studies teachers have taught about the world. Globally oriented teachers don't teach an "us-them" dichotomy that only views events or issues from the norms of American foreign policy or Eurocentric tradition. Instead they focus on the commonalities of the human experience as much as they do on cultural differences. A major goal is developing tolerance and an appreciation of diversity at home and abroad. Global educators also emphasize their students' own interconnections across time and space, and their roles in the world today and tomorrow. A global view of past civilizations and present global systems is related to contributions, issues, and concerns in the students' own community.

The teaching of global perspectives enriches the social studies curriculum because students learn to appreciate the complexities of multiple perspectives, global systems, and global issues. By infusing global perspectives into the social studies curriculum, teachers prepare their students to deal effectively with tradition and change. Global education empowers students to take their place in the dynamic world of today and tomorrow.

Table 1

Aspects of Global Education in the Social Studies

1. HUMAN VALUES
   - universal and diverse human values
   - perspective consciousness and multiple perspectives
   - relationships between people's values and actions
   - recognition of one's own values and world views

2. GLOBAL SYSTEMS
   - economic, political, ecological, technological systems
   - knowledge of global dynamics
   - procedures and mechanisms in global systems
   - the nature of global transactions
   - interconnections across different global systems

3. GLOBAL ISSUES AND PROBLEMS
   - state of the planet awareness
   - peace and security issues
   - development issues (e.g., poverty, sustainable agriculture, women in development, technology transfer)
   - food and hunger issues
   - human rights issues
   - global movement of people (e.g., refugees, migration)
   - environmental issues (e.g., pollution, use of natural resources, extinction of species, disposal of toxic wastes)
   - energy issues (e.g., resources, conservation)
   - education and literacy issues
   - global health and population issues
   - economic issues (e.g., the global assembly line, trade practices, water rights, national and international debt)
   - issues related to distribution (e.g., of wealth, technology and information, food, resources, weapons)
   - urbanization issues
   - transportation and communication issues
   - issues related to dependency
   - military issues (e.g., weapons sales, use of space, arms control, military aid, terrorism)
   - interrelationships across issues & problems

4. GLOBAL HISTORY
   - acceleration of interdependence over time (J-curves)
   - antecedents to current issues
   - origins and development of cultures
   - contact and borrowing among cultures

Table 1 *(continued)*
Aspects of Global Education in the Social Studies

- evolution of global systems
- changes in global systems over time

5. CROSS-CULTURAL AWARENESS
   - recognition of the complexity of cultural diversity
   - the role of one's own culture in the world system
   - skills and experiences in seeing one's own culture from other perspectives
   - experiences in learning about another culture and the world from another viewpoint
   - cultural values and worldviews

6. AWARENESS OF HUMAN CHOICE
   - by individuals, organizations, local communities, nations, regions, economic or political alliances
   - past and present actions and future alternatives
   - recognition of the complexity of human behavior

7. DEVELOPMENT OF ANALYTICAL AND EVALUATIVE SKILLS
   - abilities to collect, analyze, and use information
   - critical thinking skills (e.g., ability to detect bias, identify underlying assumptions)
   - recognition of the role of values in inquiry
   - recognition of the role of contextual factors in inquiry

8. STRATEGIES FOR PARTICIPATION AND INVOLVEMENT
   - experiences in other cultures
   - opportunities for making and implementing decisions
   - experience with addressing real-life problems

CHAPTER TWELVE

Teaching Social Issues: Implementing an Issues-Centered Curriculum[1]

Ronald W. Evans

Social studies, as a broadly defined and interdisciplinary field devoted to the examination of issues and problems, seems to be in danger of dying. The history of efforts to reform social studies is replete with false starts, curricular fads, blind alleys, and heroic efforts amid ongoing ideological conflicts over what should be taught in schools. The neoconservative revival of history and geography is plainly an attempt to lay social studies in its grave.

During the 1980s social studies became a scapegoat for neoconservative critics who sought to revive the near monopoly of history and geography. The California History and Social Science Framework, the formation of the Bradley Commission on History in the Schools and subsequent founding of the National Council for History Education, the report of the National Commission on Social Studies and other allied efforts spurred ongoing debate over the nature of social studies.

In an effort to incorporate criticism and insure its continued survival, the National Council for the Social Studies drafted a definition and mission statement. Unfortunately, the definition, while it may be a step in the right direction, does not provide a sufficiently powerful alternative to the critics of social studies. Nor does it move the field beyond its perennial dilemma as a derivative conglomeration of the social sciences and history, and the alternative of social studies as a unitary field of study built around the in-depth investigation of perennial human issues.

Ultimately, the current chapter in the long-standing squabble over social studies represents, at its root, a battle over purposes and the ideological direction of the curriculum, a battle between

197

competing worldviews. On the one hand, advocates of a disciplines-based approach to social studies tend to think of knowledge gain as a test of learning. Advocates of a reflective approach, however, tend to emphasize thoughtfulness and social criticism. Embedded in these opposing views are competing assumptions on what counts as knowledge and which knowledge will receive priority. Of course, the alternatives described above are not simple either-or choices, but rich alternatives, often overlapping, which represent major competing strands in curriculum theory and practice.

In developing an alternative conception for social studies curricula that holds the potential for real improvement I will discuss the following concerns:

1. Why is an interdisciplinary approach to social studies necessary, even imperative?
2. What makes an issues-centered focus the most promising alternative for the creation of an interdisciplinary curriculum?
3. What would an issues-centered curriculum look like? What are some practical examples of lessons, units, and curricula?
4. How might we realize this vision in schools in the years to come?

All of this is undertaken in the belief that it matters what our children study in school, that it matters what form their studies take, and what messages are implicit in school structure and in the curriculum. The stakes are very high. If social studies is to survive as a viable alternative to the trend toward history and geography as core, we must come up with a bold vision of a dynamic yet workable curriculum.

Interdisciplinary Social Studies

Why is an interdisciplinary approach to social studies necessary, even imperative? Interdisciplinarity is currently fashionable among educators, at least in the rhetoric of educators. Yet several factors make interdisciplinarity and extradisciplinarity important qualities of social studies education. At the heart of social studies education is the need to prepare thoughtful, knowledgeable, clear-thinking citizens. None of the established disciplines has this purpose—the preparation of citizens—at its core.

Prior to making a case, it is important to consider what is meant by the term *interdisciplinary*. Multiple meanings are possible, ranging from *correlation* of two or more discipline-based subjects to *open core* education in which students and teacher are free to select the problems on which they wish to work, or *prestructured core* in which students and teacher study predetermined problems and subject matter from the disciplines and other sources are "brought in as needed in working on the problems" (Wraga, in press). For purposes of this analysis, *interdisciplinary* means some form of core in which subject matter is brought in as part of an in-depth investigation and dialogue. As I shall argue in the pages that follow, issues provide a natural focus for in-depth, interdisciplinary study.

The central purpose of social studies, preparation of citizens, is quite different from the central purposes of the university-based disciplines. Certainly some overlap exists (the disciplines are educative of citizens), but the knowledge and concepts included, and the means of inquiry, are fundamentally structured by the foundational aspects of the discipline and the boundaries that separate the world of social inquiry into specialized compartments.

A second major reason that social studies must be interdisciplinary is that inquiry into any real-world matter related to citizenship is naturally holistic. Social inquiry requires a search for knowledge that cannot be bound by the rules or boundaries of any university academic discipline. It requires multiple sources of relevant evidence from all useful sources, including books, periodicals, videos, and other forms of media, relevant works of art, music, and literature, the community, and students' lives. Meaningful social inquiry values the knowledge students bring to school and maintains awareness of the context of their experiences. Some advocates of a discipline-based approach argue that certain disciplines are inclusive and naturally interdisciplinary. Historians, for instance, frequently champion interdisciplinarity in making a case for their discipline as the core school subject. However, the version of interdisciplinarity they suggest is bound by a chronological structure and an emphasis on historical context, rather than the context of students' experience.

A third important argument is related to the reality that students must take action in the social world based on their personal synthesis of knowledge from a wide array of sources, their values and beliefs, and the meaning they make of their world. The beliefs students hold about their world are necessarily formative and tentative. While learning, exploring, and gaining new knowledge and experience, students are making decisions that necessarily require a synthesis of sources, decisions that will benefit from knowledge of history, geography, and the social sciences only as that knowledge is meaningfully and consciously connected to the reflective process.

Some students make connections on their own. Unfortunately, many do not. Connections, implications, and meaning must be explicitly discussed and alternatives considered in order to make social studies instruction meaningful. A discipline-based approach is inadequate for conscious development of the well-rounded synthesis needed for quality decision-making and active social participation.

An Issues-Centered Focus

Why issues? What makes an issues-centered focus the most promising alternative for creation of an interdisciplinary and vital social studies curriculum? Issues are the proper focus for social studies because they pose real-life problems, raise areas of doubt, motivate reflection, stimulate the need to gain knowledge, and highlight problematic areas of culture. The focus of an issues-centered approach is on cultural dilemmas and institutional obstacles to social improvement. Exploration and in-depth investigation of issues, and the dialogue that process entails, necessarily cause students to examine and reflect on the basic assumptions underlying our social institutions and lifestyles. It leads students to raise fundamental questions, the kinds of questions that must be addressed if students are to develop depth of social understanding.

Perhaps most important, given the failings of the typical discipline-based curriculum, it emphasizes the connection of social study to life in the world, connecting individual choices to public policy issues and to the ongoing and fundamental dilemmas of human existence. This is important because in far too many classrooms students see no connections between the subjects they study and the real world in which they live.

One caveat. It should be clear by now that an issues-centered approach is not simply a focus on current events, but on perennial human issues that permeate the curriculum. Let me offer a definition: by issues-centered education, I mean an approach to education centered around reflective questions, that emphasizes open-ended questions, questions which have no "right" answer. It is an approach to education that emphasizes thoughtfulness and depth, weighing evidence, values, and consequences. Students examine social practices using the ideals of democracy as criteria, clarifying and testing alternatives to determine which are preferable. Thus, an issues-centered approach should include knowledge, concepts, and means of inquiry from the disciplines and other sources. The method is both discipline-based and interdisciplinary, with primary emphasis on the problems and dilemmas confronted by citizens. Inherently, issues-centered approaches have both personal and public dimensions in which ethics, questions of right and wrong, and consideration of a diversity of views are at the center of the curriculum.

Thus, issues education is built around situations and dilemmas that pose problems, that make us ponder what to do in matters of public policy as well as in private courses of action, that require us to reflect on our values and aspirations, and the possible consequences of our decisions. Issues-centered education seeks to develop citizens who are well informed, who can thoughtfully reflect on the evidence, project possible consequences, weigh values, and arrive at supportable and consistent beliefs.

Too frequently citizens are swayed by fashion, propaganda, and unreasonable fears, by lack of knowledge rather than informed thought. An issues-centered approach seeks to develop citizens who model authentic behavior in which values, beliefs, and a skeptical and reasoned approach to all kinds of relevant evidence go into the development of quality decisions and healthy lifestyles. Implicitly, this approach to teaching and learning requires ethical direction. It is guided by reflection on utopian visions and the consideration of alternative values and beliefs, actions and policies that will make the world a better place to live, and ours a society in which we can all get along.

This approach to social studies is not neutral. It has its origins in the tradition of progressive reform that aims to improve society (Evans 1987; Saxe 1992), but at the same time it is nondoctrinaire in terms of suggesting preferred solutions. Issues-centered study is built upon a long history among social studies reformers. This has been one of the strongest traditions in social studies, but has been somewhat diffused by an emphasis on reflective thinking in almost any form. In my opinion, the object of reflection, the subject matter selected, is also an important choice. By ignoring this, advocates of reflective teaching and learning run the risk of being simply incorporated, and often lost, in curricular approaches and courses that tend not to be issues-oriented.

Though I tend to agree with Shaver (1992) that teachers and groups of teachers must come up with their own reasons for choosing an issues-centered approach, I believe there are several key rationales. First, the issues are important and cry out for out attention. Issues represent current manifestations of perennial dilemmas of public policy, and dilemmas of private and personal decision-making. Issues provide teachers and students with a way to thoughtfully consider the web of individuals and institutions that make up our society and the modern world. Issues give us a meaningful way of using knowledge from relevant sources, including especially the disciplines of history and the social sciences, in a larger attempt to find better ways to live. The aim of social improvement is a central rationale. Thus, I see issues-oriented social education as implicitly social reconstructionist in orientation.

Second, issues are motivational because of the competing interpretations and value orientations they inspire and the emotions that are attached to deeply held beliefs. A dilemma with several feasible alternatives, in the hands of a thoughtful and creative teacher, can create cognitive dissonance (a feeling of doubt), a spark of intellectual impetus, and a desire to know enough to resolve a dilemma. In social studies education, motivation is a key and perennial problem (Goodlad 1984; Shaver, Davis, and Helburn 1979). An issues-centered approach has the potential to enhance student motivation and inspire reflection in a meaningful context connected to the fabric of life and to our desire for liberty, equality, and a socially just community. It has the potential to promote classroom thoughtfulness and depth of understanding. Finally, it may enhance the chances for a teacher to survive in the classroom (Massialas 1989), and it offers a natural need for continual renewal.

Designing a curriculum to facilitate this possibility is a challenge I will examine in the following pages.

Alternative Structures and Models: A Bold Vision

What would an issues-centered curriculum look like? Previous advocates of an issues-centered social studies have developed alternative visions of an issues-centered curriculum. For the most part, these visions have conceived of issues education as an approach that would be implemented across the social studies curriculum and infused within traditional course offerings, organized chronologically or conceptually. A second alternative for the implementation of issues-centered approaches would create issues-centered units within discipline-based courses. A third alternative would create courses built around issues and issue areas, and an issues-centered alternative to the typical scope and sequence. Included among previous thinkers who have advocated an issues-centered approach are Rugg (1939), Hunt and Metcalf (1955), Oliver and Shaver (1966), Engle and Ochoa (1988), and others.

Reflective Teaching Strategies

Reflective, dialogical teaching strategies are central to issues-centered approaches. In what follows I will provide some basic understandings of what that encompasses.

1. All issues-centered lessons are built around the investigation of open-ended questions (probing questions), which pose a problem for students to solve. Every lesson must be conceived in this fashion. "Topics or episodes which cannot be conceived in this way would be dropped from the curriculum" (Engle and Ochoa 1988). Probing questions include a wide variety of problem-posing questions, including: definitional questions—What do we mean by issues-oriented?; evidential questions—What evidence can we find to support or refute the value of issues education?; policy questions—Should educational organizations endorse an issues-centered approach?; value questions—Which is more important, generating interest or covering factual knowledge?; speculative questions—What might happen if most teachers adopted an issues-centered approach?; and explanatory questions—How might we best explain the limited acceptance of problem-posing approaches in schools?

2. While predefined structures for investigation and discussion of an issue are helpful, the approach is necessarily flexible, not linear. It may jump around from hypothesizing and arguing over explanations to evaluating new evidence or analogous cases, and back and forth. Conclusions are necessarily somewhat tentative.

3. An issues-centered approach is heavily dependent on reflective discussion, using multiple formats: including Socratic seminar, group work, role-playing, and simulation, student research, and a

variety of formats for large and small group discussion. It is an approach that seeks to create a critical dialogue, a problem-posing form of education in the classroom as opposed to a banking approach (Freire 1970).

4. The approach tends to discourage spending a long time—days or weeks, even years—giving students background information on a topic prior to a reflective discussion. Instead, the emphasis is on *creating a sense of doubt* and a desire to find relevant information that will help in the process of resolving the question or issue. How much initial information or knowledge is needed to create a sense of doubt? On most topics and issues, especially the perennial ones embedded in the curriculum, it can usually be done in a relative short period of time—fifteen to twenty minutes. Once students are interested, curious, and motivated, it is time to begin a search for relevant evidence from as many data sources as possible, with the teacher providing initial data and guiding students to search for additional sources. This approach requires more data, not less, more books and journals, not fewer, and more background information, but the information is handled differently than in traditional approaches to teaching.

5. The approach emphasizes use of evidence to make judgments and the weighing of value dilemmas. It also relies on careful use of analogies to test the possible consequences of a particular course of action. It aims toward the reflective examination of student beliefs and values as part of a larger process of social, emotional, and intellectual growth.

Demonstration: "New Report on Urban Unrest"

Drawn from Engle and Ochoa's *Education for Democratic Citizenship* (1988), and Dewey's *How We Think* (1933), I have developed two alternative templates for issues-centered lessons, depending on the type of probing question being explored. Using a newspaper story as a springboard, I will demonstrate two possible discussions that could ensue. The first is an example of what I term an *inquiry* discussion, or a discussion that seeks understanding via consideration of alternative explanations for some phenomenon or event. The second, a variation on the same theme, is a *decision-making* lesson, asking students to choose a course of action.

A news story that appeared in the *Los Angeles Times* on February 28, 1993, was entitled, "New Report Echoes 'Two Societies'

Warning of 1968 Kerner Commission." The story describes a report
from the Milton S. Eisenhower Foundation, issued on the twenty-
fifth anniversary of the 1968 Kerner Commission report on civil
disorders. It states that the conclusion of that report, that America
was moving toward "two societies, one black, one white," has grown
more relevant in the wake of the previous year's Los Angeles riots
and the failure of the government to respond. As a remedy, the
foundation called for the nation to focus on improving the lot of the
urban hard-core poor, "the roughly 10 percent of the population
who live in urban areas of concentrated long-term poverty, and
whose violence and suffering has a disproportionate effect on
American life, class tension, and race tension." The report recommended that federal officials scrap or reform a number of unsuccessful high-profile programs and move away from experimental
efforts in favor of programs that have demonstrated success.

Example of an *Inquiry* Lesson

First, let me illustrate how a teacher might create an "inquiry"
lesson built around probing questions based on this story.
Define the Problem-Focus Question. How do you explain the
unrest in Los Angeles last spring? After discussing the news story
described above, the teacher might show a brief video on the unrest
in Los Angeles, then ask the focus question. The format for this
portion of the lesson could range from large group discussion to
dyads or small group brainstorming with butcher-paper reports,
with students asked to rank their explanations.
Develop Hypotheses. What are the major alternative explanations for the unrest? Alternatives might range from disrespect for
laws and the property of others to oppression and alienation due to
years of poverty and injustice. After the class takes some time
to mull over possible explanations, the teacher will probably want
to lead the class to distill these into three or four major interpretations through a full class discussion.
Collect and Analyze Additional Evidence. What additional evidence do we need to decide which of these explanations is most
helpful? Where can we find it? This phase could last indefinitely,
could involve a unit of resources, and could include individual and
group investigation as well as whole class and small group discussion. Realistically, it is important for the teacher to provide some
materials and resources, but the investigation can prove most

meaningful if students are also involved in locating and sharing relevant evidence and resources. In any event, the sources and materials used must provide evidence for each of the major perspectives.

Evidence on the history of race relations and government policy vis-à-vis race and class may be found in most United States history textbooks. Obviously, a thoughtful teacher could select cases from the past for in-depth study to shed light on the discussion, and would probably want to include an overview of the historical development of relations among the races.

Test Each Hypothesis with Evidence. For each alternative, what is the most convincing evidence? Is there counter-evidence that discredits this explanation? After a considerable amount of data is amassed, the teacher might lead an in-depth discussion of analogous cases.

Develop Reasoned Conclusion(s). Which explanation(s) for the unrest is(are) most defensible? Based on what we know now, what should we conclude? In this phase of the activity the teacher will want to encourage students to develop thoughtful conclusions based on their study of the problem. Conclusions will necessarily have a tentative quality.

Also, at this point, and at earlier stages in the discussion, the teacher will need to assess student progress and the quality of the conclusions reached. This might be accomplished through a variety of assessment techniques, but will be more meaningful if it involves writing, creating, or doing rather than simply responding to teacher-created exam questions.

Applications/Implications. What are the implications of our conclusions for the future of race relations in Los Angeles? An optional, concluding phase, yet perhaps the most important, involves asking students to make meaning of their learning and their tentative conclusions by drawing implications. The example of *decision-making* that follows might flow naturally from this discussion.

Example of a Decision-Making Lesson

Similar to the *inquiry* lesson described above, a *decision-making* lesson involves posing a problem. But in this case the problem asks for more than explanation; it calls for a policy/action decision to be reached.

Identify and Define Problem—State Decision Needed. What should we do about the "slide toward a divided nation" described in the report? The opening phase will involve discussion of possible solutions, and might be built on the group's conclusions developed above.

Identify Alternatives. What are the alternative courses of action? Alternative solutions might range from "do nothing" to "use governmental power to stimulate job creation," "provide a guaranteed income for all," "follow the Eisenhower Foundation's recommendations," or "provide tax incentives to encourage interracial marriage and housing."

Collect and Analyze Additional Evidence. What additional evidence do we need to make a decision on this issue? Where might we find it? The teacher may want to lead students to examine previous attempts to address the problems of racial and economic inequality, and evidence on the success and relative merits of previous efforts. Of course, such examination must include in-depth discussion of the context in which earlier efforts were implemented, taking account of similarities and differences. A creative teacher could develop an entire unit centered around the topic "Racial Justice in American Life" in almost any social studies course. The entire history of race and ethnicity would be relevant to such a unit. It could be handled through a strand of development approach, studying the chronology of racial and ethnic relations in the United States, and focusing on particular cases in depth. Selection of cases would be made on the basis of their relevance to the focus problem stated above.

Weigh Consequences. What consequences might result from each alternative course of action? What evidence can we have to demonstrate the likelihood of this consequence? This discussion would involve examining the cases selected for study in phase three, and developing analogies, arguments, and evidence for key alternative courses of action.

Consider Values. What values are involved in a decision? What is the central dilemma faced? Values are multiple and complex. Values to be considered in this unit might include human welfare vs. property rights; respect for racial and ethnic diversity vs. freedom of association and freedom of speech. The point of the discussion of values would be to clarify which values are being chosen or prized by each of the alternatives, and to lead students to reflect on the consistency of their position on the issue with their value position.

Make Decision. Given what we know at this point, what alternative should be choosen? Which alternative is most consistent with our values? Which alternative is most likely to lead to a preferred consequence? In this phase of the activity, each student might be asked to write a position paper discussing alternatives and supporting a particular course of action.

Debrief. What happened in this case? Which alternative did our government choose? Why? What were the results? What are the implications? What is the significance of that choice for the future of our lives together?

In each approach described above, a series of lessons or a unit could be developed by using a problem or issue as the starting point, with problem resolution as the goal. Most of the evidence, the "stuff" of history and the social sciences that students would learn, would be discovered during the course of the investigation. Some would come from textbooks and the teacher (even in the form of brief lectures). Much of the evidence would be found in alternative, supplementary sources.

A similar approach to unit development could be adapted to any of the social studies courses currently taught in schools. It holds the potential for making those courses come alive with controversy and student interest. In the lower grades, similar questions might be investigated, but resources would be selected with greater attention to readability. An elementary teacher would make use of a wide array of children's literature. (See Evans 1992, and Evans and Saxe (1996) for additional examples of issues-centered approaches.)

The Dream of an Issues-Centered Curriculum

The future offers possibility for alternative visions for the social studies which are not bound by the typical scope and sequence found in schools today (Evans and Saxe, 1996). As we move into the twenty-first century and beyond, we need to explore new educational formats, experiment with various forms of curricula, and develop a dynamic vision of social studies that can empower teachers and students to develop ever-more creative and meaningful ways of preparing for thoughtful citizenship. The key question guiding this exploration is the degree to which the goals of quality decisions, a thoughtful citizenry, and authentic behavior are realized.

I believe the mediocre state of practice in the field—whether we call it history, social studies, or indoctrination to American life—requires that the alternative vision we propose be innovative and dynamic. It must propose a unitary field of study that is fully issues-centered and interdisciplinary rather than a field that is merely derivative. We must craft a vision that will lead to the kind of border crossing that Henry Giroux espouses, overcoming the boundaries of the traditional disciplines and school subjects (Giroux 1992).

Thoughtfulness, reflection, problem-solving, valuing, and social criticism should be at the heart of social study. These processes must be central to any social studies program in which knowledge will be truly integrated. Social studies should be built around the investigation of persistent issues and social realities, studied in great depth. Meaningful social studies will require knowledge from many sources, not only interdisciplinary but extradisciplinary. We need a bold vision of a dynamic curriculum that can inspire deep dreams of justice and fair play, that can help us move further in the direction of social transformation, that can help us enliven social studies education, and come closer to realizing the full potential of the American dream.

Instead of building curriculum around courses based in the academic disciplines, I believe a more powerful vision for the future of social studies might be built around social realities and the ethical questions and possibilities they raise. Imagine a semester-long high school course entitled *Race and Ethnicity in American Life;* another entitled *Social Class, Stratification, and Social Responsibility;* another on *Gender in Social Life and Culture;* another entitled *Power in America;* another on *Ideology, Government, and Economic Life;* still another, *The Border Mentality: Nationalism and International Relations;* another on *Philosophy in Personal and Public Life;* another on *Media and Social Understanding;* another entitled *Utopian Visions and Competing Ideologies;* yet another on *Technology, Society, and the Environment;* another entitled *Sex, Marriage, and Family Life;* and of course *The School as an Institution.* . . . This incomplete list could go on. The main criterion, the course must be centered outside any of the disciplines cited at the university. A shift to semester-long courses might also help break dependence on massive textbooks and encourage use of multiple sources.

Each of these courses would be interdisciplinary by necessity, and each would have strands reflecting what we currently think of as the major sources of knowledge; each would include cross-national perspectives. The length may vary; some might be required, others elective. The curriculum might begin with an Introduction to Problems and Issues, and conclude with Philosophy and Life. It might also include a course entitled Social Research in which students engage in in-depth research on a community or school issue, most likely a manifestation of a national or global problem. Most courses could include research components, and time for individual and committee study while consulting with teachers.

Most importantly, the starting point for each course would be present manifestations of persistent issues and dilemmas, something students can have firsthand knowledge of, and may be able to study directly, both within the school and out in the community. Each course would be built around the reflective investigation of central questions, problems, and issues. Each course would also allow for the kind of in-depth study required for meaningful social education. Perhaps the key element in all of this would be giving teachers both the freedom and the time to reconceptualize the curriculum and create these courses.

It might be helpful to explore the possibilities for a particular course following this approach, and then compare and contrast it with a discipline-based course. Take American foreign policy as an example. In the typical high school today, our nation's role in the world is addressed primarily in courses on United States history. Typically, the issue is not explicitly addressed, at least not directly, except in the occasional forays into current events. Yet relevant evidence on the issue is covered as part of the chronological survey of history. In a classroom in which an issues-approach is infused, the issue would at least be addressed each time the chronology dictates (Monroe Doctrine, Spanish American War, etc.). In the alternative vision I have sketched above, our nation's role in the world would receive in-depth treatment through a separate course. The course could begin and end with the question—What role should the U.S. play in the world? It would examine alternatives for the future as well as our changing role in the world over time. The course might include units on various aspects of the central issue—for example, the defense budget, world government—as well as in-depth study of key episodes in history and examination of the chronological development of U.S. foreign relations. It would, in the end, help to prepare students who are conversant on the issue, knowledgeable about its history, relevant scholarship, and evidence that might help us develop a saner and more sophisticated understanding.

The alternative vision described above has implications for the way schools are structured, the way time is allocated, the ways school buildings are constructed, and the ways in which resources and materials are conceptualized and distributed. Of course, this sort of alternative vision would not preclude retaining traditional, discipline-based courses as well, but would offer students more choice of curricula and a more exciting educational introduction to society. To allow such an alternative vision to enter mainstream practice we will need to lobby for academic freedom and against national testing in social studies. We will need to educate teachers, parents, administrators, and the public regarding the need for a more dynamic curriculum, and the possibilities of alternative visions.

Finally, and most pointedly, we will need to offer a sufficiently powerful alternative to traditional curricula to convince educational policymakers of the folly of setting national standards, and of the benefits of curricular freedom and experimentation that could allow thousands of creative school courses bloom.

From Vision to Reality

How might we realize this vision in schools in the years to come? Though many social studies professionals and would-be reformers have given up hope of ever having a major impact on social studies classrooms, reformers have had some success over the years. The recent success of the revival of history, the development of the Problems of Democracy course early in this century, and the wide, though superficial impact of the New Social Studies movement of the 1960s and 70s are evidence that reformers can have an impact, making negativism unwarranted. Yet the hopes of would-be reformers must be tempered by a realistic assessment of classroom constancy documented by Larry Cuban's descriptions of the classrooms of the past (Cuban 1984).

Given the range of factors that have limited attempts to reform social studies, a multilayered approach to reform seems warranted. Advocates of issues-oriented education would probably be wise to continue promoting an issues-centered focus within present offerings. We must educate teachers on the possibilities, increasing awareness of the issues-centered vision and how it might be implemented. This might include a variety of dissemination efforts including inservice education, methods textbooks, demonstration videos, and creation of issues-centered curricular materials and textbooks for current course offerings as well as for innovative issues-centered courses such as those described above. Dissemination, combined with lobbying and educating parents, teachers, and policymakers, and support for academic freedom and teacher-led curricular development could be most effective if it is well organized and well financed.

Of course, as others have suggested (Gross 1989; Shaver 1989), the chances for large-scale change are slight. We must recognize the contextual constraints and set realistic goals. Despite the realities of classroom constancy and the slight impact of many previous efforts at reform, the future offers possibility and the hope for a better tomorrow. In social studies education, that hope is for an engaging, issues-oriented curriculum, built on the legacy of previous reform efforts.

Persistence, timing, and the national political climate can all make a difference in the success of our efforts. We must continue to look forward with the knowledge that it matters, that our work could potentially have a profound impact on teachers and students, and on the future of our lives together. As anthropologist Margaret Mead once wrote, "Never doubt that a small group of committed individuals can change the world. Indeed, it is the only thing that ever has."

CHAPTER THIRTEEN

Assessment in Social Studies: Moving toward Authenticity

Sandra Mathison

Assessment, Not Tests and Measurement

For many years, psychometricians have controlled the ways we thought about, and our practices, for evaluating students, teachers, and curriculum. Early in the century, E. L. Thorndike set the path for the development of tests and measurement as a quantitative one: "Whatever exists at all exists in some amount. To know it involves knowing its quantity as well as its quality" (Thorndike 1918, p. 16).

In a field such as education, seeking to be scientific and rigorous, the technology of testing and measurement has been enviable and seen as the physics of the field. Our envy has given way, however, to skepticism and uncertainty about whether the exactitude of psychometrics gets us where we want to go in education.

Our skepticism has been fueled also by recent interest in ideas such as teacher empowerment, local control of education, and teachers-as-researchers. Tests and measurement are created outside schools, edicts to be adopted by teachers and schools, an idea out of synch with the contemporary views of teaching as a profession, one which should rightly be controlled by teachers, not psychometricians.

More frequently now, we talk of assessment, and tests and measurement are a means toward this end, but by no means the only means. What differences are implied by talking about assessments, rather than tests and measurements? Measurement surely implies that we can know with precision *how much of something* there is. For example, when we bake a cake we measure two cups of flour, and there is very little room for interpretation or misinterpretation—two cups is two cups, and flour is flour. When we measure something, we assign it a numeric value based on some pre-established standard. In education we might say this student is reading at a grade level of 5.6, a statement which automatically raises questions. First, what is meant by reading—Is it low-level comprehension requiring only recall? Is it critical analysis? And so on. Second, what do I know if a student has a reading level of grade 5.6—What is a grade? How do I understand a number, which is really an interpolation, not an actual measurement? And so on.

While we are confident of the precision of many measurements (temperature, distance, volume), the standards used in education (grade point average, grade equivalent score, normal curve equivalent) leave substantial room for interpretation and misinterpretation. So we look beyond measurement to determine the quality or value of something.

Tests, in a general sense, are a way of *trying* something out, such as in testing a light bulb by screwing it into a fixture to see if it works. In education, tests have become less a means of trying something out, than a means for measuring something that is predetermined. Tests are associated with standardized, formal ways of *finding* something out. They have been stripped of the connotation of tentativeness implied by other uses of the word *test*.

Assessment, on the other hand, is an activity that may use tests and measurement, but relies more on the idea of tests as a means of trying out, and it demands less faith in the exactitude of the measurement resulting from that test. I am reminded of a recent conversation with my sister, the owner of a small farm, whose property had recently been reassessed resulting in a higher property tax. Property assessments include an *estimated* dollar value expressed in quantitative terms, but delivered without guarantees or even probabilities. My sister could not, for example, hold the county to her assessed property value if she were unable to sell her property for that assessed dollar value. Additionally, property assessments often rely on qualifications along with the property dollar values. In the case of my sister's farm, they might note she has a new Victorian-style home and an electric fence around the property. These qualifications suggest that assessments involve an inexact measurement, but also include nonnumerical qualitative indicators.

Assessment also implies a relationship between the assessor and the assessed:

An "assessment" is where one "sits with" the learner. It is something we do "with" and "for" the student, not something we do "to" the student. Such a "sitting with" suggests that the assessor has an obligation to go the extra mile in determining what the student knows and can do. The assessor must be more tactful, respectful, and responsive than the giver of tests. [Wiggins 1993a]

Assessments, therefore involve the student in substantive ways, and are not solitary acts performed by them.

In education, we speak more of assessments, now, which depend on tests and measurements, but they also relate to other educational ideas such as curriculum, instruction, standards, and policy. Additionally, the current emphasis in assessment is on performance assessment in contrast with more traditional standardized, close-ended tests. This shift in emphasis can be revealed by a closer look at both the technical and social aspects of assessment.

The Technical and Social Aspects of Assessment

In schools, as in other American institutions, efficiency is highly valued. Until the performance assessment movement of the 1990s, testing was a mark of efficiency in the educational system. The development of large-scale standardized testing programs was a technological response to the ever-increasing numbers of people taking tests and the increased emphasis on using test scores as policy instruments (Madaus 1993). G. F. Madaus discusses the historical development of testing as a series of changes, each responding to a contemporary constraint on testing, and each of which enhanced the efficiency of testing—that is, the ability to test more people at less cost and in less time. For example, in the mid 1800s, Horace Mann replaced the oral examinations then given in Boston schools with written examinations. These "allowed examiners to pose an identical set of questions simultaneously, under similar conditions, in much less time to a rapidly expanding student body, thereby producing comparable scores" (Madaus 1993, p. 17). Early in the twentieth century, studies showed the unreliability of scoring essay tests and the multiple choice test item was created. And in 1955 Lindquist's invention of the optical scanner, combined with the use of multiple-choice test items, created the possibilities for the developments in large-scale testing over the past thirty years.

While these technical developments in testing and measurement increased the efficiency of testing, concomitant developments in the uses of testing occurred. Sometimes these technological changes were intended to facilitate certain uses, sometimes new uses were made possible by the changes. An example of the former is the not very concealed intention of getting rid of certain headmasters in the Boston schools, which motivated Horace Mann's introduction of written examinations. By using common written examinations, Mann reasoned that any differences in student scores could be attributable to nothing other than the ability of the teachers. If poor performance occurred, this was reason for dismissal. It helped that Mann thought it likely that those headmasters who were resisting his attempts to abolish corporal punishment would have the lowest scores. An example of the latter type of use has been the ever-increasing use of testing as a policy implementation strategy for controlling what is taught and how in schools (Madaus 1988; Mathison 1991). In the search for greater efficiency it is doubtful that measurement experts saw the potential use of testing as a means of curricular control, but the power of testing which was efficient became apparent. A good historical example of this is the New York State Regents Examinations, which still effectively control the secondary education of many students in New York state.

Not all technological changes in testing have been embraced by the American educational community though, even when these changes add some type of efficiency. A good example of this is a strategy used by the National Assessment of Educational Progress (NAEP) for reporting on the status of achievement in American schools. NAEP uses matrix sampling, a strategy that minimizes the testing burden for individuals and the system as a whole, but allows for fairly good indicators of achievement. Matrix sampling has not been widely adopted by states, for example, which profess to be interested primarily in system accountability. For example, in New York state, relatively new statewide performance tests in social studies are given to all sixth-graders, even though the test is called the "Social Studies Program Evaluation Test." The Bureau of Social Studies (and the Bureau of Science with a similar test) did not even consider using matrix sampling when these tests were adopted in the late 1980s (Mathison 1991). And, although a sophisticated matrix sampling procedure has been used in the California Assessment Program, it was abandoned in favor of comprehensive testing.

The rejection of some technological advances, such as matrix sampling, suggests that not only is efficiency an important value, but so too are individuality and competitiveness. American culture cannot resist thinking in terms of individuality, individual accomplishment, and failure, and matrix sampling disallows the assignment of value or disvalue to individuals—the most important unit of analysis.

Another challenge to the primacy of efficiency has also occurred in the testing industry. While standardized, machine-scored multiple-choice tests have made it possible to test many people in many places at one time at relatively low cost, there is an increasing dissatisfaction with the value of such practices. There has been ample research suggesting the deleterious effects of such testing, especially in high-stakes situations, on teaching and curriculum (Darling-Hammond 1991; Madaus 1988; Mathison 1987; Shepard 1991; Smith 1991). And, clearly, such testing has created differential effects on particular segments of the population, including minority students, speakers of languages other than English, and females (Fass 1989; Miller-Jones 1989; O'Connor 1989).

The administrative uses of standardized tests, particularly their power to control what is taught and how, are now perceived to be a constraint. This is particularly the case because tests administered in schools are seen as impediments to school reform (Madaus 1993). Concern about international competitiveness and falling standards have occasioned multiple calls for the reform of schooling. This has led to a plethora of standard-creating activities by virtually every organization involved in education. At least eleven (five of which are in areas specific to the social studies) national professional or scholarly organizations have received federal money for the development of content and performance standards (U. S. Department of Education 1994). These standard setting activities have generally moved in the direction of what is now called performance assessment, and away from the conserving tests and measurements currently employed.

> Implementation of performance-based assessment systems based on clear and public standards can support all schools in reaching the goals recently espoused by educators and policymakers throughout the United States. [Taylor 1994, p. 259].

Performance assessment is clearly the wave of the future in all disciplines (Herman, Aschbacher, and Winters 1992; Perrone 1991; Wiggins 1989, 1993b; Wolf, Bixby, Glenn, and Gardner 1991). The most straightforward definition of performance assessment is offered by the Office of Technology Assessment (1992): performance testing is "testing that requires a student to create an answer or a product that demonstrates his or her knowledge or skills." This is to distinguish them from assessments that require choosing from given options—for example, multiple-choice test items. Performance assessment can take many forms including projects (individual or group), interviews, oral presentations, essays, experiments, demonstrations, and portfolios (Rudner and Boston 1994).

The emphasis in performance assessment shifts from whether or not students simply know the right answer to a demonstration of how they arrive at an answer. Performance assessments are also intended to be directly related to the goals of instruction and expected outcomes. For example, a traditional test might require students to match countries and their capital cities, while a performance assessment might require students to prepare a travel brochure of a region of the world, including the countries and cities to visit, the geographical relationship among the countries, and attractions to see as a traveler. In other words, the assessment task is synonymous with the instructional task. The expectation is also that performance assessments can and will examine more complex and interrelated skills and knowledge. For example, students can demonstrate they understand the issues about capital punishment, can conduct library research, and demonstrate public speaking skills by participating in a debate on the issues.

A distinction can be made between performance and authentic assessments. While all authentic assessments are performances, the reverse is not true. Many performance assessments have meaning in school contexts but do not necessarily have more general meaning or value, especially in lived experience contexts. It is the latter characteristic that distinguishes authentic assessment. If the intention is for students to learn about unionism, for example, a performance assessment might require students to write an essay about John L. Lewis, or stage a play demonstrating attempts to unionize coal miners in the south, or prepare a photo essay of working conditions in union and nonunion companies. An authentic assessment on the same topic would require students to be involved in real-life issues of unionism by, for example, organizing their own union or through some type of involvement with real unions and management.

Needless to say, most emphasis is on performance assessment, and the term *authentic assessment* is sometimes misused. Were we to seriously consider creating authentic assessment, the above example suggests the very radical changes in knowledge, authority, and domains for learning that would be required.

While standard setting groups and policy-makers recognize the problems of creating and adopting performance assessment, these are seen as technical problems to be left to experts. Psychometricians have demonstrated admirable technical advances in the past; surely they will do likewise in the future. Measurement experts are left with serious problems of validity and reliability created by the enthusiasm of policy-makers, and the literature is full of reasoned and serious discussions about these matters (Linn, Baker, and Dunbar 1991; Linn 1994; Mehrens 1992; Messick 1994). And, given the quality of these discussions, it is reasonable to expect significant advances will be made in the construction, administration, and interpretation of performance assessments.

What, however, will be the consequence of this technological advance? Just as other forms of assessment have corrupted and been corruptible, so it will be with performance assessments—in the long run. Examples already exist of performance assessments driving the curriculum in much the same way as multiple-choice standardized tests have. Little consideration has been given to the underlying meaning of these common connections between assessment (regardless of its form) and curriculum and teaching (Mathison 1991). This is not to suggest that performance assessment is not indeed an improvement over current standardized, multiple-choice testing practices, but it is to suggest that it is no panacea for the problems of education:

> The idea that any testing technique, be it a new test design or a national test or system, can reform our schools and restore our nation's competitiveness is the height of technological arrogance and conceals many of the negative possibilities of such a move under the guise of a seemingly neat technological fix. Further, by casting the debate over how to address the problems in our schools in terms of a testing solution we divert attention from systemic problems related to delivery systems such as instructional delivery, quality of textbooks, length of the school day and year, teacher training and working conditions, and gross inequalities in in-school and extra-school resources. [Madaus 1993, p. 23]

What is important is that the technological changes in testing are accompanied by social consequences, sometimes intentional and sometimes fortuitous. The challenge for social studies educators is to embrace the promise of performance assessment, aware that to do so will have consequences, and to avoid utopian thinking about the value of performance assessment.

The Social Studies and Performance Assessment

Social studies is a school subject that has received a great deal of attention in the standards-development movement. As previously mentioned, many of the national organizations that have received federal money for such activities have been working specifically in the social studies.[1] And even an innocent bystander would realize that the outcome of these efforts has fueled more, not less, debate about what scholars and practitioners believe students should know and be able to do as a result of their social education. This debate is significant since the performance-assessment movement is dependent on delineations of what students should know and be able to do. And, as indicated previously, good performance-assessment tasks become instructional activities, and therefore require reconsideration of what is taught and how. These are significant challenges to all disciplines, particularly the social studies.

An example of the state of performance assessment in the social studies is illustrated in a special issue of the *Social Science Record* (Baker 1993). (Also, see chapters by Epstein, Evans, and Fleury in this volume for illustrations of performance assessment in the social studies.) In this special issue, after an introduction by Grant Wiggins, several accounts are given of assessment practices in New York schools. Jones (1993) gives examples of assessment items for elementary grades and Browne and Shultz (1993) give examples for secondary grades. These are useful examples for thinking about the promise and challenge of adopting performance assessment in the social studies.

In these discussions, many examples of instructional activities that would be performances or demonstrations of what students have learned are given. For example, a sample task for a global studies student portfolio is:

> Conduct an oral history on a topical but historically interesting issue: recent American immigrants [or] veterans of Desert Storm, Vietnam, and World War II on "America as policeman in the world." [Wiggins 1993, p. 6]

A sample task for a middle-school English and social studies portfolio is:

> The principal has asked the class to be responsible for one of the school's showcases for the year. S/he has requested that they be changed monthly and reflect various periods in American history. Each student will become part of a task force that will effectively design and create displays for a showcase. [Wiggins 1993, p. 7]

Jones (1993) suggests the following for a fifth-grade social studies portfolio:

1. A student self-assessment: What I have learned in fifth-grade this year and what advice I would give to next year's students.
2. Videotape or slide set with a cassette of a project (e.g., demonstration of a Native American craft).
3. A research project, such as "How People Make a Living in Argentina."
4. A draft of a story based on an Inuit tale or legend.
5. A summary of a group activity in which the student participated (e.g., a decision-making activity on each of five cities to visit: Toronto, Atlanta, San Diego, Caracas, Rio de Janeiro).
6. A letter to a pen-pal in another country, in which the student describes the characteristics of American culture.
7. A journal entry in which the student describes the advantages of democratic government. [p. 21]

There are many more examples, but these illustrate the nature of the suggested assessment practices in social studies.

An examination of these examples illustrates both the promise of and challenges in adopting p: formance assessment. Notable characteristics of these examples are that they describe learning activities that require active participation by students, that varied forms of representation are encouraged, and that students need to draw on multiple domains of knowledge and skill in doing the activity. As assessment tasks (and as learning activities) these are significant improvements over textbook-driven instruction where students are assessed using tests or quizzes with matching, multiple-choice, or fill-in the blank items. This transformation is no small accomplishment. It occurs in the face of a long tradition of teaching social studies as lists, truncated facts, and predetermined answers (McNeil 1988).

At the same time, these examples also demonstrate some of the challenges faced by social studies educators in the move toward performance assessment. The examples are presented without reference to why students should do these particular activities, even though a thoughtful reader could easily make reasonable inferences. These writers may have been constrained by space in their discussions, but often the move to adopt performance assessment leads to the creation of activities or tasks that result in a performance without first thinking about the fundamental goal to be demonstrated by that performance (Mathison 1994). The activity for the social studies and English portfolio, for example, would be more sensible and richer if we knew the intention was for students to, let's say, "identify and use key concepts such as chronology, causality, change, conflict, and complexity to explain, analyze and show connections among patterns of historical change and continuity" (NCSS 1994, p. 34). The design and creation of a showcase would then be pedagogically purposeful and related to foundational goals of social studies curriculum, and not activity for its own sake.

The examples are also fairly specific in terms of the subject matter and form of the performance. For example, the global studies example specifically delineates not only how students will do the performance (an oral history) but also about whom (immigrants or veterans). There is little apparent opportunity for students to exercise choice about how and through what content to demonstrate they have acquired certain knowledge or skills.

Referring back to the earlier distinction made between performance and authentic assessments, these examples illustrate the performance aspect specifically in ways associated with school-relevant knowledge. One needs obviously to think about the desirability of authenticity in creating instructional tasks/performance assessments, which includes considerations about the role and nature of social studies content and students' roles in assessment. Given the emphasis in the social studies on creating civic-minded individuals (NCSS 1994), and the real-life nature of civic responsibility, authenticity is probably a critical element of performance assessments that truly lead to the achievement of social studies goals.

Such are the promises of and challenges to creating and adopting performance assessment in social studies. The National Council for the Social Studies *Curriculum Standards for Social Studies* provide a good starting place for thinking about such reformation. These standards avoid a rigid specification of particular content (for example, the Civil War or the American Revolution must be taught at such and such a time) and although they are organized around ten thematic areas, the focus is on well-articulated skills and knowledge. The examples provided also illustrate how the Standards can be translated in classroom practices.

What the Standards do not provide is a vision of the curriculum planning that will facilitate the move toward more authentic learning tasks and assessments. Scholars and practitioners alike need to think carefully about how this development work will be done.

The danger of mapping an existing curriculum (for example, the history of Native Americans in the fourth grade) onto something like the NCSS Standards without thinking simultaneously about the more foundational goals conveyed by the Standards will be an exercise in compliance, not reformation. It is complex to think about generic skills and knowledge, and disciplinary content simultaneously. Mostly, disciplinary knowledge has won out. While content knowledge is important (and there is nothing wrong with fourth graders learning about Native Americans), it provides little direction in the formulation of learning and assessment tasks. This is much more related to the more basic and generic ideas outlined in the Standards. Clearly such work has begun, as is illustrated by the special issue of the *Social Science Record*.

Conclusion

In social studies, as in other school subject areas, the emphasis is to move away from what have until recently been the tried and true means of assessing student knowledge and skills. No longer are traditional tests and measurements adequate for the many purposes to which we put assessments. Assessment reform (and the concomitant curricular and instructional reform) face many roadblocks, perhaps the least of which is the array of technical problems performance assessments present (Mathison 1995). In fact, any such reform faces a series of dilemmas that will inevitably require compromise. But if considered during the reform process, they will increase the likelihood that social studies teaching and learning will move in a direction that creates the opportunities for

students to indeed become good citizens. Briefly these dilemmas
are:

1. *State/national versus local control.* A perennial problem in any educational reform, including assessment.
   Performance assessment intensifies the tension by calling for a more active role for students in their own
   assessment. Discussions about who has authority over
   social studies curriculum and assessment are necessary.
2. *Adding on versus reformulation.* Adopting new forms of
   assessment is often done in addition to those assessment already done by the district, state, or other agencies. The testing burden is already too heavy in schools.
   Therefore serious interest in performance assessment
   demands reconsideration of the whole program of
   assessment.
3. *Limited resources versus accomplishing the ideal.* There
   will never be enough resources (especially time) to create the performance assessment—and therefore social
   studies curriculum—that we might want. This dilemma
   is particularly real, given that good performance assessments, especially those that are authentic, must be
   created at the local level. This places demands on the
   time and talent of an already overworked and undervalued teaching corps. The ideal cannot be realized, but
   might be approximated if there were a serious reconsideration of uses of teacher time.
4. *Disciplines/activities versus goals/objectives.* So much
   of what counts as school knowledge has become fossil-
   ized, making it hard to give up or discard what is currently done. While what is currently taught and by what
   means may be perfectly appropriate for a new social
   studies, it must be at least open to question in face of
   considerations about what the goals and objectives for
   teaching and learning in the social studies are.
5. *Political versus technical solution.* As has already been
   indicated, the performance-assessment movement is both
   a political and technical solution to perceived problems
   in teaching and learning. Balancing the efforts between
   the two foci is critical to avoid the co-optation of performance assessment for crass political ends or in the name
   of technical sophistication.

Notes

Chapter One

1. The balance of this section draws directly upon E. W. Ross (in press), Diverting democracy: The curriculum standards movement and social studies education, *International Journal of Social Education*. I am indebted to the work of William H. Schubert for the historical analysis in this section, see his (1991), Historical perspective on centralizing the curriculum, in M. F. Klein (ed.), *The politics of curriculum decision-making* (pp. 98–118). Albany: State University of New York Press.

2. This sections draws upon E. W. Ross (1994), Teachers as curriculum theorizers, in E. W. Ross (ed.), *Reflective practice in social studies* (pp. 35–41). Washington, D.C.: National Council for the Social Studies.

Chapter Two

1. Ravitch's argument, in somewhat abbreviated form, has been repeated in both Bradley Commission reports, *Building a History Curriculum* (1988) and *Historical Literacy* (1989). Thus, it may be thought of as the "unofficial" position of the most prominent advocates of a history-centered curriculum.

2. Many scholars, of course, perhaps most notably John Dewey, consider this a false dichotomy. See, for example, Dewey's *School and Society* (1899).

3. The fact that many students left school in the 8th or 9th grade was the principal reason for the division of the curriculum into junior and senior cycles, but this division also reflects the influence of early research about child development.

4. Much of what the Social Studies Committee said about history education is based on the ideas of James Harvey Robinson, a professor of history at Columbia University who served on the Committee and was quoted repeatedly and at length in the Committee's final report. See Robinson's The New History (1912).

5. Ironically, many of the leading advocates of a history-centered curriculum also support the movement to establish national standards for his-

tory education. In fact, the National Center for History in the Schools is directing the twenty-nine organizations, including the American Historical Association, the Organization of American Historians, the National Council for History Education, and the Organization of History Teachers, that are participating in the National History Standards Project.

Chapter Four

1. This essay was an invited address presented to the Research in Social Studies Education Special Interest Group at the annual meeting of the American Educational Research Association in San Francisco, April 1992. It also appeared in *Theory and Research in Social Education*, Spring 1992, *20* (3), pp. 230–241.. It is reprinted here with permission of the author and *Theory and Research in Social Education*.

Chapter Six

1. Special funding and technical support for this essay were provided by Colgate University in the form of two working research grants. Similar support was offered to me in the form of a department of speech communication visiting fellowship by the University of Illinois at Urbana-Champaign in the 1992–93 academic year. The initial outlines of this essay emerged in a conversation I had with Abdul JanMohamed and Decric Robinson on the topic of race and identity at the Humanities Research Institute at the University of California at Irvine in the spring of 1992. I am indebted to Abdul and Cedric for their wise counsel, and to Jan for the invitation to give a talk at the Institute. I would also like to thank Robin Small-McCarthy, Warren Crichlow, Lawrence Grossberg, Michael Apple, Lisa Reilly, Mike Dyson, Stephen David, K. E. Supriya, Gregory Byschenk, Jonathan York, Alicia Rodriguez, Kathleen Weiler, Roxana Ng, Joe Onosko, Melissa Orlie, Louis Heshusius, Patrick Solomon, Fazal Rizvi, Jim Ladwig, Vivki Crawley, and Susan Huddleston Edgerton for their insightful comments on early drafts of this chapter.

2. Besides the matter of Elridge's misrecognition of the music produced by "members of his race," Gate's comments here poignantly raise another issue: the matter of the inherent tension between text (in this case a musical text) and reception. Gate's comments point specifically to the difficulty of guaranteeing any "preferred reading" of a given text (see Hall 1980b). Authors, even master musicians such as Roy Elridge, do not have a final hold on the meaning or the audiences that their work engenders. This is particularly true with respect to producers of black popular culture. The history of black popular arts is marked by the central paradox of massively aggressive white consumption, white interpretation, and white cultural appropria-

tion of these art forms, even when, as in the case of the blues, black producers and black audiences for these art forms have attenuated or declined (Gilroy 1990). It is the case, for instance, that the more Afrocentric and neo-nationalist rap music becomes, the more it is bought, consumed, and imitated by middle-class white youth. For example, rap artist Ice-T contends that some 70 to 80 percent of his records are sold to white youth consumers (Light 1992). Of course, there is also considerable nonwhite consumption of white popular cultural forms such as country music (Wood 1991).

3. Contrary to the claims of neoconservative writers like D'Souza, Afrocentrism and multiculturalism are marginalized discourses in the curriculum field.

4. The language of "cultural deprivation" associated with 1960s U.S. educational theorists' explanations of black underacheivement is a powerful example of mainstream pathologization of minority youth. The deeply racialized discourse of "educational subnormality" used disproportionately by English educators to classify underachieving black youth is another example (Toyna and Hatcher 1992; Ogbu).

5. Black middle-class parents' investment in the private school system as a strategy for procuring intergenerational mobility for their children continues apace in the 1990s (West 1993).

6. The work of Gamoran and Berends (1986) and Oakes (1992) strongly corroborates Spring and Grant's claims of a powerful black-white differential with respect to access to instructional opportunity.

Chapter Seven

1. In New York state the debate over multicultural education has focused, I think unfortunately, on whether multicultural education would promote self-esteem in minority students. Given that increased knowledge of the social world and the social inequalities that minorities, women, and the poor have faced, students may gain a better and more realistic understanding of the struggles ahead, leading to expanding social debate and action, but not necessarily better self-esteem. The debates over "Curriculum of Inclusion," the report of the New York State Task Force on Minorities: Equity and Excellence (1989) are chronicled in Catherine Cornbleth and Dexter Waugh, *The Great Speckled Bird: Multicultural Politics and Education Policymaking*, New York: St. Martin's Press (1995).

2. Ceasar McDowell and Patricia Sullivan's, chapter in *Freedom's Plow: Teaching in the Multicultural Classroom*, describes the importance of teaching "movement history" to students. The book as a whole is an excellent resource for teachers.

3. An excellent resource on teaching about Columbus and Native Americans is *Rethinking Columbus*, published by and available from *Rethinking Schools*, 1001 East Keefe Ave., Milwaukee, WI 53212, 414–964–9646.

4. African-American cultural critic bell hooks provides accessible examples of how such analyses might be carried out. See her *Yearning: Race, Gender, and Cultural Politics*.

5. This is a revised version of an article that originally appeared in the *Social Science Record*. It is reprinted here with permission.

Chapter Twelve

1. This chapter is drawn from a chapter included in M. Nelson (ed.), *The Future of Social Studies*. Boulder, Colo.: Social Science Education Consortium.

Chapter Thirteen

1. These organizations include the National Center for History in the Schools, UCLA; the Center for Civic Education; the National Council for Geographic Education (in cooperation with the Association of American Geographers, the National Geographic Society, and the American Geographical Society); the National Council on Economic Education; and the National Council for the Social Studies.

References

Chapter One

Apple, M. (1986) *Teachers and texts*. New York: Routledge.

Barr, R. D., Barth, J. L., and Shermis, S. S. (1977) *Defining the social studies*. Arlington, Va: National Council for the Social Studies.

Ben-Peretz, M. (1989) *The teacher-curriculum encounter*. Albany: State University of New York Press.

Black, H. (1967) *The American schoolbook*. New York: William Morrow.

Bowler, M. (1978) The making of a textbook. *Learning, 6* (March), 38–42.

Brooks, M. G. (1991) Centralized curriculum: Effects on the local school level, in M. F. Klein (ed.), *The politics of curriculum decision-making* (pp. 151–66). Albany: State University of New York Press.

Committee of Seven. (1899) American Historical Association. *The study of history in schools*. New York: Macmillan.

Committee of Ten. (1893) National Education Association. *Report of the committee on secondary school studies*. Washington, D.C.: United States Bureau of Education.

Committee on Social Studies. (1916). National Education Association. *The social studies in secondary education*. Washington, D.C.: United States Government Printing Office.

Cornbleth, C. (1985) Social studies curriculum construction and reconstruction. *Social Education, 49*, 554–56.

Cornbleth, C., and Waugh, D. (1995). *The great speckled bird*. New York: St. Martin's Press.

Cornett, J. W., Chase, K. S., Miller, P., Schrock, D., Bennett, B. J., Goins, J., and Hammond, C. (1992) Insights from the analysis of our own theorizing: The viewpoints of seven teachers, in E. W. Ross, J. W. Cornett, and G. McCutcheon (eds.), *Teacher personal theorizing: Connecting curriculum practice, theory and research*. Albany: State University of New York Press.

Dewey, J. (1904) The relation of theory to practice in education, in *The relation of theory to practice in the education of teachers: Third yearbook of the National Society for the Scientific Study of Education*, Part I. Bloomington, Ill: Public School Publishing Co.

Engle, S. (1963) Decision making: The heart of social studies instruction. *ocial Education, 24*(7), 301–4, 306.

Engle, S., and Ochoa, A. (1988), *Education for democratic citizenship: Decision making in the social studies.* New York: Teachers College Press.

Fullinwider, R. K. (1991). Philosophical inquiry and social studies, in J. P. Shaver (ed.), *Handbook of research on social studies teaching and learning* (pp. 16–26). New York: Macmillan.

Hunt, M. P., and Metcalf, L. E. (1955) *Teaching high school social studies: Problems in reflective thinking and social understanding.* New York: Harper & Row.

Kilpatrick, W. H. (1918) *The project method.* New York: Teachers College, Columbia University.

Kleibard, H. M. (1987) *The struggle for the American curriculum, 1893–1958.* New York: Routledge.

Kohlberg, L. (1973) Moral development and the new social studies. *Social Education, 14*(1), 35–49.

——— (1975) The cognitive-developmental approach to moral education. *Phi Delta Kappan, 56*(10), 670–77.

Krug, E. A. (1969) *The shaping of the American high school, 1880–1920.* Madison: University of Wisconsin Press.

Loewen, J. W. (1995) *Lies my teacher told me.* New York: New Press.

Longstreet, W. S. (1985) Citizenship: The phantom core of social studies curriculum. *Theory and Research in Social Education, 13*(2), 21–29.

Marker, G., and Mehlinger, H. (1992) Social studies, in P. W. Jackson (ed.), *Handbook of research on curriculum* (pp. 830–51). New York: Macmillan.

Mathison, S. (1991) Implementing curricular change through state-mandated testing: Ethical issues. *Journal of Curriculum and Supervision, 6*, 201–12.

McCutchen, S. P. (1963) A discipline for the social studies. *Social Education, 52*, 444–46.

McCutcheon, G. (1995) *Developing the curriculum.* White Plains, NY: Longman.

Morrissett, I., and Haas, J. D. (1982) Rationales, goals, and objectives in social studies, in *The current state of social studies: A report of Project SPAN* (pp. 1–80). Boulder, CO: Social Science Education Consortium.

Newmann, F. (1977) *Clarifying public controversy: An approach to teaching social studies.* Boston: Little, Brown.

National Council for the Social Studies. (1994) *Expectations of excellence: Curriculum standards for social studies.* Washington, D.C.: Author.

Oliver, D., and Shaver, J. P. (1966) *Teaching public issues in the high school.* Boston: Houghton Mifflin.

Parker, W. C. (1987) Teachers' mediation in social studies. *Theory and Research in Social Education, 15,* 1–22.

Parker, W. C., and McDaniel, J. (1992) Bricolage: Teachers do it daily, in E. W. Ross, J. W. Cornett, and G. McCutcheon (eds.), *Teacher personal theorizing: Connecting curriculum practice, theory and research.* Albany: State University of New York Press.

Ravitch, D. (1989) The plight of history in American schools, in P. Gagnon and the Bradley Commission on History in Schools (eds.), *Historical literacy: The case for history in American education* (pp. 51–68). New York: Macmillan.

———. (1990) Multiculturalism, E pluribus plure. *American Scholar* (Summer), 337–54.

Ross, E. W. (1992) Educational reform, school restructuring and teachers' work. *International Journal of Social Education, 7,* 83–92.

———. (1994) Teachers as curriculum theorizers, in E. W. Ross (ed.), *Reflective practice in social studies.* Washington, D.C.: National Council for the Social Studies.

———. (in press). Diverting democracy: The curriculum standards movement and social studies education. *International Journal of Social Education.*

Ross, E. W., Cornett, J. W., and McCutcheon, G. (1992) *Teacher personal theorizing: Connecting curriculum practice, theory and research.* Albany: State University of New York Press.

Saxe, D. W. (1991) *Social studies in schools: A history of the early years.* Albany: State University of New York Press.

Schlesinger, A. M., Jr. (1991) *The disuniting of America.* Knoxville, TN: Whittle Direct Books.

Schubert, W. H. (1991) Historical perspective on centralizing curriculum, in M. F. Klein (ed.), *The politics of curriculum decision-making* (pp. 98–118). Albany: State University of New York Press.

Shaver, J. P. (1977). The task of rationale-building for citizenship education, in J. P. Shaver (ed.), *Building rationales for citizenship education* (pp. 96–116). Arlington, VA: National Council for the Social Studies.

Shaver, J. P., Davis, O. L., and Helburn, S. W. (1980) An interpretive report on the status of precollege social studies education based upon three NSF-funded studies in *What are the needs in precollege science, mathematics, and social studies education.* Washington, D.C.: National Science Foundation.

Stanley, W. B., and Nelson, J. L. (1994) The foundations of social education in historical context, in R. Martusewicz and W. Reynolds (eds.), *Inside/out: Contemporary critical perspectives in education* (pp. 266–84). New York: St. Martin's Press.

Stanley, W. B. (1985) Recent research in the foundations of social education: 1976–1983, in W. B. Stanley (ed.), *Review of research in social studies education: 1976–1983* (pp. 309–99). Washington, D.C.: National Council for the Social Studies.

Superka, D. P., and Hawke, S. (1982) *Social roles: A focus for social studies in the 1980s.* Boulder, CO: Social Science Education Consortium.

Thornton, S. J. (1991) Teacher as curricular-instructional gatekeeper in social studies, In J. P. Shaver (ed.), *Handbook of research on social studies teaching and learning* (pp. 237–48). New York: Macmillan.

———. (1994) The social studies new century's end: Reconsidering patterns of curriculum and instruction. *Review of Research in Education, 20,* 223–54.

Whelan, M. (1992) History and the social studies: A response to the critics. *Theory and Research in Social Education, 20*(1), 2–16.

Wirth, A. G. (1992) *Education and work in the year 2000.* San Francisco: Jossey-Bass.

Chapter Two

Barth, J. L., et al. (1991) Social studies as a discipline. *International Journal of Social Education, 6*(2), 7–87. (Articles in the Special Edition included J. L. Barth, Beliefs that discipline the social studies, 19–24; W. S. Longstreet, Reflections on a discipline of the social studies, 25–32; J. L. Nelson, Discipline, knowledge, and social education, 41–50; S. P. Wronski, A discipline of the social studies: Forward to the basics, 57–68; and C. W. Keller, It is time to abolish the mythology that social studies constitute a discipline, 69–77.)

Bradley Commission on History in Schools. (1988) *Building a history curriculum*. New York: Educational Excellence Network.

Committee of Seven. (1899) American Historical Association. *The study of history in schools*. New York: Macmillan.

Committee of Ten. (1893) National Education Association. *Report of the Committee on Secondary School Studies*. Washington, D. C.: United States Bureau of Education.

Committee on Social Studies. (1916) National Education Association. *The Social Studies in Secondary Education, Bulletin No. 28*. Washington, D. C.: Government Printing Office.

Cuban, L. (1991) History of teaching in social studies, in J. P. Shaver (ed.), *Handbook of research on social studies teaching and learning*. New York: Macmillan.

Dewey, J. (1899) *School and society*. Chicago: University of Chicago Press.

Downey, M. T., and Levstik, L. S. (1988) Teaching and learning history: The research base. *Social Education*, *52*(6), 336–42.

Downey, M. T., and Levstik, L. S. (1991) Teaching and learning history, in J. P. Shaver (ed.), *Handbook of research on social studies teaching and learning* (pp. 400–410). New York: Macmillan.

Engle, S. H. (1990) The commission report and citizenship education. *Social Education*, *54*(7), 431–34.

Evans, R. W. (1989a) A dream unrealized: A brief look at the history of issue-centered approaches. *The Social Studies*, *80*(5), 178–83.

———. (1989b) Diane Ravitch and the revival of history: A critique. *The Social Studies*, *80*(3), 85–88.

———. (1989c) The future of issue-centered education. *The Social Studies*, *80*(5), 176–77.

———. (1992) Misunderstanding social studies: A rejoinder to Whelan. *Theory and Research in Social Education 20*(3), 313–17.

Franklin, B. M. (1990) Something old, something new, something borrowed: A historical commentary on the Carnage Council's Turning Points. *Education Policy*, *5*(3), 265–72.

Gagnon, P. and The Bradley Commission on History in Schools. (1989) *Historical literacy: The case for history in American education*. New York: Macmillan.

Goodlad, J. I. (1984) *A place called school: Prospects for the future*. New York: McGraw-Hill.

Grob, G. N., and Billias, G. A. (eds.). (1987) *Interpretations of American history: Patterns and perspectives. Vol. 1 and 2.* New York: Free Press.

Hertzberg, H. W. (1981) *Social studies reform, 1880–1980.* Boulder, CO: Social Science Education Consortium.

Hirsch, E. D., Jr. (1987) *Cultural literacy: What every American needs to know.* Boston: Houghton Mifflin.

Jackson, K. T., and Jackson, B. B. (1989) Why the time is right to reform the history curriculum, in Paul Gagnon and the Bradley Commission on History in Schools (eds.), *Historical literacy: The case for history in American education* (pp. 3–15). New York: Macmillan.

Kammen, M. (1980) *The past before us: Contemporary historical writing in the United States.* Ithaca, N.Y.: Cornell University Press.

Kliebard, H. M. (1986) *The Struggle for the American Curriculum 1893–1954.* Boston: Routledge and Kegan Paul.

Leming, J. S. (1989) The two cultures of social studies education. *Social Education, 53*(6), 404–8.

Lybarger, M. B. (1991) The historiography of social studies: Retrospect, circumspect, and prospect, in J. P. Shaver (ed.), *Handbook of research on social studies teaching and learning* (pp. 3–15). New York: Macmillan.

Nelson, J. L. (1990) Charting a course backwards: A response to the national commission's nineteenth century social studies program. *Social Education, 54*(7), 434–37.

———. (1992) Social studies and history: A response to Whelan. *Theory and Research in Social Education, 20*(3), 318–24.

Ravitch, Diane. (1985) From history to social studies: Dilemmas and problems, in *The schools we deserve: Reflections on the educational crises of our times* (pp. 112–32). New York: Basic Books.

———. (1989a) The plight of history in American schools, in Paul Gagnon and the Bradley Commission on History in Schools (eds.), *Historical literacy: The case for history in American education* (pp. 51–68). New York: Macmillan.

———. (1989b). The revival of history: A response. *The Social Studies, 80*(3), 89–91.

Saxe, David Warren (1991) *Social studies in schools: A history of the early years.* Albany: State University of New York Press.

———. (1992a) An introduction to the seminal social welfare and efficiency prototype: The founders of 1916 social studies. *Theory and Research in Social Education, 20*(2), 156–78.

———. (1992b) Framing a theory for social studies foundations. *Review of Educational Research, 62*(3), 259–77.

Shaver, J. P. (1987) Implications from research: What should be taught in social studies? in V. Richardson-Koehler (ed.), *Educator's handbook: A research perspective* (pp. 112–38). New York: Longman.

Shaver, J. P., Davis, O. L., Jr, and Helburn, S. W. (1980) An interpretive report on the status of precollege social studies education based on three NSF-funded studies, in *What are the needs in precollege science, mathematics and social science education? Views from the field.* Washington, D. C.: National Science Foundation.

Superka, D. P., Hawke, S., and Morrissette, I. (1980) The current and future status of the social studies. *Social Education, 44*(4), 362–69.

Thornton, S. J. (1991) Teacher as curricular-instructional gatekeeper in social studies, in J. P. Shaver (ed.), *Handbook of research on social studies teaching and learning* (pp. 237–48). New York: Macmillan.

Whelan, M. (1991) James Harvey Robinson, the new history and the 1916 social studies report. *The History Teacher, 24*(2), 191–202.

———. (1992) History and the social studies: A response to the critics. *Theory and Research in Social Education, 20*(1), 2–16.

Wiley, K. B. (1977) *The status of precollege science, mathematics and social science education, 1955–1975: Vol. 3. Social science education.* Washington, D. C.: Government Printing Office (GPO Stock No. 038–000–00363–1).

Chapter Three

Dewey, J. (1926) Individuality and experience. *Journal of the Barnes Foundation.*

Engle, S., and Ochoa, A. (1988) *Education for democratic citizenship.* New York: Teachers College Press.

Evans, R. W., and Saxe, D. W. (1996) *Handbook for teaching social issues.* Washington, D.C.: National Council for the Social Studies.

Hirsch, E. D., Jr. (1996) *The schools we need.* New York: Doubleday.

Chapter Four

Abbott, Edwin A. (1952) *Flatland*. New York: Dover.

Beecher, Catherine. (1977) *A treatise in domestic economy*. New York: Schocken Books. Original published in 1842.

Brock-Utne, Birgit. (1985) *Educating for peace: A feminist perspective*. New York: Pergamon Press.

Chodorow, Nancy. (1978) *The reproduction of mothering*. Berkley: University of California Press.

Day, Dorothy. (1952) *The long loneliness*. San Francisco: Harper & Row.

Elshtain, Jean Bethke. (1987) *Women and War*. New York: Basic Books.

Gilligan, Carol J. (1982) *In a different voice*. Cambridge: Harvard University Press.

MacIntyre, Alasdair. (1984) *After virtue*. Notre Dame: University of Notre Dame Press.

Noddings, Nel. (1984) *Caring: A feminine approach to ethics and moral education*. Berkley and Los Angeles: University of California Press.

———. (1991/92) Feminist fears in ethics. *Journal of Social Philosophy 21*(2 and 3), pp. 25–33.

———. (1992). *The challenge to care in schools*. New York: Teachers College Press.

Reardon, Betty A. (1985) *Sexism and the war system*. New York: Teachers College Press.

Taylor, Laurie. (1986) Provoked reason in men and women: Heat-of-passion manslaughter and imperfect self-defense. *UCLA Law Review 33*, 1679–735.

Tetreault, Mary Kay Thompson. (1986) Integrating women's history: The case of United States history high school textbooks. *The History Teacher 19*(2), 211–62.

Walker, Alice. (1983) *In search of our mothers' gardens*. San Diego: Harcourt Brace Jovanovich.

Chapter Five

Anyon, J. (1983) Intersections of gender and class: Accommodation and resistance by working-class and affluent females to contradictory sex-role ideologies, in S. Walker and L. Barton (eds.), *Gender, class and education* (pp. 19–37). Sussex: Falmer Press.

Bahmueller, C. (ed.). (1991) *Civitas: A framework for civic education*. Washington, D.C.: National Council for the Social Studies.

American Association of University Women. (1992) *How schools shortchange girls*. Washington, D.C.: AAUW Education Foundation.

Banks, J. (1994) *An introduction to multicultural education*. New York: Allyn and Bacon.

Bernard-Powers, J. (1992) *The girl question in education: Vocational education for young women in the progressive era*. London: Falmer.

———. (1994) Lucy Laney, in M. Seller (ed.), *Women educators in the United States: A biographical and bibliographical sourcebook*. Boulder, CO: Greenwood Press.

Biklen, S., and Pollard, D. (1993) *Gender and education: Ninety-second yearbook of the National Society for the Study of Education*. Chicago: University of Chicago Press.

Boulding, E. (1988) *Building a global civic culture: Education for an interdependent world*. New York: Teachers College Press.

Boxer, B. (1993) *Strangers in the senate: Politics and the new revolution of women in America*. Washington, D.C..: National Press Books.

Brown, C. S. (1990) *"Ready From Within": A first person narrative, Septima Clarke and the Civil rights movement*. Lawrenceville, N.J.: Africa World Press.

Buss, H. (1991) Reading for the doubled visioned discourse of American women's autobiography. *a/b Autobiography Studies, 5* (1), 95–108.

Campbell, D. (1988) Letter to the editor. *Social Education 52*(6), 403.

Connell, R. W. (1993) Disruptions: Improper masculinities and schooling, in L. Weis and M. Fine (eds.), *Beyond silenced voices: Class, race and gender in United States schools* (pp. 191–208). Albany: State University of New York Press.

Cornbleth, C., and Waugh, D. (1995) The great speckled bird: Multicultural politics and education policymaking. New York: St. Martin's Press.

Education Commission of the States. (1973) *Political knowledge and attitudes*. Washington, D.C.: United States Government Printing Office.

Evans, T. (1988) *A gender agenda*. Sydney: Allen & Unwin.

Faludi, S. (1992) *Backlash*. New York: Crown.

Fox-Genovese, E. (1991) *Feminism without illusion: A critique of individualism*. Chapel Hill: University of North Carolina Press.

Gabriel, S., and Smithson, I. (eds.) (1990). *Gender in the classroom: Power and pedagogy.* Urbana: University of Illinois Press.

Gagnon, P. (1988) *Democracy's untold story: What world history textbooks neglect.* Washington, D.C.: American Federation of Teachers.

Gillespie, D., and Spohn, C. (1987) Adolescents' attitudes toward women in politics: The effect of gender and race, *Gender and Society 1*(2), 208–18.

Gilligan, C. (1993) Joining the resistance: Psychology, politics, girls and women, in L. Weis and M. Fine (eds.), *Beyond silence voices: Class, race and gender in United States schools.* Albany: State University of New York Press.

Gilligan, C., Lyons, N., and Hanmer, T. (eds.). (1990) *Making connections: The relational worlds of adolescent girls at Emma Willard School.* Cambridge: Harvard University Press.

Grambs, J. (ed.). (1976) *Teaching about women in the social studies.* Washington, D.C.: National Council for the Social Studies.

Grundfest, E. (1989) Women and gender in geography courses in the United States. *Journal of Geography in Higher Education 13* (1), 112–14.

Hahn, C., and Bernard-Powers, J. (1985) Sex equity in social studies, in S. Klein (ed.), *A handbook for achieving sex equity through education* (pp. 280–97). Baltimore: Johns Hopkins University Press.

Harwood, A., and Hahn, C. (1992) Civic learning in young adolescents. Paper presented at the American Education Research Association, April.

Hirsch, E. D., Jr. (1987) *Cultural literacy: What every American needs to know.* Boston: Houghton-Mifflin.

Hirsch, M., and Fox-Keller, E. (1990) *Conflicts in feminism.* New York: Routledge.

Ivins, M. (1994) Clinton sticks gig in Congress. *San Francisco Chronicle,* January 28, 1994, p. A23.

Johnson, L. (1989) Feminist or gender geography in Australia. *Journal of Geography in Higher Education 13* (1), 85.

Jones, J. (1985) *Labor of love, labor of sorrow: Black women, work and the family from slavery to the present.* New York: Basic Books.

Kingston, M. H. (1989) *The Woman Warrior.* New York: Vintage.

Kwon, Y. (1993) Ahead of their time: Earliest feminist writers of modern Korea. Paper presented at the Western Association of Women Historians Annual Meeting, May.

Ladson-Billings, G. (1993) Review of A. S. Schlesinger, *The disuniting of America: Reflections of a multicultural society. Theory and Research in Social Education, (21)*3, 84–92.

Light, B., Staton, P., and Bourne, P. (1989) Sex equity content in history textbooks. *The History and Social Science Teacher, (25)*1, 18–21.

MacIntosh, P. (1985) Countering the reactionary federal program for education. Paper presented at the Annual Conference of the National Association of Independent Schools, Washington, D.C. (ERIC Document No. ED 348 288).

Marker, G. and Mehlinger, H. (1991) Social studies, in P. Jackson (ed.), *Handbook of research on curriculum.* New York: Macmillan.

Martin, J. R. (1995) The radical future of gender enrichment, in J. Gaskell and J. Willinsky (eds.), *Gender in/forms curriculum* (pp. 157–173). New York: Teachers College Press.

McKenna, K. (1989) An examination of sex equity in the *1986 Curriculum guidelines for history and contemporary studies. History and Social Science Teacher 25*(1), 21–24.

Mills, K. (1993) *This little light of mine: The life of Fannie Lou Hamer.* New York: Dutton.

Minnich, E. K. (1982). Liberal arts and civic arts: Education for "the free man"? *Liberal Education 68,* 311–321.

Morrison, T. (1970) *The bluest eye.* New York: Holt.

National Commission on Social Studies in the Schools. (1989) *Charting the course: Social studies for the twenty-first century.* Washington, D.C.: National Council for the Social Studies.

Ninth Circuit Task Force on Gender Bias. (1993) Executive summary of the preliminary report of the Ninth Circuit Task Force on Gender Bias. *Stanford Law Review 45* (6), 2153.

Noddings, N. (1992) Social Studies and feminism. *Theory and Research in Social Education, 20*(3), 230–241.

Pagano, J. (1991) Relating to students. *Journal of Moral Education, (20)*3, 26–31.

Peake, L. (1989) The challenge of feminist geography. *Journal of Geography in Higher Education 13*(1), 85.

Ravitch, D. and Finn, C. (1987) *What do our seventeen year-olds know?* New York: Harper & Row.

Rhode, D. (1990) *Theoretical perspectives on sexual differences.* New Haven: Yale University Press.

Robinson, T.L., and Ward, J.V. (1991) A belief in self far greater than anyone's disbelief: Cultivating resistance among African American female adolescents. *Women and Therapy, 2.*

Sadker, M. and Sadker, D. (1994) *Failing at fairness: How America's schools cheat girls.* New York: Scribner.

Sadker, M., Sadker, D., and Steindam, S. (1989) Gender equity and educational reform. *Educational Leadership, 46*(6), 44.

Schlesinger, A. M., Jr. (1986) *The cycles of American history.* Boston: Houghton Mifflin.

Seager, J. (1992) Women deserve spatial consideration, in C. Karmare and D. Spender (eds.), *The Knowledge explosion: Generations of feminist scholarship* (pp. 213–22). New York: Athene.

Shakeshaft, C. (1985) Strategies for overcoming the barriers to women in educational administration, in S. Klein (ed.), *Handbook for achieving sex equity through education.* Baltimore: Johns Hopkins University Press.

Shaver, J. (ed.). (1991) *Handbook of research on social studies teaching and learning.* New York: Macmillan.

Smith, R. (1995). Schooling and the formation of male students' gender identities. *Theory and Research in Social Education 24,* 54–70.

Tetreault, M. K. (1986) Integrating women's history. *The History Teacher* (*19*)2, 212–62.

Thorne, B. (1990) Children and gender, in D. Rhode (ed.), *Theoretical perspectives on sexual difference.* New Haven: Yale University Press.

Waugh, D. (1991) California's history textbooks: Do they offend? *California Journal* (22) 3, 121–27.

Walter, J. C. (1991) Gender and transformation, in J. Butler and J. C. Walter (eds.), *Transforming the curriculum.* Albany: State University of New York Press.

Weis, L., and Fine, M. (1993) *Beyond silenced voices: Class, race and gender in United States schools.* Albany: State University of New York Press.

Woolf, V. (1938) *Three Guineas.* London: Hogarth.

Chapter Six

Ahmad, A. (1992) *In theory: Classes, Nations, Literatures.* New York: Verso.

Althusser, A. (1971) Ideology and ideological state apparatuses (Notes towards an investigation, in L. Althusser *Lenin and philosophy and other essays* (pp. 121–73). New York: Monthly Review.

Aronowitz, S., and Giroux, H. A. (1991) The politics of clarity. *Afterimage*, *19*(3) 5, 17.

Asante, M. (1987) *The Afrocentric idea*. Philadelphia: Temple University Press.

Baldwin, J. (1963) *The fire next time*. New York: Dell.

Bell, R. (1975) Lower class Negro mothers' aspirations for their children, in H. Stub (ed.), *The sociology of education: A sourcebook* (pp. 125–36). Homewood, IL: Dorsey Press.

Bhabha, H. (1986) Signs taken for wonders: Questions of ambivalence and authority under a tree outside Delhi, May 1817, in H. L. Gates, Jr. (ed.), *"Race," writing, and difference*. Chicago: University of Chicago Press.

Bowles, S., and Gintis, H. (1976) *Schooling in capitalist America*. New York: Basic Books.

Burawoy, M. (1981) The capitalist state in South Africa: Marxist and sociological perspectives on race and class, in M. Zeitlin (ed.), *Political power and social theory* (vol. 2, pp. 279–335). Greenwich, CT: JAI Press.

De Lauretis, T. (1984) *Alice doesn't: Feminism, semiotics, and cinema*. Bloomington: Indiana University Press.

D'Souza, D. (1991) *Illiberal education: The politics of race and sex on campus*. New York: Free Press.

Edari, R. (1984) Racial minorities and forms of ideological mystification, in M. Berlowitz and R. Edari (eds.), *Racism and the denial of human rights: Beyond ethnicity* (pp. 7–18). Minneapolis: Marxist Educational Press.

Fine, M. (1990) *Framing Dropouts*. Albany: State University of New York Press.

Fusco, C. (1988) Fantasies of oppositionality. *Screen, 29*(4), 80–95.

Gamoran, A., and Berends, M. (1986) *The effects of stratification in secondary schools: Synthesis of survey and ethnographic research*. Madison: National Center on Effective Secondary Education, University of Wisconsin-Madison.

Gates, H. (1991) "Authenticity," or the lesson of little tree. *New York Times Book Review*, November 24, p. 1.

Gilroy, P. (1988/89) Cruciality and the frog's perspective: An agenda of difficulties for the black arts movement in Britain. *Third Text, 5*, 33–44.

————. (1990) Art of darkness, black art and the problem of belonging to England. *Third Text, 10*, 45–52.

Giroux, H. A. (1992) Border crossings: Cultural workers and the politics of education. New York: Routledge.

Grant, L. (1984) Black females' "place" in desegregated classrooms. *Sociology of Education, 57*, 98–111.

————. (1985) Uneasy alliances: Black males, teachers, and peers in desegregated classrooms. Unpublished manuscript, Southern Illinois University, Department of Sociology, Carbondale.

Hall, S. (1980a) Race, articulation and societies structured in dominance, in UNESCO, *Sociological theories: Race and colonialism* (pp. 305–45). Paris: UNESCO.

————. (1980b) Encoding and decoding, in S. Hall, D. Hobson, A. Lowe, and P. Willis (eds.), *Culture, media, language* (pp. 128–39). London: Hutchinson.

————. (1981) Teaching race, in A. James and R. Jeffcoate (eds.), *The school in the multicultural society* (pp. 58–69). London: Harper & Row.

————. (1986) Gramsci's relevance to the analysis of race. *Communication Inquiry, 10*, 5–27.

————. (1989) Cultural identity and cinematic representation. *Framework 36*, 66–81.

Henriques, J. (1984) *Changing the subject*. London: Methuen.

Hicks, E. (1981) Cultural Marxism: Nonsynchrony and feminist practice, in L. Sargeant (ed.), *Women and revolution* (pp. 219–238). Boston: South End Press.

Hirsch, E. D. (1987) *Cultural literacy*. Boston: Houghton Mifflin.

Institute for the Study of Social Change. (1991) *The diversity project: Final report to the Chancellor*. Berkeley: University of California Press.

Jackobowitz, C. (1985) State and ethnicity: Multiculturalism as ideology, in F. Rizvi (ed.), *Multiculturalism as educational policy* (pp. 43–63). Geelong, Victoria: Deakin University Press.

JanMohamed, A., and Lloyd, D. (1987) Introduction: Minority discourse—What is to be done? *Cultural Critique, 7*, 5–17.

Jaschik, S. (1990) Scholarships set up for minority students are called illegal. *Chronicle of Higher Education, 37*(15), A 1.

Jensen, A. (1984) Political ideologies and educational research. *Phi Delta Kappan, 65*(7), 460.

Kunjufu, J. (1990) *The conspiracy to destroy black boys*. Chicago: African American Images.

Light, A. (1992) Ice (an interview with Ice-T). *Rolling Stone*, August 20, 29–32, 60.

McCarthy, C. (1990) *Race and curriculum*. London: Falmer Press.

McCarthy, C., and Crichlow, W. (eds.). (in press). *Race, identity, and representation in education*. New York: Routledge.

Nkomo, M. (1984) *Student culture and activism in black South African universities*. Westport, CT: Greenwood Press.

Oakes, J. (1992) Can tracking research inform practice? Technical, normative, and political considerations. *Educational Researcher, 21*(4), 12–21.

Ogbu, J. (1978) *Minority education and caste*. New York: Academic Press.

Omi, M, and Winant, H. (1991) Contesting the meaning of race in the post-civil rights period. Paper presented at the Annual Meeting of the American Sociological Association, August 23–27.

Orr, E. (1987) *Twice as less*. New York: W. W. Norton.

Roman, L. (in press). White is a color! White defensiveness, postmodernism, and anti-racist pedagogy, in C. McCarthy and W. Crichlow (eds.), *Race, identity, and representation in education*. New York: Routledge.

Said, E. (1992) Identity, authority and freedom: The potentate and the traveler. *Transition, 54*, 4–18.

Sandoval, C. (1991) U. S. third world feminism: The theory and method of oppositional consciousness in the postmodern world. *Genders, 10*, 1–24.

Spring, J. (1991) *American education* (5th ed.). New York: Longman.

Sullivan, M. (1990) *Getting paid: Youth crime and work in the inner city*. Ithaca, N.Y.: Cornell University Press.

Tiedt, I., and Tiedt, P. (1986) *Multicultural teaching: A handbook of activities, information and resources*. Boston: Ally and Bacon.

Toyna, B., and Hatcher, R. (1992) *Racism in children's lives*. London: Routledge.

Wallace, (1990) *Invisibility blues*. New York: Verso.

Waters, M. (1990) *Ethnic options: Choosing identities in America*. Berkeley: University of California Press.

West, C. (1993) *Race matters*. Boston: Beacon Press.

Will, G. (1989) Eurocentricity and the school curriculum. *Baton Rouge Morning Advocate*, December 18, 3.

Wood, J. (1991) Cultural consumption, from Elvis Presley to the young black teenagers. *Voice Rock and Roll Quarterly*, 10–11.

Wright, E. O. (1978) *Class, crisis and the state*. London: New Left Review.

Chapter Seven

Anyon, J. (1980) Social class and the hidden curriculum of work. *Journal of Education, 162*, 67–92.

Apple, M. (1979) *Ideology and curriculum*. London: Routledge and Kegan Paul.

Banks, J. (1991) A curriculum for empowerment, action, and change, in Sleeter, C. (ed.), *Empowerment through multicultural education* (pp. 125–42). Albany: State University of New York Press.

Bowles, S., and Gintis, H. (1976) *Schooling in capitalist America*. New York: Basic Books.

Bigelow, B. (1990) Once upon a genocide. A review of Christopher Columbus in children's literature. *Rethinking Schools*, 5(1),8–9, 12.

Brickman, P., Rabinowitz, V., Kazura, J., Coates, D., Cohen, E., and Kidder,L. (1982) Models of helping and coping. *American Psychologist, 37*, 368–84.

Britzman, D. (1991) *Practice makes practice*. Albany: State University of New York Press.

Brown, C.S. (1990) *Like it was: A complete guide to writing oral history*. New York: Teachers and Writers Collaborative.

Carby, H. (1990) The politics of difference. *MS.*, September/October, 84–85.

Crichlow, W. (1990) Theories of representation: Implications for understanding race in the multicultural curriculum. Paper presented for the Bergamo Conference, Oct. 17–20, Dayton, Ohio.

Fine, M. (1991) *Framing dropouts: Notes on the politics of an urban public high school*. Albany: State University of New York Press.

Giroux, H. (1987) Critical literacy and student empowerment: Donald Grave's approach to literacy. *Language Arts, 64*(2), 175–81.

Grant, L. (1984) Black females "place" in desegregated classrooms. *Sociology of Education, 57*, 98–111.

hooks, b. (1990) *Yearning: Race, gender, and cultural politics.* Boston: South End Press.

Kohl, H. (1991) The politics of children's literature: The story of Rosa Parks and the Montgomery bus boycott. *Rethinking Schools*, Jan./Feb., 10–13.

McCarthy, C. (1990) *Race and curriculum.* London: Falmer Press.

McDowell, C.L., and Sullivan, P. (1993) To fight swimming against the current: Teaching movement history, in Perry, T., and Fraser, J. (eds.), *Freedom's plow: Teaching in the multicultural classroom.* New York: Routledge.

McLaren, P. (1989) *Life in schools.* New York: Longman.

McNeil, L. (1986) *Contradictions of control: School structure and school knowledge.* New York: Routledge and Kegan Paul.

New York State Social Studies Review and Development Committee. (1991) *One nation, many peoples: A declaration of cultural interdependence.* Albany: New York State Education Department.

Rethinking Schools. (1991) *Rethinking Columbus.* Milwaukee: Rethinking Schools.

Rose, M. (1989), *Lives on the boundary: A moving account of the struggles and achievements of America's educational underclass.* New York: Free Press.

Simon, R.I., and Dippo, D. (1987) What schools can do: Designing programs for work education that challenge the wisdom of experience. *Journal of Education, 169,* 101–16.

Sleeter, C. (ed.). (1991) *Empowerment through multicultural education.* Albany: State University of New York Press.

Tetreault, M.K.T. (1987) Rethinking women, gender, and social studies. *Social Education,* 51(3). 170–78.

Walker, A. (1985) *The color purple.* New York: Pocket Books.

Chapter Eight

Apple, M., and Christian-Smith, L. (eds.). (1991) *The politics of the textbook.* New York: Routledge.

Asante, M.K. (1991) The Afrocentric idea in education. *Journal of Negro Education, 60,* 170–80.

Au, K., and Jordan, C. (1981) Teaching reading to Hawaiian children: Finding a culturally appropriate solution, in H. Trueba, G. Guthrie, and

K. Au (eds.), *Culture and the bilingual classroom: Studies in classroom ethnography* (pp. 139–52). Rowley, MA: Newbury House.

Cazden, C., and Legett, E. (1981) Culturally responsive educations: Recommendations for achieving Lau remedies II, in H. Trueba, G. Guthrie, and K. Au (eds.), *Culture and the bilingual classroom: Studies in classroom ethnography* (pp. 69–86). Rowley, MA: Newbury House.

Cuban, L, (1973) Ethnic content, white instruction, in J. Banks (ed.), *Teaching ethnic studies* (pp. 91–99). Washington, D.C.: National Council for the Social Studies.

Erickson, F., and Mohatt, G. (1982) Cultural organization and participation structures in two classrooms of Indian students, in G. Spindler (ed.), *Doing the ethnography of schooling* (pp. 131–74). New York: Holt, Rinehart & Winston.

Foster, M. (1989) "It's cookin' now:" A performance analysis of the speech events of a black teacher in an urban community college. *Language in Society, 18,* 1–29.

Giroux, H., and Simon, R. (1989) Popular culture and critical pedagogy: Everyday life as a basis for curriculum knowledge, in H. Giroux and P. McLaren (eds.), *Critical pedagogy, the state, and cultural struggle* (pp. 236–52). Albany: State University of New York Press.

Gomez, M.L., Graue, M.E., and Bloch, M.N. (1991). Reassessing portfolio assessment: Rhetoric and reality. *Language Arts, 68,* 620–28.

Goodlad, J. (1984) *A place called school.* New York: McGraw-Hill.

Goodman, Y. (1989) Roots of the whole language movement. *Elementary School Journal, 90,* 113–27.

Hirsch, E.D. (1987) *Cultural literacy: What every American needs to know.* Boston: Houghton Mifflin.

Irvine, J. (1990) *Black students and school failure.* Westport, CT: Greenwood Press.

Jordan, C. (1985) Translating culture: From ethnographic information to educational program. *Anthropology and Education Quarterly, 16,* 105–23.

Ladson-Billings, G. (1990a), Culturally relevant teaching: Effective instruction for Black students. *The College Board Review, 155,* 20–25.

———. (1990b) Like lightning in a bottle: Attempting to capture the pedagogical excellence of successful teachers of Black students. *The International Journal of Qualitative Studies in Education, 3,* 335–44.

———. (1991) Returning to the source: Implications for educating teachers of Black students, in M. Foster (ed.), *Readings on equal education:*

Qualitative investigations into schools and schooling (Vol. 11, pp. 227–44). New York: AMS Press.

———. (1992a) Culturally relevant teaching: The key to making multicultural education work, in C. Grant (ed.), *Research and multicultural education* (pp. 106–21). London: Falmer Press.

———. (1992b) Liberatory consequences of education: A case of culturally relevant instruction for African American students. *The Journal of Negro Education, 61,* 378–91.

———. (1992c) Reading between the lines and beyond the pages: A culturally relevant approach to literacy teaching. *Theory into practice, 31,* 312–20.

———. (1995). Making math meaningful in cultural contexts, in W. Secada, E. Fennema, and L. Byrd, (eds.), *New directions for equity in mathematics* (pp. 126–145). New York: Cambridge University Press.

Mohatt, G., and Erickson, F. (1981) Cultural differences in teaching styles in an Odawa School: A sociolinguistic approach, in H. Trueba, G. Guthrie, and K. Au (eds.), *Culture and the bilingual classroom: Studies in classroom ethnography* (pp. 105–19). Rowley, MA: Newbury House.

Newmann, F. (1988) Can depth replace coverage in the high school curriculum? *Phi Delta Kappan ,69,* 345–48.

Ravitch, D. (1988) Tot sociology. *American Educator, 12*(3), 39.

Ravitch, D., and Finn, C. (1987) *What do our 17-year-olds know?* New York: Harper & Row.

Shulman, L. (1987) Knowledge and teaching: Foundations of the new reform. *Harvard Educational Review, 57,* 1–22.

Spradley, J. (1979) The ethnographic interview. Troy, MO: Holt, Rinehart, & Wilson.

Vogt, L., Jordan, C., and Tharp, R. (1987) Explaining school failure, producing school success: Two cases. *Anthropology and Education Quarterly, 18,* 276–86.

Chapter Nine

Asante, M. (1991) The Afrocentric idea in education. *Journal of Negro History, 60,* 170–180.

Bishop, W. (1990) *Released into language.* Urbana, IL: National Council for Teachers of English.

Botkin, B. (1945) *Lay my burden down*. Chicago: University of Chicago Press.

Blassingame, J. W. (1979) *The slave community: Plantation life in the antebellum south* (rev. ed.). New York: Oxford University Press.

Bruner, J. (1985) Narrative and paradigmatic modes of thought, in E. W. Eisner (ed.), *Learning and teaching the ways of knowing: Eighty-fourth yearbook of the National Society for the Study of Education, Part II* (pp. 97–115). Chicago: University of Chicago Press.

———. (1986). *Actual minds, possible worlds*. Cambridge: Harvard University Press.

Craig, G. (1989) History as a humanistic discipline, in P. Gagnon (ed.), *Historical literacy: The case for history in American education*. New York: Macmillan.

Dewey, J. (1934) *Art as experience*. New York: Minton, Balch & Co.

Douglass, F. (1982) *The narrative of the life of Frederick Douglass, an American slave*. New York: Penguin Books.

DuBois, W. E. B. (1973) *The souls of black folk*. New York: Kraus-Thomson Organization, Limited.

Eisner, E. W. (1982) *Cognition and curriculum*. New York: Longman.

———. (1985) Aesthetic ways of knowing, in E. W. Eisner (ed.), *Learning and teaching the ways of knowing: Eighty-fourth yearbook of the National Society for the Study of Education Part II* (pp. 23–36). Chicago: University of Chicago Press.

Epstein, T. E. (1990) Equity in educational experiences and outcomes. *Magazine of History, 4*, 35–40.

———. (1994) Sometimes a shining moment: High school students' creations of the arts in historical contexts. *Social Education 58,* 136–141.

———. (1994) The arts of history: An analysis of secondary students' interpretations of the arts in historical context. *Journal of Curriculum and Supervision. 9,* 174–194.

Garcia, J. (1993) The changing image of ethnic groups in textbooks. *Phi Delta Kappan, 75,* 29–35.

Gardner, H. (1983) *Frames of mind: The theory of multiple intelligences*. New York: Basic Books.

Gates, H. L., Jr. (1988) *Figures in black: Words, signs and the "racial" self.* New York: Oxford University Press.

Goodlad, J. (1984) *A place called school*. New York: McGraw-Hill.

Goodman, N. (1978) *Ways of worldmaking*. Indianapolis: Hackett.

Handlin, O. (1979) *Truth in history*. Cambridge: Harvard University Press.

Holt, T. (1990) African-American history, in E. Foner (ed.), *The new American history*. Philadelphia: Temple University Press.

Huggins, N. (1990) *Black odyssey*. New York: Vintage.

Langer, S. (1942) *Philosophy in a new key*. Cambridge: Harvard University Press.

———. (1953) *Feeling and form*. Cambridge: Harvard University Press.

Levine, L. W. (1978) *Black culture and black consciousness: Afro-American folk thought from slavery to freedom*. New York: Oxford University Press.

Michael, J. (1983) *Art and adolescence*. New York: Teachers College Press.

Nash., G. B. (1992) The great multicultural debate. *Contention, 1*, 1–28.

New York State Social Studies Review and Development Committee. (1991) *One nation, many peoples: A declaration of cultural interdependence*. Albany, Department of Education.

Ravitch, D. (1990) Multiculturalism: E pluribus plures. *American Scholar,* 337–54.

Ravitch, D., and Finn, Jr., C. E. (1987) *What do our 17-year olds know? A report of the first national assessment of history and literature*. New York: Harper & Row.

Rosenblatt, L. M. (1978) *The reader, the text, the poem*. Carbondale: Southern Illinois University Press.

Southern, E. (1983) *The music of black Americans* (2nd ed.). New York: W. W. Norton.

Chapter Ten

Appenbrink, D., and Hounshell, P. (1981) *Physical science*. Englewood Cliffs, N.J.: Prentice-Hall.

Barnet, R. (1994) Lords of the global economy. *The Nation*, December 19, pp. 754–57.

Barr, R. D., Barth, J. L., and Shermis, S. S. (1977) *Defining the social studies*. Arlington, Va.: National Council for the Social Studies.

Bruner, J. S. (1960) The process of education. Cambridge: Harvard University Press.

Bush, V. (1945) *Science: The endless frontier.* (reprint 1960). Washington, D.C.: National Science Foundation.

Carter, C. (1991) Science-technology-society and access to scientific knowledge. *Theory into Practice, 30*(4), 273–79.

Charles, C., and Samples, B. (eds.). (1978) *Science and society: Knowing, teaching, learning.* Washington, D.C.: NCSS.

Cheek, D. (1992) *Thinking constructively about science, technology and society education.* Albany: State University of New York Press.

Cummings, H. H. (Ed.). (1957) *Science and the social studies.* Washington, DC: National Council for the Social Studies.

Dewey, J. (1939) *Experience and education.* New York: Macmillan.

Duschl, R. (1988). Abandoning the scientistic legacy of science education. *Science Education, 72*(1), 51–62.

England, J. M. (1982) *A patron for pure science: The National Science Foundation's formative years, 1945–1957.* Washington, D.C.: National Science Foundation.

Fleury, S. C., and Bentley, M. L. (1991) Educating elementary science teachers: Alternative conceptions of the nature of science. *Teaching Education,* 3(2), 58–67.

Freedman, K. (1989) Dilemmas of equity in art education: Ideologies of individualism and cultural capital, in W. G. Secada (ed.), *Equity in education* (pp.103–17). New York: Falmer.

Freese, L. (Ed.). (1980) Theoretical methods in sociology: Seven Essays. Pittsburgh: University of Pittsburgh Press.

Freire, P. (1989) *Pedagogy of the oppressed* (trans. by M. Ramos). New York: Seabury Press. (Original work published 1970).

Greene, G. (1995) The war at home: Review of *Cancer Wars: How politics shape what we know and don't know about cancer. The Nation,* May 19, 768–69.

Handlin, O. (1979) *Truth in history.* Cambridge: Harvard University Press.

Heath, P. A. (1988) *Science/technology/society in the social studies.* Bloomington, IN: ERIC Clearinghouse for Social Studies/Social Science Education.

Hurd, P. D. (1991) Closing the educational gaps between science, technology, and society. *Theory into Practice,* 30(4), 251–59.

Kaplan, A. (1964) *The conduct of inquiry.* San Francisco, CA: Chandler.

Leming, J. S. (1989) The two cultures of social studies education. *Social Education*, 404–8.

Marker, G. W. (1992) Integrating science-technology-society into social studies education. *Theory into Practice, 21*(1), 20–26.

May, W. T. (1992) What are the subjects of STS-really? *Theory into Practice, 31*(1), 73–83.

McNeil, L. M. (1986) *Contradictions of control: School structure and school knowledge.* New York: Routledge.

Moyer, R., & Bishop, J. (1986) *General science.* Columbus, OH: Merrill.

Mills, C. W. (1959) *The sociological imagination.* New York: Oxford Press.

Odets, W. (1995) The fatal mistakes of AIDS education. *Harpers, 290,* 13–17.

Parenti, M. (1995) *Democracy for the few.* (6th ed.) New York: St. Martin's Press.

Patrick, J. J., & Remy, R. C. (1985) *Connecting science, technology, and society in the education of citizens.* Boulder, CO: Social Science Education Consortium.

Popkewitz, T. S. (1991) *A political sociology of educational reform: Power / knowledge in teaching, teacher education, and research.* New York: Teachers College Press.

Reichenbach, H. (1951) *The rise of scientific philosophy.* Berkeley: University of California Press.

Remy, R. (1990) The need for science/technology/society in the social studies. *Social Education, 54,* 203–7.

Rosenthal, D. (1989) Two approaches to science-technology-society (S-T-S) education. *Science Education, 73,* 581–89.

Ross, L., and Lepper, M. (1980) The perseverance of beliefs: Empirical and normative considerations, in R. Shweder (ed.), *Fallible judgment in behavioral research: New directions for methodology of social and behavioral science.* San Francisco: Jossey Bass.

Sagan, C. (1977) *The dragons of Eden.* New York: Random House.

Snyder, M., and Swann, W., Jr. (1978) Hypothesis testing in social interaction. *Journal of Personality and Social Psychology, 36,* 1202–12.

Snyder, M., and White, P. (1981) Testing hypotheses about other people: Strategies of verification and falsification. *Personality and Social Psychology Bulletin, 7*(1), 39–43.

Splittgerber, F. (1991) Science-technology-society themes in social studies: Historical perspectives. *Theory into Practice, 30*(4), 242–50.

Stake, R., and Easley, J. (1978) *Case studies in science education.* Urbana, IL: Center for Instructional Research and Curriculum Evaluation, University of Illinois.

Steelman, J. R. (1947) *Science and public policy.* Washington, D.C.: U.S. Government Printing Office.

Tanner, D. (1990) The curriculum frontier. *Social Education 54,* 195–197.

Wesley, E. (1967) The waxing of the social studies and the waning of history. Paper presented at the annual meeting of the National Council for the Social Studies, Seattle, November.

Wraga, W. G., and Hlebowitsh, P. S. (1990) Science, technology, and the social studies. *Social Education,* 54(4), 195–98.

Wraga, W. G. (1993) The interdisciplinary imperative for citizenship education. *Theory and Research in Social Education,* 21(3), 201–31.

Yeager, R. E. (1990) The science/technology/society movement in the United States: Its origin, evolution, and rationale. *Social Education,* 54(4), 198–201.

Chapter Eleven

(1) Conceptualization and Practice of Global Education

Alger, C., and Hoovler, D. (1978) You and your community and the world. Occasional paper. Columbus, OH: The Mershon Center, Ohio State University.

Alger, C. F., and Harf, J. E. (1986) Global education: Why? For whom? About what?," in R. E. Freeman (ed.), *Promising practices in global education: A handbook with case studies* (pp. 1–13). New York: National Council on Foreign Language and International Studies.

Anderson, C. A. (1990) "Global education and the community," in K. A. Tye (ed.), *Global education. From thought to action* (pp. 125–41). Alexandria, VA: Association for Supervision and Curriculum Development.

Anderson, L. (1979) *Schooling for citizenship in a global age: An exploration of the meaning and significance of global education.* Bloomington, IN: Social Studies Development Center.

Becker, J. M. (ed.) (1979) *Schooling for a global age.* New York: McGraw-Hill.

Case, R. (1991) *Key elements of a global perspective* (EDGE series). Vancouver, British Columbia: Centre for the Study of Curriculum and Instruction, Faculty of Education, University of British Columbia.

Hanvey, R. G. (1975) *An attainable global perspective.* New York: Center for War/Peace Studies.

Kniep, W. M. (1986) Defining a global education by its content. *Social Education, 50,* 437–66.

―――. (ed.). (1987) *Next steps in global education: A handbook for curriculum development.* New York: American Forum.

Lamy, S. L. (1987) *The definition of a discipline: The objects and methods of analysis in global education.* New York: Global Perspectives in Education.

Lamy, S. L. (1990) Global education: A conflict of images, in K. A. Tye (ed.), *Global education. From thought to action* (pp. 49–63). Alexandria, VA: Association for Supervision and Curriculum Development.

Levak, B. A., Merryfield, M. M., and Wilson, R. C. (1993). Global connections: An interdisciplinary approach. *Educational Leadership 51*(1), 73–75.

Martin, G. O. (1988 November). Factors that support change in teachers' use of new materials and teaching strategies. Paper presented at the meeting of the National Council for the Social Studies, Orlando, FL.

Merryfield, M. M. (1993) Responding to the Gulf war: A case study of teacher decision-making. *Social Education, 57,* 33–41.

―――. (1992 April) Teacher decision-making and global perspectives: The dynamism of guiding principles and contextual factors. Paper presented at the meeting of the American Educational Research Association, San Francisco, CA.

―――. (1992 June). Teaching about the world in multicultural classrooms: Teacher beliefs and student diversity. Paper presented at the meeting of the Social Science Educational Consortium, San German, Puerto Rico.

Mulloy, P. A. (1990) Joshua Eaton Elementary School. In K. A. Tye (Ed.), *Global education: School-based strategies* (pp. 41–52). Orange, CA: Interdependence Press.

National Council for the Social Studies. (1982) Position statement on global education. Washington, D.C.: Author.

Shaver, J. P., Davis, O. L., and Helburn, S. W. (1979) The study of social studies education: Impressions from three NSF studies. *Social Education, 43,* 150–153.

Swift, J. (1990) Adlai Stevenson High School, in K. A. Tye (ed.), *Global education: School-based strategies* (pp. 117–30). Orange, CA: Interdependence Press.

Torney-Purta, J. (1989 April). A research agenda for the study of global/international education in the United States. Paper presented at the meeting of the American Educational Research Association, San Francisco.

Tucker, J. L. (1983) Teacher attitudes towards global education: A report from Dade County. *Educational Research Quarterly, 8*(1), 65–77.

Tye, B. B., and Tye, K. A. (1992) *Global education: A study of school change.* Albany: State University of New York Press.

Tye, K. A. (ed.). (1990) *Global education: From thought to action.* Alexandria, VA: Association for Supervision and Curriculum Development.

———. (ed.). (1990) *Global education: School-based strategies.* Orange, CA: Interdependence Press.

Wilson, A. (1983) A case study of two teachers with cross-cultural experience: They know more. *Educational Research Quarterly, 8*(1), 78–85.

———. (1982) Cross-cultural experiential learning for teachers. *Theory Into Practice, 21*, 184–92.

Woyach, R. B. (1984) Using the local community to teach about the global community, in M. C. Schug and R. Beery (eds.), *Community study: Applications and opportunities* (pp. 15–28). Washington, D.C.: National Council for the Social Studies.

Woyach, R. B., and Remy, R.C. (1982) A community-based approach to global education. *Theory Into Practice, 21*, 177–183.

(2) Organizations that Produce and Disseminate Instructional Materials in Global Education

American Forum for Global Education, 120 Wall Street, Suite 2600, New York, NY, 10005, publishes the global education newsletter *ACCESS* that notes upcoming conferences, new resources, and other facets of global education. The American Forum also develops materials such as *Exploring Global Art* and *Evaluating Global Education.*

Center for Teaching International Relations (CTIR), University of Denver, Denver, CO, 80208, develops global education materials such as *Teaching about Food and Hunger.*

Foreign Policy Association, 729 Seventh Avenue, New York, NY, 10019, is known for *Great Decisions*, their annual publication of current foreign policy issues, as well as other publications, such as *Political Tides in the Arab World.*

Mershon Center, 1501 Neil Avenue, Columbus, OH, 43210, develops materials on national security, including *World Geography and National Security* and *Approaches to World Studies: A Handbook for Curricular Planners.*

Social Science Education Consortium (SSEC), 3300 Mitchell Lane, Suite 240, Boulder, CO, 80301, develops materials such as *Global Geography* and *A Look at Japanese Culture through the Family.*

Social Studies Development Center (SSDC), 2805 E. Tenth Street, Bloomington, IN, 47405, develops materials such as *Lessons from Africa* and *Internationalizing the U.S. Classroom: Japan as a Model.*

Social Studies School Service, 10200 Jefferson Boulevard, Room 1021, PO Box 802, Culver City, CA, 90232–0802, disseminates many types of materials through their global education catalog.

Stanford Program on International and Cross-Cultural Education (SPICE), Littlefield Center, Room 14, Stanford University, Stanford, CA, 94305, develops a wide range of materials on cultures and global issues including the Eastern Europe Series, *Discovery Box: Exploring Japan through Artifacts* and *Heelotia: A Cross-Cultural Simulation.*

World Bank, Washington, DC, 20433, produces materials on developing countries and development issues, including *The Development Data Book* and poster kits on population, life expectancy, and GNP per capita.

Worldwatch Institute, 1776 Massachusetts Avenue, N.W., Washington, D.C., 20036, develops materials on global environmental issues such as their annual *State of the World.*

Chapter Twelve

Cuban, L. (1984) *How teachers taught.* New York: Longman.

Dewey, J. (1933) *How we think.* Boston: Heath.

Engle, S. H., and Ochoa, A. S. (1988) *Education for democratic citizenship: Decision making in the social studies.* New York: Teachers College Press.

Evans, R. W. (1987) Defining the worthy society: A history of the societal problems approach in the social studies, 1895–1985. Unpublished doctoral dissertation. Stanford University.

———. (1992) Resources and materials for issues-centered social studies. *The Social Studies, 83*: 118–19.

Evans, R. W., and Saxe, D. W. (eds.). (1996). *Handbook on teaching social issues.* Washington, D.C.: National Council for the Social Studies.

Freire, P. (1970) *Pedagogy of the oppressed.* New York: Continuum.

Giroux, H. (1992) *Border crossings: Cultural workers and the politics of education*. New York: Routledge.

Goodlad, J. (1984) *A place called school*. New York: McGraw-Hill.

Gross, R. E. (1989) Reasons for the limited acceptance of the problems approach. *The Social Studies, 80*: 185–86.

Hunt, M. P., and Metcalf, L. E. (1955) *Teaching high school social studies: Problems in reflective thinking and social understanding*. New York: Harper & Row.

Massialas, B. (1989) The inevitability of issue-centered discourse in the classroom. *The Social Studies, 80*: 173–75.

Michener, J. (ed.). (1939) *The future of the social studies: Proposals for an experimental social studies curriculum*. Curriculum Series #1. Washington, D.C.: National Council for the Social Studies.

Oliver, D. O., and Shaver, J. P. (1966) *Teaching public issues in the high school*. Boston: Houghton-Mifflin.

Rugg, H. O. (1939) Curriculum design in the social sciences: "What I believe . . . ," in J. A. Michener (ed.), *The future of the social studies*. Curriculum Series #1. Washington, D.C.: National Council for the Social Studies.

Saxe, D. W. (1992) Framing a theory for social studies foundations. *Review of Educational Research, 62*: 259–77.

Shaver, J. P. (1989) Lessons from the past: The future of an issues-centered social studies curriculum. *The Social Studies, 80*: 192–96.

———. (1992) Rationales for issues-centered social studies education. *The Social Studies, 83*: 95–99.

Shaver, J. P., Davis, O. L., and Helbrun, S. (1979) The status of social studies education: Impressions from three NSF studies. *Social Education, 43*: 150–53.

Wraga, W. G. (1993). The interdisciplinary imperative for citizenship education. *Theory and Research in Social Education, 21*, 201–301.

Chapter Thirteen

Baker, P. (ed.). (1993) Special section on authentic assessment. *Social Science Record, 30*(2).

Browne, D., and Shultz, N. (1993) A visit with Ibn Battuta: Prince of travelers. *Social Science Record, 30*(2), 29–33.

Darling-Hammond, L. (1991) The implications of testing policy for educational quality and equality. *Kappan, 73*, 220–25.

Fass, P. (1989) *Outside in: Minorities and the transformation of American education.* New York: Oxford University Press.

Herman, J. , Aschbacher, P., and Winters, L. (1992) *A practical guide to alternative assessment.* Alexandria, VA: Association for Supervision and Curriculum Development.

Jones, D. H. (1993) Using authentic assessment in elementary social studies. *Social Science Record, 30*(2), 17–24.

Linn, R. L., Baker, E. L., and Dunbar, S. B. (1991) Complex, performance-based assessment: Expectations and validation criteria. *Educational Researcher, 20*(8), 15–21.

Linn, R. L. (1994) Performance assessment: Policy promises and technical measurement standards. Paper presented at the annual meeting of the American Educational Research Association, New Orleans.

Madaus, G. F. (1988) The influence of testing on the curriculum, in L. Tanner (ed.), *Critical issues in curriculum.* Chicago: University of Chicago Press.

———. (1993) A national testing system: Manna from above. *Educational Assessment, 1*(1), 9–26.

Mathison, S. (1987) The effects of standardized testing on teaching and curricula. Unpublished doctoral dissertation. Champaign: University of Illinois.

———. (1991) Curricular change through state-mandated testing: Ethical issues. *Journal of Curriculum and Supervision, 6*(3), 201–12.

———. (1994) *An evaluation of the Shenendehowa integrated social studies and English curriculum testing variance.* Albany, NY: Author.

———. (1995) Using student portfolios in mathematics: Issues in the reform of assessment. *LINKAGES: Reviews of Research and Practice, 2.*

McNeil, L. (1988) *Contradictions of control: School structure and school knowledge.* London: Routledge.

Mehrens, W. A. (1992) Using performance measurement for accountability purposes. *Educational Measurement: Issues and Practice, 11*(1), 3–9,20.

Messick, S. (1994) The interplay of evidence and consequences in the validation of performance assessments. *Educational Researcher, 23*(2), 13–23.

Miller-Jones, D. (1989) Culture and testing. *American Psychologist, 44*(2): 360–66.

National Council for the Social Studies (1994) *Expectations of excellence: Curriculum standards for social studies.* Washington, D.C.: Author.

O'Connor, M. C. (1989), Aspects of differential performance by minorities on standardized tests: Linguistic and socio-cultural factors, in B. Gifford (ed.), *Test policy and the politics of opportunity allocation: The workplace and the law*. Boston: Kluwer-Nijhoff.

Office of Technology Assessment, Congress of the United States. (1992) *Testing in American schools: Asking the right questions*. Washington, D.C.: Government Printing Office. ED 340 770.

Perrone, V. (1991) (ed.) *Expanding student assessment*. Alexandria, VA: Association for Supervision and Curriculum Development.

Rudner, L. M., and Boston, C. (1994) Performance assessment. *ERIC Review*, *3*(1): 2–12.

Shepard, L. A. (1991) Will national tests improve student learning? *Kappan*, *73*(3), 232–38.

Smith, M. L. (1991) Meanings of test preparation. *American Educational Research Journal*, *28*(3), 521–42.

Taylor, C. (1994) Assessment for measurement or standards: The peril and promise of large-scale assessment reform. *American Educational Research Journal*, *31*(2), 231–62.

Thorndike, E. L. (1918) The nature, purposes, and general methods of measurement of educational products, in G. M. Whipple (ed.), *The measurement of educational products*. Bloomington, IL: Public School Publishing Company.

U.S. Department of Education. (1994) U.S. Department of Education Funds Standards Groups. *ERIC Review*, *3*(1): 15.

Wiggins, G. (1989) A true test: Toward more authentic and equitable assessment. *Kappan*, *70*(9), 703–13.

———. (1993a) Assessment to improve performance, not just monitor it: Assessment reform in the social sciences. *Social Science Record*, *30*(2), 5–12.

———. (1993b) *Assessing student performance: Exploring the purpose and limits of testing*. San Francisco: Jossey-Bass.

Wolf, D. P., Bixby, J., Glenn, J., and Gardner, H. (1991) To use their minds well: Investigating new forms of student assessment. *Review of Research in Education*, *17*, 31–74.

Contributors

Jane Bernard-Powers is Associate Professor of Elementary Education at San Francisco State University. She is a founding member of the Special Interest Group for Gender and Social Justice (National Council for the Social Studies) and is interested in women's educational history and multicultural, gendered social studies education. Her publications include *The Girl Question in Education: Vocational Education for Young Women in the Progressive Era* (Falmer).

Terrie L. Epstein is an Assistant Professor of Education at the University of Michigan where she teaches courses in social studies and curriculum theory. A recent recipient of a National Academy of Education Postdoctoral Fellowship, her current research examines differences in African American and European American adolescents' perspectives on United States history.

Ronald W. Evans teaches in the School of Teacher Education at San Diego State University. He has authored numerous articles and book chapters and is co-editor of the *Handbook on Issues-Centered Education,* a bulletin of the National Council for the Social Studies. He is currently writing a history of social studies education.

Stephen C. Fleury is Associate Professor of Education and Associate Dean of the School of Education at the State University of New York at Oswego. The themes of his professional writings and presentations in social studies education, science education, teacher education, and educational philosophy emanate from his interest in the epistemological impact of science on society, especially pertaining to education for democracy.

David Hursh has been working to reform universities and elementary and secondary schools for almost three decades. He is currently working on two reform projects. One project aims to develop critical teachers through a magnet program on teaching in an urban high school. A second project focuses on teachers researching their own practices in four elementary schools. He writes about critical social education, teacher research, and school reform. Hursh is an Associate Professor and Chair of the Teaching and Curriculum Program in the Warner Graduate School of Education and Human Development at the University of Rochester.

Gloria Ladson-Billings is Associate Professor in the Department of Curriculum and Instruction at the University of Wisconsin-Madison. Ladson-Billings has written numerous articles and book chapters about her research on successful teachers for African American students and other work in multicultural education that has appeared in journals such as *American Educational Research Journal, The Journal of Negro Education, Teachers College Record, Theory Into Practice, The Journal of Education,* and *Social Education.* She is the author of *The Dreamkeepers: Successful Teachers for African American Children* (Jossey-Bass).

Sandra Mathison is Associate Professor in the Department of Educational Theory and Practice at the State University of New York at Albany. Mathison conducts research on curriculum evaluation with particular emphasis on issues such as epistemology, justice, and democracy as they relate to evaluation theory and practice. She has conducted many evaluations on both local and national levels, and views reflection on practice a critical approach to research on evaluation. She has published in many scholarly journals including *Educational Researcher, Cambridge Journal of Education, Evaluation and Program Planning, and Journal of Curriculum and Supervision.* She is co-editor of *Evaluation Studies Review Annual, Volume 7,* and *A Casebook for Teaching Ethics in Qualitative Research.*

Cameron McCarthy is a member of the Institute for Communication Research at the University of Illinois at Urbana-Champaign. He is the author of *Race and Curriculum* (Falmer) and the co-editor of *Race Identity and Representation in Education* (Routledge).

Merry M. Merryfield is Associate Professor of Social Studies and Global Education at The Ohio State University. Merryfield has taught high school social studies and Latin in Atlanta, Georgia, and geography and African literature in Segbwema, Sierra Leone. She has researched social studies education in Kenya, Malawi, and Nigeria and developed junior secondary social studies curricula in Botswana. Her research in American global studies has focused on teacher education in global perspectives and the contexts of teacher thinking and decision-making in K-12 classroom instruction and school/university collaboration. Her most recent books include *Teaching About International Conflict and Peace, Making Connections Between Multicultural and Global Education,* and *Preparing Teachers to Teach Global Perspectives: A Handbook for Teacher Educators.* Merryfield is currently involved in developing case studies of ten teacher education programs in the U.S.A. and Canada that have different theoretical and programmatic approaches to preparing teachers for equity and diversity in an interconnected world.

Nel Noddings is the Lee L. Jacks Professor of Child Education at Stanford University. She has published widely in education, ethics and feminist educational philosophy. Her books include *Caring, A Feminine Approach to Ethics and Moral Education* (University of California Press), *Educating for Intelligent Belief and Unbelief* (Teachers College Press), *Women and Evil* (University of California Press), *Awakening the Inner Eye: Intuition in Education* (Teachers College Press), and *Philosophy of Education* (Westview).

E. Wayne Ross is Associate Professor in the School of Education and Human Development at the State University of New York at Binghamton. His scholarly interests are in teacher education and curriculum studies. His research focuses on the intersection of theory and practice in curriculum work and the lives of teachers. He has published in numerous scholarly journals and edited several books, including *Teacher Personal Theorizing: Connecting Curriculum Practice, Theory and Research* (State University of New York Press), and *Reflective Practice in Social Studies* (National Council for the Social Studies). He is currently editor of the journal *Theory and Research in Social Education.*

David Warren Saxe teaches social studies education at The Pennsylvania State University. He is the author of *Social Studies in*

Schools: A History of the Early Years (State University of New York Press) and is the co-editor of the *Handbook on Issues-Centered Education,* a bulletin of the National Council for the Social Studies.

Michael Whelan is Associate Professor of History and Social Studies Education at The College at New Paltz, State University of New York. He has published widely on the history of social studies as a school subject, with articles and reviews appearing in journals such as *The American Journal of Education, The History Teacher,* and *Theory and Research in Social Education.*

Name Index

Ahmad, A., 96
Alger, C., 183, 187
Althusser, A., 97
Anderson, C., 187
Anderson, L., 187
Anyon, J., 84, 113, 114, 115
Appenbrink, D., and Hounshell, P., 170
Apple, M., 113, 114, 115
Apple, M., and Christian-Smith, L., 133
Aronowitz, S., and Giroux, H. A., 95
Asante, M., 95, 128, 142
Au, K., and Jordan, C., 123

Bagley, W. C., 12, 44
Baker, P., 220
Balch, E. G., 60, 63. *See also* Textbooks: representations of women
Banks, J., 74, 115
Barnard, H., 10
Barnet, R., 181–182
Barr, R. D., Barth, J. L., and Shermis, S., 6–7, 171
Barth, J. L., 22
Becker, J., 187
Beecher, C., 64
Bell, R., 96
Ben-Peretz, M., 17
Bernard-Powers, J., 80, 86
Bhabha, H., 95
Bigelow, B., 109, 117
Bishop, W., 163

Black, H., 163
Blassingame, J. W., 146
Botkin, B., 145
Bowler, M., 13
Bowles, S., and Gintis, H., 96, 113, 114, 115
Boyd, C. D., 129
Brickman, P., 112
Britzman, D., 118
Brocke-Utne, B., 60
Brooks, M. G., 11
Brown, C. S., 119
Browne, D., and Shultz, N., 220
Bruner, J., 138–139, 176
Burawoy, M., 98
Buss, H., 86–87

Campbell, D., 74
Carby, H., 107–108
Carter, C., 179
Case, R., 187
Cazden, C., and Legett, E., 123
Charles, C., and Samples, B., 177
Chavez, C., 60
Cheek, D., 180
Chodorow, N., 65
Churchill, W., 36
Clark, S., 87
Coerr, E., 129
Columbus, C., 109, 117
Connell, R., 78
Cornbleth, C., 9
Cornbleth, C., and Waugh, D., 11, 13, 74

Cornett, J. W., 18
Craig, G. 139
Crichlow, W., 118
Cuban, L., 31, 125, 211
Cummings, H. H., 176

Darling-Hammond, L., 217
Day, D., 60. *See also Catholic Worker*; Textbooks: representations of women
DeGarmo, C., 10
de Lauretis, T., 97
Dewey, J., 12, 18, 41–42, 44, 138, 160, 171, 174, 204
Douglass, F., 146, 147
Downey, M. T., and Levstik, L. S., 31
D'Souza, D., 96
DuBois, W. E. B., 80
Duschl, R., 169

Edari, R., 96
Eisner, E. W., 159
Eliot, C., 10
Elshtain, J. B., 61
England, J. M., 175
Engle, S., 31, 34, 171
Engle, S., and Ochoa, A., 8, 54, 203, 204
Epstein, T. L., 8, 141, 220
Erickson, F., and Mohatt, G., 123
Evans, R. W., 8, 21, 27, 30–31, 78, 201, 208, 220
Evans, R. W., and Saxe, D. W., 54, 208
Evans, Terry, 83

Faludi, S., 73
Fass, P., 217
Fine, M., 104, 110, 112, 117, 119
Fleury, S. C., 220
Fleury, S. C., and Bentley, M. L., 171
Foster, M., 126
Fox-Genovese, E., 74–75

Franke, A., 87
Frankline, B. M., 31
Freedman, K., 172
Freese, L., 180
Freire, P., 179, 204
Fullinwider, R. K., 6
Fusco, C., 95, 106

Gagnon, P., 74
Garcia, J., 141, 143
Gardner, H., 140
Gates, H. L., 92, 146, 147
Gillespie, D., and Spohn, C., 85
Gilligan, C., 63, 86, 87
Giroux, H. A., 106, 118, 209
Giroux, H. A., and Simon R. I., 124
Gomez, M. L., Graue, M. E., and Bloch, M. N., 134
Goodlad, J. I., 31, 125, 141, 153, 202
Goodman, N., 163
Goodman, Y., 129
Grambs, J., 71
Gramsci, A., 44
Grant, L., 92, 102–103, 114
Greene, G., 166
Griffin, A., 171
Grob G. N., and Billias, G. A., 33
Gross, R. E., 212
Grundfest, E., 82

Hahn, C., and Bernard-Powers, J., 78
Hall, S., 95, 104
Hamer, F. L., 87
Handlin, O., 139, 140, 154, 172
Hanvey, R., 187
Harrington, M., 60
Harris, A. K., 75–76
Harris, W. T., 10
Harwood, A., and Hahn, C., 85–86
Heath, P. A., 165, 167, 177, 178
Henriques, J., 97
Herman, J., Aschbacher, P. and Winters, L., 217

Hertzberg, H. W., 21, 25
Hicks, E., 98
Hirsch, Jr., E.D., 43, 44, 54, 75, 96, 135
Hirsch, M., and Fox-Keller, E., 76
Holt, T., 142, 154
Huggins, N., 142
Hunt, M. P., and Metcalf, L. E., 203
Hurd, P. D., 174, 175
Hye-Sok, N., 87

Irvine, J., 123
Ivins, M., 86

Jackobowitz, C., 96
Jackson, K. T., and Jackson, B. B., 27
Jaschik, S., 99
Jensen, A., 96
Johnson, L., 81
Jones, D. H., 220–221
Jones, J., 80
Jordan, C., 123

Kammen, M., 33
Kaplan, A., 170
Kilpatrick, W. H., 12
Kingston, M. H., 87
Kleibard, H. M., 10, 25
Kniep, W., 187
Kohl, H., 108–109, 117
Krug, E. A., 11
Kunjufu, J., 95, 96

Ladson-Billings, G., 74, 123, 125, 126, 132
Lamy, S., 187
Laney, L., 80
Langer, S., 139, 163
Leming, J. S., 22, 171, 173
Levine, L. W., 146, 148
Lewis, A. (pseudonym), 126, 128–132, 133, 134
Light, B., Staton, P., and Bourne, P., 79

Linn, R. L., 219
Linn, R. L., Baker, E. L., and Dunbar, S. B., 219
Loewen, J. W., 13
Longstreet, W. S., 6
Lybarger, M. B., 21
Lyons, N., 86

MacIntyre, A., 62, 63
Madaus, G. F., 215, 216, 217, 219
Mann, H., 215–216
Marker, G. W., 167, 177, 178
Marker, G., and Mehlinger, H., 6, 7, 9, 10, 12–13, 14, 17, 79
Martin, J. R., 88
Martin-Kniep, G., 187
Massialas, B., 202
Mathison, S., 11, 216, 217, 219, 222, 223
May, W. T., 178–179
McCarthy, C., 98, 114, 115
McCarthy, C., and Crichlow, W., 106
McCutchen, S. P., 6
McCutcheon, G., 12
McIntosh, P., 74
McKenna, K., 78
McMurry, F., 10
McNeil, L., 115, 117, 222
Mead, M., 212
Mehrens, W. A., 219
Mencken, H. L., 36
Merryfield, M. M., 187
Merton, T., 60
Messick, S., 219
Metcalf, L. E., 171
Michael, J., 163
Mikel, L., 86
Miller-Jones, D., 217
Mills, C. W., 171
Mills, K., 87
Minnich, E. K., 88
Mohatt, G., and Erickson, F., 123
Morrissett, I., and Haas, J. D., 6, 7
Moyer, R., and Bishop, J., 170

Nash, G. B., 141
Nelson, J. L., 21, 30
Newmann, F., 128
Nkomo, M., 98, 103
Noddings, N., 62, 63, 67, 88

O'Connor, M. C., 217
Odets, W., 167
Oliver, D. O., and Shaver, J. P., 203
Omi, M., and Winant, H., 92, 93, 96, 99, 103
Orr, E., 96

Pagano, J., 86
Parenti, M., 171
Parker, W. C., 16
Parker, W. C., and McDaniel, J., 18
Parks, R., 108–109, 111, 117
Patrick, J. J., and Remy, R. C., 173
Peake, L., 81, 82
Perrone, V., 217
Popkewitz, T. S., 168, 172

Ravitch, D., 5, 8, 21, 23–25, 27, 74, 94, 135, 141, 142
Ravitch, D., and Finn, C., 74–75, 135, 141, 153
Reagan, R., 73, 74, 77
Reardon, B. A., 60
Reichenbach, H., 172
Remy, R. C., 165, 167, 173, 177, 178, 187
Robinson, T. L., and Ward, J. V., 81
Roman, L., 106
Rose, M., 112
Rosenberg, R., 75–76
Rosenblatt, L. M., 152
Rosenthal, D., 179
Ross, E. W., 11, 14, 15
Ross, E. W., Cornett, J. W., and McCutcheon, G., 9

Ross, L., and Lepper, M., 170
Rudner, L. M., and Boston, C. 218
Rugg, H. O., 177, 203

Sadker, M., and Sadker, D., 72, 84
Sadker, M., Sadker, D., and Steindam, S., 74
Sagan, C., 180
Sandoval, C., 106
Saxe, D. W., 5, 8, 17, 24–25, 27, 201
Schlesinger Jr., A. M., 8, 17
Schubert, W. H., 10, 12, 13, 14, 17
Schwab, J., 176
Seager, J., 82
Shakeshaft, C., 83
Shaver, J. P., 6, 31, 176, 202, 203
Shaver, J. P., Davis Jr., O. L., and Helburn, S. W., 16, 17, 29, 31, 171, 202
Shepard, L. A., 217
Shulman, L., 124–125, 135
Simon, R. I., and Dippo, D., 118
Sleeter, C., 108, 110, 116, 117
Smith, M. L., 217
Smith, R., 78
Snyder, M., and Swann Jr., W., 170
Snyder, M., and White, P., 170
Southern, E., 142, 148, 150
Sowell, T., 99
Splittgerber, F., 176
Spradley, J., 126
Spring, J., 92, 100–101, 103, 104
Stake, R., and Easley, J., 169
Stanley, W. B., 6
Stanley, W. B., and Nelson, J., 3, 5, 7, 8–9
Steele, S., 99
Sullivan, M., 104
Superka, D. P., Hawke, S., and Morrissette, I., 31

Tanner, D., 177
Taylor, C., 217

Taylor, L., 63
Tetreault, M. K. T., 59, 79, 116–117
Thorndike, E. L., 213
Thorne, B., 76, 83
Thorton, S. J., 6, 15, 16, 29, 30
Tiedt, I., and Tiedt, P., 97
Torney-Purta, J., 187
Tucker, J., 187
Tye, B., and Tye, K., 187

Vogy, L., Jordan, C., and Tharp, R., 123

Walker, A., 67, 109
Wallace, 97, 98
Walter, J. C., 80–82
Washington, B. T., 80
Waugh, D., 74
Weis, L., 84
Weis, L., and Fine, M., 84
Wesley, E., 171

West, C., 95
Whelan, M., 5, 8, 9, 18, 28
Wiggins, G., 215, 217, 220, 221
Wiley, K. B., 31
Will, G., 94
Williams, M., 99
Wilson, A., 187
Winston, G. (pseudonym), 126–128, 132, 133, 134
Wirth, A. G., 11
Wolf, D. P., Bixby, J., Glenn, J., and Gardner, H., 217
Won-ju, K., 87
Woolf, V., 87
Woyach, R., 187
Wraga, W. G., 178
Wraga, W. G., and Hlebowitsh, P. S., 173, 178
Wright, E. O., 98

Yeager, R. E., 179

Subject Index

Affirmative action, 99
Afrocentricism, 91, 94–95, 97;
   panethnic unity, 97
African American culture, 124,
   126–132, 137, 141–144
A Nation at Risk, 124
A Political Sociology of Educational Reform, 168
Amazing Grace, 129
American Association for the
   Advancement of Science Cooperative Committee, 175
American Association of University Women (AAUW), 77, 83, 89
American Historical Association
   (AHA) Commission on Social
   Studies, xi. *See also* Committee
   of Seven
Arts: complex understandings of,
   138–140; -based curriculum, 142
Assessment, 213–215; authentic,
   218–219, 223; performance, 217–223; reform, 223–224; technical
   and social aspects of, 215–220
Assimilationist teaching, 124

Backlash, 73. *See also* gender
   equity
"Bias Against Girls is Found Rife
   in Schools, With Lasting
   Damage", 77. *See also* gender
   equity
Bluest Eyes, 76. *See also* gender
   equity

Bradley Commission on History in
   the Schools, 21, 171, 197
Bush Report, 175. *See also*
   knowledge: forms of

California Assessment Program, 216
California History-Social Science
   Framework, 78–79, 197
Canadian Committee on Women's
   History, 88
*Caring: A Feminine Approach to
   Ethics and Moral Education*, 65.
   See also Noddings, N.
Catholic Worker, 60–61. *See also*
   Day, D.; textbooks: representations of women
The Challenge to Care in Schools,
   65. *See also* Noddings, N.
Charlie Pippin, 129
Citizenship, 28, 39, 54, 64, 83,
   170–173, 208; expanded notion
   of, 64
Citizenship education, 6, 24, 28,
   44–45; gender studies, 83–88;
   study of autobiography and
   biography, 86–88
Citizenship transmission, 6, 7. *See
   also* social studies: purposes of
Civic competence, 8, 39–41, 44–47;
   history courses, 44; socialization,
   49–50; teaching, 49–54. *See also*
   citizenship education
Civics courses, 26. *See also*
   citizenship education

The Color Purple, 109. *See also* Walker, A.

Columbus and the World, the World in Columbus. 183. *See also* Christopher Columbus

Commission on Excellence in Education, 124. *See also A Nation At Risk*

Committee of Seven (American Historical Association), 5, 10, 23–25, 28–29

Committee of Ten (National Education Association), 5, 10, 23–25, 28–29

Committee on the Social Studies 1916 Report (National Education Association), xi, 5, 10, 22, 23–29, 31–33

Contradictions of Control, 172. *See also* McNeil, L.

Critical pedagogy, 124. *See also* Culturally relevant teaching; Pedagogy, Teaching

Cultural literacy, 75, 96. *See also* Hirsh Jr., E. D.; Multicultural education and canon controversy

Cultural studies, 7

Cultural synchronization, 123. *See also* Culturally relevant teaching

Cultural transmission, 6–7

Culturally relevant teaching, 123; aspects of, 132–135; context of, 125; examples of, 126–135

Curriculum: alignment, 11; arts-based, 143–144; canon controversy, 74; change, 211–212, 223–224; conceptions, 9; control, 9–15, 48; feminist influence on, 59, 63, 116–117; interests served by, 61–70; hidden, 169; interdisciplinary, 12; issues-centered, 208–211; social diversity, 119; standards, 4, 9, 14–15, 18–19, 32, 222–223. *See also* Social studies; Textbooks

Curriculum centralization, 4, 9, 10–15, 19, 224; government and non-government policy, 10–12; published materials, 12–14. *See also* Textbooks

Curriculum development: grassroots, 4, 9, 12, 14, 19, 47, 224; parents' roles, 68; teachers' roles in, 4, 9, 14, 16–18, 29, 31–32, 47, 48, 55, 59, 151–154

Disciplines: assessment of, 224; role in social studies, 36–37, 65; structure of, 14, 168–169, 173. *See also* Geography; History; Historical scholarship; Knowledge; Social Studies: history-centered

Diversity, 73, 107, 119. *See also* Afrocentricism, African American Culture, Culturally relevant teaching; Ethnic affiliation; Ethnic studies; Multiculturalism

Economic inequality, 113–114. *See also* Social inequality

Education Commission of the States, 85

Education for Democratic Citizenship, 204. *See also* Engle, S. and Ochoa, A.

Equal Rights Amendment, 72, 73

Equity in education, 100, 114, 140–141, 150–151

Ethnic affiliation, 92–98; white ethnicity, 93–94

Ethnic studies, 7, 63

Eurocentricism, 91. *See also* Afrocentricism; Diversity, Multiculturalism

Evaluation: of historical artwork, 161–165; of students, 213. *See also* Assessment

Expectations of Excellence: Curriculum Standards for Social

Studies, 223. *See also* Curriculum: standards; National Council for the Social Studies

Falling Down, 93. *See also* ethnic affiliation
Feminism without Illusions, A Critique of Individualism, 74
Feminism, 59, 61–62. *See also* Gender equity
Feminist scholarship, 75–76, 79–83, 97; in geography 81–83. *See also* Gender studies
Flatland, 68
Framing Dropouts, 110. *See also* Fine, M.; Gender equity

Gay/lesbian studies, 7. *See also* Diversity
Gender: codes, 77; resources for teaching, 88–89; racial experiences, 102–104, 114–115: and social education, 71
Gender and Education, 75
Gender equity, 72–77; citizenship education, 83–88; curriculum frameworks, 78–79; teacher education, 78; teaching methods, 77, 116–117; textbooks, 79. *See also* Non-sexist education.
Gender studies, 63; in geography, 81–83; in history, 116–117
Geography, 81–83
Global education: courses, 192–193; infusion in social studies, 190–193; nature of, 187–190, 194–195; purposes, 183–186

Heritage Foundation, 171
Historical inaccuracies: in children's books, 108–109, 154
Historical narratives: 146; interpretations of, 139, 154
Historical scholarship: African Americans, 80–81; methods of,

33–34; representation of women, 59–61
History: empathic representations, 155–158; oral, 119, 144; social inquiry, 172; social passivity, 108–109; student interpretations of, 144–151; textbooks, 109; women's, 116–117
History-centered social studies: 5, 21–22, 29–37, 46; civic competence, 44; critiques of, 24–25, 30–31; didactic teaching, 46; organization, 34–36
How We Think, 204. *See also* Dewey, J.
Huckleberry Finn, 67

Ideology and Curriculum, 113. *See also* Apple, M.
Institute for the Study of Social Change, 93
Issues-centered social studies, 7–8, 21–22, 24, 27, 174, 179, 197, 200–203; examples of lessons, 204–208

Journal of Geography in Higher Education, 8. *See also* Gender equity

Kerner Commission, 205
Knowledge: conceptions of, 132; forms, 138–140, 168; linking over time and space, 192; technocratization, 173–179

Liberal-democratic thinking, 55
Liberalism, 62
Like it Was: A Complete Guide to Writing Oral History, 119. *See also* history: oral; teaching methods

Man: A Course of Study (MACOS), 14, 17, 176–177. *See also* knowledge: forms of

Milton S. Eisenhower Foundation, 205
Multicultural education, 67–68, 97; aims, 108–111, 119; the arts, 141–143; canon controversy, 74–75; human relations approach, 110–112; in social studies, 107; social class, 109–110, 113; social history, 108, 137–138, 144–151
Multiple intelligences, 140–141

National Assessment of Educational Progress (NAEP), 177, 216
National Association of Independent Schools, 88
National Commission on Social Studies, 74
National Council for History Education, 197
National Council for the Social Studies (NCSS), 9, 72, 73, 165, 171, 176, 177, 183–184, 197, 222, 223
National Defense Education Act (1958), 13
National Education Association (NEA), xi, 5, 10
National education system, 112
National Endowment for the Humanities, 73
National Organization for Women (NOW), 72. See also gender equity
National Science Foundation (NSF), 175–177
National Women's History Project, 88
National Women's Studies Association, 88
Nationalistic education, 5
New Social Studies, 14, 17, 171, 211
New York State Bureau of Social Studies, 216

New York State Social Studies Review and Development Committee, 143
Non-sexist education, 112. See also Gender equity

Office of Technology Assessment, 218

Pacifism, 61. See also Peace studies
Peace studies, 60–61
Pedagogy 124–126. See also Teaching; Teaching methods
Performance assessment, 217–223. See also Assessment
Perkins Vocational and Applied Technology Act of 1990, 11
Portfolios. See Performance assessment
Positivism, 169–170
Primary sources: cognitive and contextual appropriateness, 151; historically significant themes, 152; selecting for instruction, 151–155
Problem-posing education, 179, 204, 206–208
Progressive Education Association, 174
Project method, 12

Racial authenticity, 92–93
Racial experiences: Black professional middle class, 100, 102; Black Suburbia, 99–102, 105; class antagonism, 102, 115; class dynamics, 100, 103–104; educational expectations, 100; gender, 102, 103–104, 114–115; nature of, 98–103; social order, 107; upward mobility, 100
Racial inequality: 91–92, 96–98, 114; process of nonsynchrony, 98
Race relations and education, 103–106

Race and Curriculum, 114. *See also* McCarthy, C.
Ready From Within, 87
Reflective inquiry, 7, 205–206; teaching, 203–204
Reflective thinking, 6–7, 53
Roe v. Wade, 72. *See also* Gender equity
Romeo and Juliet, 68

Sadako and the Thousand Cranes, 129
Schooling in Capitalist America, 113. *See also* Bowles, S., and Gintis, H.; social inequality
Science and social knowledge, 179–182
Science and Society: Knowing, Teaching, and Learning, 177. *See also* Charles, C., and Samples, B.; National Council for the Social Studies
Science and the Social Studies, 176. *See also* Cummings, H. H.; National Council for the Social Studies; Science-Technology-Society
· Science education, 169–170
Science-Technology-Society (STS), 165, 167, 173, 177–180, 182. *See also* social studies and school science
Scientific Research Board, 175. *See also* National Science Foundation
Social education, 5, 166–167; intergenerational life, 65; love, 68–69; mathematics, 68. *See also* Social studies.
Social improvement, 61; communitarians, 62; classical liberals, 61–62
Social inequality, 107, 111–114. *See also* Racial inequality.

Social studies in schools: arts-based, 137–164; civics-centered, 7, 44–45; civic competence, 40–41, 47; core knowledge, 43; course offerings, 10–11, 26, 31, 53–54; culturally relevant, 125–126; disciplinary knowledge, 8; feminism, 59–70; as history-centered, 5, 21–22, 29–37; global education, 190–193; interdisciplinary, 5, 7, 21, 197–200; issues-centered, 7, 8, 21–22, 24, 27, 174, 179, 197, 200–203; origins, 4–5, 21–29; multicultural, 107–108; performance assessment, 220–223; purposes, 4, 6–9, 21, 46–47, 55, 61, 183–184, 197–198; science education, 167–169; Science-Technology-Society, 177; social control, 172–173; social improvement, 51; spiritual life, 66–67; studies of self, 65–66, 78, 117–119; subject-centered, 7, 46, 167–168, 173–174
The Social Studies in Secondary Education, xi. *See also* Committee on the Social Studies 1916 Report (National Education Association)
Sears and Roebuck vs. Equal Employment Opportunity Commission, 75–76. *See also* Gender equity
SEED Project, 88. *See also* Gender equity
Smith-Hughes Act of 1917, 11
Social Education, 177. *See also* National Council for the Social Studies
Social Science Education Consortium, 165
Social Science Record, 220, 223
Stanford Summer Institute in Women's History, 73

Steelman Report, 175, 180. *See also* Knowledge: forms
Student culture, 112
Students: African American, 123–125; in global context, 191–192; interpretations of historical sources, 144–161; as passive learners, 113–115; paranoid thinking, 181–182; public presentations of private conceptions, 158–159, 160–161; as sources of learning, 117–118

Teacher: beliefs, 16; as curriculum conduit, 14, 16; empowerment, 48. *See also* Teaching; Teaching Methods, Curriculum Development
Teaching: roles of freedom and control, 40–44; social skills, 51–52; thought and action, 52–53. *See also* Teaching methods.
Teaching About Women in the Social Studies, 71
Teaching methods: with art, 137; autobiography and biography, 86–88, 109, 117–118; civic competence, 47–48; didactic, 46, 51; decision-making, 206–208; educationally conservative practices, 43; engaging students in analysis, 116–117, 119; gender equity, 77; that make knowledge inaccessible, 115–116; inquiry, 52–53, 205–206; oral history, 119, 144; primary sources, 137–139, 150–155.
Tests and measurement, 213–215, 223. *See also* Assessment
Textbooks: adoption by states, 13; curriculum centralization, 12–13; ideological interests, 13; inductivist fallacy, 170; positivism, 169–170; perpetuation of racism and colonialism, 109; representations of African

Americans, 59; representations of women, 59–61, 73, 76–79
This Little Light of Mine, 87
Title VII, 72. *See also* Gender equity
Title IX, 72, 73, 74. *See also* Gender equity
Transforming the Curriculum, Ethnic Studies, and Women's Studies, 80. *See also* Walter, J. C.
Treatise on Domestic Economy, 64. *See also* Beecher, C.

United States Bureau of Education, 25
United States Department of Education, 217
United States Ninth Circuit Court Task Force on Gender Bias, 85. *See also* Gender equity
Upper Midwest Women's History Center, 88

Western Association of Women's Historians, 88
White Palace, 93. *See also* Ethnic affiliation
The Woman Warrior, 87
Women: histories of, 116–117; reasonable person standard in law, 63; representations in textbooks, 59–61, 73, 76–79
Women's culture, 70
Women's Educational Equity Act, 72, 73
Women's International League for Peace and Freedom (WILPF), 60. *See also* Textbooks: representation of women
Women's studies, 7. *See also* Gender studies; Diversity, Feminism
Women in World Area Studies, 88
Work education, 11–12
Wuthering Heights, 69

YWCA, 80